PRAISE FOR *LEA*
AND TOURISM ᴋᴇᴛᴀɪʟ

'A timely, thought-provoking and powerful book that is essential reading for everyone with a stake in the international visitor economy. Through well-developed and clearly written examples of strategies and tactics, it goes deep into how both mature and emerging brands can make the most of new opportunities. Global disruption to international travel highlighted the vital and exceptional economic contribution of shopping tourism. Sacha Zackariya shows how the industry can come fighting back, inscribing its value to the global economy and deliver for customers and businesses alike.'
Helen Brocklebank, CEO, Walpole

'Sacha Zackariya dives into the most important trends of the past decades influencing both travel and its effect on retailing around the globe. A must read!'
Georg Muzicant, CEO, Colliers International, Austria

'Today's travellers, especially in the luxury and ultra-luxury market, have new expectations. Hotels have had to adapt and it is good to learn more about those new travel patterns. Today, more than ever, relationship hospitality is key to success. It is human connections, personalized and intuitive experiences that will help differentiate and create desire for travellers. Sacha Zackariya has written a book which is timely, especially now we are in a period that is seeing an unprecedented recovery in travel after a very troubled pandemic period.'
Vincent Billiard, Managing Director, Hôtel de Crillon, Paris

Leading Travel and Tourism Retail

How businesses can sustainably capture
new profits in shopping tourism

Sacha Zackariya

KoganPage

First published in Great Britain and the United States in 2023 by Kogan Page Limited

2nd Floor, 45 Gee Street
London
EC1V 3RS
United Kingdom
www.koganpage.com

8 W 38th Street, Suite 902
New York, NY 10018
USA

4737/23 Ansari Road
Daryaganj
New Delhi 110002
India

Kogan Page books are printed on paper from sustainable forests.

ISBNs
Hardback   978 1 3986 0952 5
Paperback   978 1 3986 0950 1
Ebook   978 1 3986 0951 8

British Library Cataloguing-in-Publication Data
A CIP record for this book is available from the British Library.

Library of Congress Cataloging-in-Publication Data
Names: Zackariya, Sacha, author.
Title: Leading travel and tourism retail : how businesses can sustainably
  capture new profits in shopping tourism / Sacha Zackariya.
Description: 1 Edition. | New York, NY : Kogan Page Inc, [2023] | Includes
  bibliographical references and index.
Identifiers: LCCN 2022060930 (print) | LCCN 2022060931 (ebook) | ISBN
  9781398609501 (paperback) | ISBN 9781398609525 (hardback) | ISBN
  9781398609518 (ebook)
Subjects: LCSH: Retail trade. | Tourism. | Marketing.
Classification: LCC HF5429 .Z33 2023 (print) | LCC HF5429 (ebook) | DDC
  658.8/7–dc23/eng/20230105
LC record available at https://lccn.loc.gov/2022060930
LC ebook record available at https://lccn.loc.gov/2022060931

Typeset by Integra Software Services, Pondicherry
Print production managed by Jellyfish
Printed and bound by CPI Group (UK) Ltd, Croydon CR0 4YY

CONTENTS

FOREWORD

Over the next decade, the demands and expectations of travellers will change as they continue to seek unique and personalized experiences. The travel and tourism sector has been adapting, embracing new technologies and better ways to satisfy customer needs. Retail will need to adapt too. As traveller numbers grow globally, retail could be one of the biggest beneficiaries. This is an immense opportunity.

For over three decades, the World Travel and Tourism Council (WTTC) has been quantifying the economic impact of travel and tourism, highlighting the importance of the sector globally. Its annual research for 2022 covers 185 countries and economies, and 26 regions of the world. These insights reveal both the impact of the Covid-19 pandemic on the sector and its strong recovery so far.

Before the pandemic, travel and tourism was one of the world's biggest and fastest growing sectors. It accounted for one in four of all new jobs created and 10.3 per cent of global gross domestic product (GDP), with international traveller spending accounting for $1.8 trillion in 2019. It helped to reduce poverty and contributed to socio-economic development in some of the world's poorest countries. Opportunities opened up to get women, ethnic minorities and young people into the workforce. Retail tourism grew and flourished alongside it.

The pandemic halted this growth. Businesses were shuttered, borders were closed and planes were grounded. In 2020 alone, 62 million jobs were wiped out, the sector suffered losses of almost $4.9 trillion, and its contribution to GDP declined by 50.4 per cent year-on-year. The impact was felt across the sector, but small and medium-sized businesses, which make up 80 per cent of it, suffered most, with travel retailers heavily affected.

Almost three years on from the beginning of the pandemic the travel and tourism sector is rebuilding – 2021 saw the first green shoots of recovery with borders reopening and people ready to travel again. In that year alone, the sector's contribution to GDP increased by $1 trillion to reach $5.8 trillion, representing a 22 per cent increase year-on-year. Meanwhile, 18.2 million jobs were recovered.

Projections for growth over the next decade are strong. The sector is expected to grow, on average, by 5.8 per cent annually in that time, racing ahead of the global economy as a whole. By the end of 2032, the WTTC predicts the recovery to 2019 levels will be complete, with a further 126 million jobs created.

We, at the WTTC, believe that the best policy and planning decisions are made with reliable and accessible data. We will continue to work with the public and private sectors, providing data that enables leaders all over the world to rebuild the sector in an inclusive and sustainable manner.

As travel and tourism recovers and grows, retail will play an important role in it, creating jobs and contributing to socio-economic development across the world. In 2023, the WTTC will release a report on retail tourism together with Hong Kong Polytechnic University and 'The Bicester Collection', which will explore the many ways how.

The growth of travel and tourism over the next decade represents an opportunity for retail, which it must seize. For those looking for expertise on how this can be done, they should look no further than the pages of this book.

Julia Simpson
CEO and President of the World Travel and Tourism Council (WTTC)

LIST OF INTERVIEWS

Sir Tony Blair, former British Prime Minister, UK

Pierre-Hugues Schmit, Chief Commercial and Operations Officer at Vinci Airports Group, France

Ravi Thakran, Group Chairman of LVMH Asia, Singapore

Michael Ward, Managing Director of Harrods, UK

Jacques Stern, CEO of Global Blue, Switzerland

Vasiliki Petrou, CEO of Unilever Prestige, UK

Andrea d'Avack, President of the Chanel Foundation, France

Pallak Seth, CEO of PDS Apparel Manufacturing, India

Louis de Bourgoing, International Chairman of WHSmith, UK

Jose-Antonio Lasanta Luri, CEO of Prosegur Cash, Spain

Dan Cockerell, former Vice President of Disney's Magic Kingdom, United States

Tine Arentsen Willumsen, CEO of Above & Beyond Group, founder of The Diversity Council, Denmark

Paul Samuels, Executive Vice President of AEG Entertainment Group, UK

Hugo Brady, Vice President of AEG Entertainment Group, UK

Malik Fernando, Director of Dilmah Tea, MJF Hotels and Holdings, Sri Lanka

Jonathan Chippendale, CEO of Holition Technologies, UK

Ben Zifkin, President of Hubba, Canada

Desirée Bollier, Chair and Chief Merchant of Value Retail, UK

Stewart Wingate, CEO of London Gatwick Airport, UK

Craig Robins, founder and owner of Miami Design District Development, United States

Taylor Safford, President and CEO of Pier 39, San Francisco, United States

Frances O'Grady, Secretary General of the Trades Union Congress, UK

Christine Comaford, leadership guru (SmartTribes Institute) and leading author of *Power Your Tribe*, United States

Baroness Nicky Morgan, former Secretary of State for Digital, Culture, Media and Sport, UK

Professor Ian Woodward, INSEAD, Singapore

Professor Steve Jarding, Harvard University, United States

Lesley Batchelor OBE, Director General of the Institute for Export and International Trade, UK

Jason Holt, Chair of the Apprenticeship Ambassador Network, Chairman of Holts Group, UK

List of additional contributors

Julia Simpson, CEO and President of the World Travel and Tourism Council

Vicki Stern, Managing Director at Barclays Investment Bank, UK

Tina Beattie, co-founder of ESG One, former Global Head of Debt and Equity Research ABN AMRO Bank, the Netherlands

Andreas Keese, Director and General Manager Sacher Hotel, Austria

Thierry Lebeaux, Secretary General of ESTA, Belgium

Frederik Schreve, founder and Managing Director of Oktave, Switzerland

Dinesh Dhamija, founder of ebookers.com, UK

James Berkley, MD at Ellice Consulting Ltd and operating partner at Bosham Capital Advisers, UK

Stephen Bebis, former CEO of Brookstone, United States, and former CEO of Golftown, Canada

Massimiliano Alvisini, Senior Vice President and General Manager, Europe, CIS and Africa at Western Union, UK

Nick Davis, partner at Mishcon de Reya, UK

Introduction

Serving international customers is one of the most lucrative and yet one of the most demanding sides of retailing and hospitality. As they travel, international customers tend to value the experience of new things and are often willing to pay a premium for that. It brings in vast sums of much-needed foreign exchange revenues for wealthy and poorer economies alike. According to the US Travel Association, 75 million international visitors spend nearly $250 billion in the United States annually, benefitting American jobs across the aviation, travel and tourism sector, including hotels, restaurants, attractions, retailers and domestic air carriers (United States Department of State, 2022). For other countries the amounts they earn from international visitors can have an even bigger economic and well-being impact. It is, therefore, unsurprising that many businesses and communities worldwide are doing everything they can to attract tourists' money.

This book has been meticulously researched and contains insightful interviews with presidents and CEOs of global retailers, luxury brands, prominent landlords, politicians, union leaders and many more. It is designed to give you a 360-degree view and enable you to gain actionable ideas. I spent a great deal of time asking probing questions and teasing out information that until now has rarely, if ever, been shared with people outside their organizations. This book is designed to help foster an entrepreneurial spirit within your organization by highlighting opportunities for growth and how different areas are interconnected in ways you might not have realized.

While serving international customers has for many decades been intensely profitable, it is highly complex, and few truly excel in this area. This has been very good for the organizations that have adapted themselves to meeting the needs of people who are effectively time-poor but cash-rich. However, a lack of knowledge of international shoppers and the ecosystem that serves them has served as barriers to entry for brands.

Luckily you don't need to be located in Paris, New York or Tokyo to benefit from international shoppers. Many big and small brands make huge profits in small towns and cities around the world where there is less competition but still good infrastructure and enticing experiences to lure in tourist shoppers.

Covid-19 came as a terrible shock. Globally the travel and tourism sector generated $9.8 trillion in 2019, with approximately 1.5 billion people travelling (WTTC, 2022). Suddenly many of the gleaming new shopping malls, event venues, airports and airlines had almost no customers. I started writing pre-Covid the chapter on disaster preparedness for this book. I based it on my experiences helping guide our global group through the impacts of 9/11, the Icelandic ash cloud, the Christchurch earthquake, and various regional and global recessions. People just never imagined anything so devastating to the world economy as a two-year interruption to international travel.

Yet, now travel and tourism are back with a vengeance! Pent-up demand and the desire to travel and spend means enormous rewards for those who can make the most of the opportunities. It means opening new outlets, hiring and training new staff, encouraging bankers and investors, working with government officials, and adapting to a post-Covid world.

Spending-wise, the media said cash is dead due to the pandemic (Dickler, 2021). The same was said of retail. Newspapers said that in the future we would all shop from the comfort of our homes, no longer shake hands, no longer want to meet up or travel, but experience things virtually through 3D headsets. They were wrong. Paying by cash locally may have dropped as people opt to pay with their phones or plastic, but we have seen across the globe that cash as travel money has increased in demand. This includes countries such as Sweden and throughout the UK, which are considered leaders in cashless payments for local transactions (England, 2022). Yet people who seem to like the thrill of travel – and the uncertainty that comes with it – often at the same time seek the certainty, safety and anonymity of cash. No one wants to be stranded without some cash in their wallet. No one wants to fall victim to cyber theft and online viruses when they have just managed to dodge real viruses. This is why some of the biggest travel-cash markets are Sweden and the UK, with market research showing that 67 per cent of people in the UK take their spending money abroad in cash (Mintel, 2022).

What does that mean for retailers wanting to attract international shoppers? First, make sure your retail units are located near a prominent, well-run currency exchange branch. Tourists with foreign cash in their pockets cannot use it unless they exchange it for the local currency. Of course, they will then want to spend it. Our data shows they typically spend more than half of the cash within 200 metres of our currency exchange branches.

So make sure you accept cash! Don't be fooled into thinking cashless payments will make you richer. All you are doing is denying yourself the ability to make a sale! Why do tourists love cash so much? This can be for privacy reasons, identity theft or card-cloning concerns. Or because they often feel they can get a better price paying in cash – retailers save on credit-card fees and get paid immediately rather than having to wait several days, or worse, not getting paid at all if the transaction is disputed.

Quick disclaimer here, together with my parents, Bette and Zacky, I co-founded ChangeGroup and built it into the world's third largest foreign exchange company. My team and I travel the world seeking new locations for branches and ATMs in shopping malls, airports, train stations, city shopping streets, outlet malls, museums, and major festivals and event spaces. Together as a family, we have owned a range of retail businesses with different brands in areas such as fashion accessories, high-class jewellery, souvenir shops, and waffle and gelato shops in prime locations in various countries, which brings a lot of challenges but a great deal of insight as well. I get to see who is travelling, where they are going, how much they are spending, and where they are spending it. And yes, that means I see a lot of cash being exchanged.

Pre-Covid, the travel and tourism industry employed 10.3 per cent of the global population and generated one in four of every new job (WTTC, 2022). The near-total collapse in travel caused vast numbers of retail, hospitality and attraction companies to close, and hundreds of millions of people lost their jobs. I say lost jobs because only a very small proportion of countries offered furlough, and, even then, many companies could not afford to enact it given the co-payments required. Many had to refinance in order to survive, ChangeGroup included (Europapress, 2022). We now have a fantastic majority owner called Prosegur Cash, which is listed on the Madrid stock exchange and employs 45,000 people. It is also part of a wider group employing 160,000 people and generating annual revenues of around $4 billion (Ernst & Young, 2022). This brings us unparalleled financial strength, technology, people and resources to make use of the new opportunities.

Now that travel is back, I have this question for you. How will you also profit from all of the opportunities presented by the growth in international travel?

Coming out of the pandemic highlighted the interconnectedness of retailers, hospitality and transport. At first, shops were allowed to open but food and beverage (F&B) was not (except for takeaway). The result was most shoppers stayed away from city centres, preferring to stay closer to home rather than have a bad experience and face the problems of poor transportation to get to a shopping destination. All of this was painful and did not make customers want to linger and browse but rather shop and get out.

As if I did not have enough to do, during the pandemic I became chairperson of YPO Greater London. YPO has more than 30,000 chief executives across 142 countries with their companies producing $9 trillion in annual earnings (Ibaraki, 2021). I was thus hearing from and supporting CEOs with businesses around the world, many of whom were severely impacted by the pandemic, but it was good to see that some CEOs in retail were actually benefitting from it.

So, as the world moves on, we will also look at complex issues such as the impact of Brexit. What started out with great optimism now has many British people questioning 'What are the benefits of Brexit to me?' Previously manufacturers were set up in the UK to benefit from being located in the only English-speaking nation in the EU. From there they could access most of the Continent tariff-free. Now that is no longer true, many brands have had to look at where to relocate for cost and ease of access. Meanwhile, retailers and manufacturers in the UK do not have enough skilled and motivated staff to work the available shifts because of a lack of investment in education, apprenticeships and because of immigration controls. Like so many other companies, we have had to increase our inventories, at a cost of millions, to deal with the long EU customs delays and paperwork when transporting goods across borders with the UK.

Perhaps the most damaging item for international travellers thinking of coming to the UK has been the removal of VAT sales tax refund, which was pushed through at the same time as Brexit (Llewellyn, 2020). Its return is key to attracting back the billions of pounds spent by international visitors who have recently shifted their retail purchases to other cities such as Paris, Milan and Madrid. Importantly though, any new scheme must provide cash refunds (and not be just digital as has been proposed) because many long-haul travellers both distrust and also need to avoid refunds to credit cards or to bank accounts in their home countries.

All the above points to the need to effectively engage with and ethically lobby politicians to ensure they understand the issues affecting their constituents' jobs and livelihoods. The good news is that you can do this, and we will discuss how.

Following the war in Ukraine, the energy and fuel crisis has hit countries and consumers globally. But even before this, countries like Sri Lanka were experiencing civil unrest and devastation to their tourism-related economies because of economic mismanagement and the inability to pay for essential imports such as petrol. China has stepped in and purchased a lot of their debts. As they have done in many emerging countries with strategic locations or resources, China now has a significant influence in the country (Etsuyo, 2022). These geopolitical considerations are important. I, for one, visited Ukraine looking to open branches in Kyiv in the years prior to the war. We have significant educational and charitable operations in Sri Lanka. Chinese tourist shoppers represent a key demographic for many retailers. You simply cannot escape geopolitics in today's world.

Wouldn't it be nice if we could just be friends? Actually, that is one of my passions. I feel travel and tourism brings people together. It allows cultural understanding, it enables a transfer of wealth between rich and poor nations, and hopefully, just hopefully, enables more peace in the world.

Not to be outdone, sustainability is very much a key feature of this book. Products and services can command higher premiums if they can show additional consumer benefits, particularly to international travellers who are already worried about their environmental footprint. Some of the world's biggest brands are finding out the hard way that not considering this can be terribly destructive to profits and shareholder value. This, and the important subject of diversity, are covered here not just for appearance sake but because it is fundamentally good business sense. Great people, no matter their race, colour, creed, gender or any other separating characteristic, are simply that, great people. And great people, those with passion, energy, diverse problem-solving skills, and drive to succeed, are what I want in my business. How about you?

Can I hope you might pass on what you learn here to people who can strengthen your business? Can I hope it might give ideas on motivating your employees, encouraging new customers, invigorating your bankers and providing new ideas to your politicians? Yes, absolutely, because just maybe, by working together, you can achieve improved results for you, your community and even further.

References

Dickler, J (2021) Another consequence of Covid: a world without cash, *CNBC*, 29 January, www.cnbc.com/2021/01/29/consumers-abandon-cash-altogether-because-of-covid.html (archived at https://perma.cc/YNQ8-Q96K)

England, J (2022) Top six digital payments countries about to go cashless, *FinTech Magazine*, London, 24 May

Ernst & Young (2022) Consolidated annual accounts audited by Ernst& Young on Prosegur Compania de Seguridad S.A. and Subsidiaries for the year ended 31 December 2022, www.prosegur.com/dam/jcr:843276ef-0dc9-4b88-8b8e-c6b01142fead/Cons%20%202021.pdf (archived at https://perma.cc/LTX2-VGK8)

Etsuyo, A (2022) Sri Lanka's economic crisis: a Chinese debt trap?, *Nippon.com*, www.nippon.com/en/in-depth/d00840/ (archived at https://perma.cc/J8LU-HFZG)

Europapress (2022), Prosegur cash adquiere ChangeGroup para liderar el comercio minorista de cambio de moneda, *msn.com*, www.msn.com/es-es/dinero/empresa/prosegur-cash-adquiere-changegroup-para-liderar-el-comercio-minorista-de-cambio-de-moneda/ar-AA12MB34?ocid=ems.display.welcomeexperience (archived at https://perma.cc/2XAV-DUCD)

Ibaraki, S (2021) YPO GIIN partnership – nearly $500 trillion global wealth prioritizing impact in 2021?, *Forbes.com*, www.forbes.com/sites/stephenibaraki/2021/08/05/ypo-giin-partnership---nearly-500-trillion-global-wealth-prioritizing-impact-in-2021/?sh=63a187701fce (archived at https://perma.cc/5FTJ-T8JX)

Llewellyn, T (2020) When Boris comes to his senses on tax-free shopping, it might be too late for the watch retail industry, *The Telegraph*, www.telegraph.co.uk/luxury/watches/boris-comes-senses-tax-free-shopping-might-late-watch-retail/ (archived at https://perma.cc/WRY7-6BRB)

Mintel (2022) *Mintel Travel Cash Report 2022*, Mintel Group Ltd, London

United States Department of State (2022) Civil Air Transport Agreements, www.state.gov/civil-air-transport-agreements#:~:text=According%20to%20the%20U.S.%20Travel,retailers%2C%20and%20domestic%20air%20carriers (archived at https://perma.cc/MSW7-EKTA)

World Travel and Tourism Council (2022) Travel and Tourism Economic Impact 2022, World Travel and Tourism Council, London

1

Growing out of the pandemic

I was sitting in a hotel in early January 2020, evaluating the reports on a major mergers and acquisitions (M&A) deal to acquire one of my competitors for several tens of millions of US dollars. Something just didn't feel right about their current retail sales numbers. So even though I had already spent almost $1 million on due diligence and professional fees, and against the advice of many people, I decided we had to walk away.

With the benefit of hindsight, I am so glad that we did. Why? Because in March 2020, as my co-founder Bette and I watched CNN from Seville, Spain, where we had just opened a brand new branch, we assumed the Covid-19 lockdown was temporary. We thought this would be like SARS or 9/11. We never believed it would go on for more than two years and devastate so many industries. But, in life, timing is everything. So, although I did not get it all correct, I did at least on this M&A.

Retailers and hospitality big and small, sporting and concert events venues, attractions, airlines, airports and hotels were forced to close almost all operations for much of the pandemic. Working from home (WFH) was not an option. The damage caused to supply chains and related businesses by rolling waves of lockdowns, followed by brief periods of partial openings of the economy, was huge. So in the middle of the pandemic I thought I should interview someone who understands the challenges of leadership in growth periods as well as in crises, former British Prime Minister Tony Blair.

CONVERSATION WITH

Sir Tony Blair is one of the longest-ever serving British prime ministers, who was in office from 1997 to 2007 during a period of many challenges, including 9/11 and SARS. His influential 'Tony Blair Institute for Global Change' was founded in 2016. He is also an adviser to governments worldwide.

Sacha: From a prime minister's perspective, what advice do you have for leaders during a serious crisis? How do you stay level-headed as a leader and make good decisions when there are so many priorities and conflicting opinions?

Sir Tony: In a crisis, such as with Covid-19 or an international financial crisis, which is overwhelming all normal business, and which has huge complexity attached to it, the following is important. The leader has to have his or her head around the detail. Not necessarily so as to give the right answers, but to ask the right questions. Second, the leader has to take the best available advice, scientific and expert, and scour the world for it. Third, divide up the key challenges and put the best people in charge of meeting them. Almost always, the challenges are around logistics; not so much knowing what to do, as how to get it done. Bring in the best brains, who will often be business people – for example people who have run complicated supply chains, or procurement processes. People who take decisions and act fast.

Sacha: Travel and tourism represent 10 per cent of global GDP and were among the first sectors to be hit by Covid-19. In crises, how can governments provide effective help to businesses that really need it most, yet avoid wasting resources?

Sir Tony: Supporting business is crucial at a time like this and there is no easy formula. But you are aiming to keep as much business as possible afloat until normality returns. Each country has their own legislative and cultural issues to examine, as societies around the world increasingly depend on travel and tourism. In an ideal scenario, governments would co-ordinate all their responses, but this is not always possible.

Sacha: Retail staff, from food to essential items, are at the forefront of dealing day-to-day with the public and keeping goods and supply chains running. They cannot just work from home. Do you think they are getting recognized enough?

Sir Tony: Retail staff often do not get the recognition they deserve at the best of times. Retailers are crucial to the tourism economy and retailers were among the ones first hit as international tourism slowed down. At a crisis time like this, retail staff and businesses are vital and also to a degree at risk, if mixing with members of the public.

Sacha: How should companies consider their corporate social responsibilities during crises, especially when they need to reduce opening hours, staffing levels and their costs in order to stay solvent?

Sir Tony: Every company should be thinking how they can contribute. Even if their own business is temporarily suspended, there may be things in the local community or nationally where they can use their experience and expertise. Of course their primary focus will be staying solvent and able to employ their people, but even if it is simply in showing concern for their staff, they can help.

Sacha: As prime minister you championed education and multiculturalism and were responsible for Ireland's landmark Good Friday peace agreement. How can tourism help improve peace and understanding among the people of the world long-term?

Sir Tony: Travel and tourism retail is a vital part of creating a more peaceful as well as prosperous world. When we travel our eyes and our minds are opened; we experience new people and cultures; we learn how others live and we see how humanity has so many ties – economic, social and spiritual – that bind us together. Tourism improves understanding and understanding improves the chances of peace and co-existence.

Certainly, the words of Sir Tony speak to the heart of the challenges governments and businesses were facing as a result of Covid-19. The impact was immediate for our company, ChangeGroup, with 126 currency exchange retail stores, hundreds of ATMs and operations in 11 countries and 37 cities around the world. No one was travelling, and staff and management did not know what to do. We went from a $10 million forecasted EBITDA (earnings before interest, taxes, depreciation and amortization) to a projected loss of triple that amount. I had been challenged to always think of potential 'Black Swan' events, but soon it became apparent that this was on a totally different dimension.

With senior management and support staff at home, we decided to close our international HQ immediately and negotiated out of the property rental contract by making a payment. We contacted all our 100+ landlords and tried to get out of marginal branches, aiming to keep only our best ones. Unfortunately, we permanently closed half our branches at huge expense since many landlords refused to let us out of contracts and wanted us to pay the full rent. We also deactivated most of our ATMs. All of this took much time and effort. I even personally gave training sessions for our senior management to assist them in negotiating the many agreements that we now needed to change or exit.

Of course, almost all retailers had to do this. CEO Dag Rasmussen of the giant travel retail group Lagardère (with 4,800 stores in 42 countries) said this to the press about his airport contracts and minimum rents:

> All rents should be variable this year, and all our teams are working on this plan with each and every landlord. The idea is that minimum annual guarantees (MAGs) are there to protect landlords against bad operators. It is not supposed to be life insurance for whatever happens. It is our position that MAGs cannot apply in this situation (Davitt, 2020).

Redundancies – this was painful. Government furlough schemes to subsidize wages were simply unavailable to cover 100 per cent of costs during the global travel restrictions, which lasted more than two years in many countries. This meant we had to say goodbye to many great people, some of whom had been with us for 10 years, 20, or even longer. Cut once and cut deep is often the advice. But we tried to hold on to as many people as we could initially, only to find successive lockdowns meant this was not viable. With each new lockdown or extended travel restriction, we had to make more cuts to the workforce.

Unfortunately, it was not good that the modelling and statistics coming out of government agencies were so inaccurate throughout the pandemic. At the start of Covid-19 in early 2020, this level of inaccuracy was understandable. However, what was unacceptable was the inaccuracy at the end of 2021, where official government advisers claimed that, despite vaccinations, we would face deaths of anything from 600 to 6,000 a day in the UK alone. This caused panic, and data from South Africa was already available to show that the figures would be wrong. The reality was a peak of 262 deaths per day reported in England, and the Office of National Statistics indicated that a potentially large proportion of these were those who died from other causes but also happened to have Covid-19. Many people said that one death is a death too many. The problem is that if you just looked at Covid-19 deaths that would be one thing, but not enough people considered the vast number of deaths and illnesses caused by other factors due to lockdown. This includes other diseases that did not get properly diagnosed or treated, such as cancer, but also malnutrition and the mental effects of people unable to properly earn a living both in the West and around the world. Lockdowns in Sri Lanka, India or Brazil had a more devastating impact on people than in metropolitan centres such as London, Paris or New York. 'Bring trade, not aid' was often said by charities and governments.

But during the pandemic so much international trade and travel stopped that the consequences will take years to recover from.

Many companies in the hospitality sector stepped up to help. Restaurateur and club owner Richard Caring's foundation served over 1 million meals to hospital staff and the needy (Ridley and Nicholls, 2020). Alexander Lebedev, the Russian owner of the UK's *Evening Standard* and *Independent* newspapers, launched the Help the Hungry campaign, which served 4.3 million meals (Cohen, 2020). However, internationally, both foreign charitable aid and the all-important multi-billions in remittances from overseas workers in the travel and tourism industry quickly fell.

I found that as devastating as it was to companies like ours in the travel and tourism sector, it was important to be honest and sincere. I felt that even if I could not tell our staff more at the time, we would be open about that too. Video films of me speaking directly to our staff and memos, of course, only went so far. Sometimes I had to make trips to see key bankers and landlords whose decision to support us or not would have material consequences. I kept feeling the need to communicate, communicate, communicate, to staff, elected bodies, trade associations, lawyers, bankers, wholesalers, and of course, to my fellow shareholders as well as to my loved ones.

Early in the pandemic, I had Covid-19 for seven days. I was 49 and relatively fit, so not likely to be in any danger. Others were, of course, not so lucky. Home schooling took its toll on the family. My wife had to step up as teacher, home carer and become my executive assistant and head of corporate communications, preparing all my many presentations. I had to manage my responsibilities as head of an education charity in Sri Lanka, which I had founded in 1998 but had to cease operations (after paying out all existing scholars to meet all our commitments). At almost the same time as Covid-19 hit, I became chairperson of YPO Greater London. YPO has more than 30,000 chief executives across 142 countries with their companies producing $9 trillion in annual earnings (Ibaraki, 2021). I used this to present the UK positively as it went through Brexit, bringing together senior UK politicians and showing large corporations worldwide that the UK was still a safe place to do business. Multi-tasking was definitely one word to describe what was going on then.

The rhetoric about support from government press announcements did not always match reality. We were forced to lobby to get support, and then when that failed we had to sue governments, from Sweden to Austria. Luckily we were successful in many cases; otherwise, I would not be here writing this chapter! Some countries were terrific with their support, such as Finland and Denmark. Others, such as in the UK, where we received no grants or loans despite asking and lobbying, decidedly less so. I am fine paying taxes if we get benefits when we need them, and in Finland's case, I cannot thank them enough.

Ninety per cent of the time I have found industry associations to be talking shops but where little gets done. In a crisis, governments quickly enact legislation that cannot be properly thought through and, yet, can have a major impact on your business. Normally, this can range from changing product standards to border controls and taxation. At those times, effective lobbying is vital to ensure that your employees and businesses are subject to the same level playing field as your competitors so that you can all survive. I found this particularly the case during the pandemic. Some industry sectors were better than others in making sure their needs were taken care of with grants and subsidies.

Sometimes I felt frustrated. One of my Spanish headquartered competitors lobbied the government successfully for a special bailout of €45 million to use locally and globally – of course, well done to them for very effective lobbying. Our company applied for and received no funding from the Spanish government despite having many similar shops and employing more than 100 people there. Some members of the press questioned how taxpayer funds were being used (El Norte de Castilla, 2022).

Some companies did unscrupulous things, of course. Court filings showed how Travelex Banknotes Ltd, part of the global Bureau de Change company, took $40 million and then a little while later took another $20 million from the same bank customer. Rather than complete the currency transaction, they kept the money and used it for themselves. Travelex later admitted wrongdoing in the UK courts but said they would not be delivering the banknotes or making a refund because Travelex was in serious financial difficulty. They were eventually forced to settle (Barton, 2020). Even though the brand has a number of issues, I did buy their website url, travelex.fr, from the bankruptcy administrator in Paris.

Cash might be king in a crisis, but cash use domestically dropped during Covid-19. Unfounded hysteria was used to promote the use of contactless payments by the fintech and banking industry, which had much to gain from the customer data and retailer fees they obtained. Indeed, card processing fees charged to retailers in the UK rose by 400 per cent in 2021, costing retailers an extra £150 million per year (BRC, 2021). Funnily enough, throughout

Covid-19, and even more so today, our own premium waffle, gelato and coffee outlet at Marble Arch in London still has more than 45 per cent cash payments. We do thousands of weekly transactions from that location – just a few hundred metres from where a Royal Parks food outlet refused to accept bank notes!

While we had a very large cash reserve and strong balance sheet going into the pandemic, ChangeGroup did need to find funding to grow again and make use of the many opportunities available and the lack of competition. As people started to travel, the demand for travel money rose dramatically because people wanted both security and privacy and the protection of cash when they travelled on leisure trips. After many negotiations, we were fortunate enough that Prosegur Cash, part of a group that employs more than 160,000 people globally, has taken a majority stake in the business and boosted our balance sheet in unimaginable ways. The deal completed in July 2022 gives us access to talented management, technology and know-how, as well as financial resources that are unmatched anywhere in the industry.

Like many retailers, we have observed how there has been a dramatic change as streets that had boarded-up shop windows are now bustling again with customers. Rent levels that once were at rock bottom during the pandemic have risen dramatically once more, and commercial real estate agents cannot find the prime spaces they once were almost trying to give away.

Importantly, I noticed that when shops were allowed to open but bars, cafes and restaurants were not, there seemed to me to be a huge accentuation of the lack of a 'fun experience' associated with shopping. It was no longer a day out but a mission to go and get a predetermined item and get back home. You could not linger, browse and explore. You could not sip a coffee and recharge yourself in a cafe. This caused shops that were located near people's homes in the suburbs to have a dramatic rise in customers. But city centres had far less allure. This speaks volumes to the need to integrate our thinking of working together with landlords and local governments to create excitement once again in retail.

Coming out of the crisis, the interesting thing is how to grow as a retailer and what to focus on. Here is an opportunity to learn from a major landlord in travel and tourism, one that many businesses might aspire to work with.

CONVERSATION WITH
*Pierre-Hugues Schmit, Chief Commercial and Operations Officer at Vinci
Airports, is the world's largest private airport operator. Based in Paris, he is
responsible for their 50+ airports, including London Gatwick, Lisbon Airport
and airports from Latin America to Japan.*

Sacha: Coming out of Covid-19, how do you see air passenger numbers growing
in the next five years across the 50+ airports you own globally?

Pierre-Hugues: The outlook is quite positive over the coming years. We saw per
passenger (pax) numbers quickly bounce back in the Americas (even above
2019 in 2022), a little slower in Europe, while Asia is taking longer. There
clearly is strong appetite for travel for the coming years. People who used to
travel are back; and new passengers who were previously not flying continue
to shift to aviation. This is above the modelling we had, where we originally
expected four years to get to recovery. There are of course concerns about the
forward cost of the flights due to fuel costs and inflationary pressures. But
two segments of the markets have shown very robust demand: the visit
friends and relatives (VFR) and tourism. People like to travel to see their
families and friends, they like to visit places and they are clearly willing to
invest money for travel.

Sacha: How important is the retail offerings to your airports and their
profitability?

Pierre-Hugues: Retail is important in two ways. The passenger experience – part
of the fun of travel is not only the destination but also the feeling that
consumers will visit airport stores, have fun, see new products that might not
be easily available elsewhere. It might not always be cheap but it is about fun,
convenience, the level of experience – it is not just transactional. As an
ordinary consumer you can see products that only a very exclusive
department store would have. Now, from an airport's profit and loss (P&L)
perspective, retail represents half of all non-aeronautical revenue, so around
20–25 per cent of total revenues. In some airports the travel retail can have
much higher value than this, such as where there are a lot of Chinese tourists,
e.g. Cambodia.

Sacha: Some of our readers will be new to airport retail tenders. Why do airports
ask retailers for a very large minimum annual guaranteed (MAG) rent, and
how do you see this changing?

Pierre-Hugues: We have seen that when there is a high MAG the retailer just
tries to reduce costs to pay the MAG and lacks interest to enhance the

experiences for the customers. So we already started in 2020 to improve things for retailers and we accelerated this during the Covid-19 pandemic. Now we do rental contracts with MAG per airport passenger, so there is more risk on us to deliver the pax, which is fair. However, we expect a higher return per pax as a result, and this seems to work. We have also benefitted from our joint ventures (JVs) with Lagadère in Lyon Airport and with Aer Rianta International in Portugal. It is not possible to do this for all operations, but moving forward we expect more commitment from the retail operators, we want to see exciting modern shops with real customer engagement. We want to look at the top line, the value generated not just the MAG. Being in a JV is helping us understand this even more. We have relationships with all the big companies and so this helps us in the analysis of the tenders. Today we have both qualitative and quantitative measures, MAG is just one.

Sacha: What synergies exist by Vinci owning so many airports? For example, when you acquire new airports, how do you improve them and make a better return than previous owners?

Pierre-Hugues: Well, that is the magic sauce. There are a couple of elements that Vinci does better in our 50+ airports. We are opportunistic in our bids, we identify value, we stick to what we know we can deliver when bidding. We benefit from significant experience gathered over two decades and 50+ airports under management. This gives us room to manage them well. We believe we have better business to business (B2B) relationships with airlines, retailers and other suppliers to get a win-win. We believe in putting the money where it matters, in finding good balance in our B2B relationships and in supporting value generation for the ecosystem. Our approach allows the airlines and retailers to be in a more risk-sharing relationship. Then there is the construction or operating costs, and we have the experience to invest money where it makes a difference and not waste money on gold-plated aspects where it does not make a difference. Of course we are always compliant with safety, security, environment and all other regulations. And for the territories we serve, we are committed to enhance the connectivity.

Sacha: Do you see good opportunities to add more airports to Vinci Group? If so, in which regions and why?

Pierre-Hugues: We see many opportunities to grow, our shareholders have given us support to do so. This is why in Mexico, Cape Verde and other locations we have now won. We have even taken on quite small airports like Annecy in the French Alps as well as the big ones like Gatwick. Many parts of the world have potential as long as there are the right conditions – economic, legal and political conditions – for the long term. Having good political understanding is vital as we often want to also expand the size of the infrastructure and this takes communities and politicians as well as businesses coming together.

Sacha: What important developments do you see in the travel and tourism retail space?

Pierre-Hugues: Before Covid-19 there were discussions on how to make brands and airports more interesting. Now post-Covid, things have not changed enough – Dufry, Lagadère, DFS, Heinemann are still running the show. We want to open our territories to more brands, to switch from transactional to more engaging. We thought the pandemic would have enabled this but it is absent, the big companies stay in their safe space. If you were a younger brand, good luck trying to get a shelf space in their airport stores. They are too risk averse. You need to show them great success in the high street or online before the big retailers will talk to you. If airports are one of the key places where customers really engage physically as opposed to being online, then travel and tourism retail needs to reinvent itself. My vision at Vinci is to open our airports to be more blended between F&B and retail and to keep innovating the experience, be more than a gateway between curbside and the aircraft.

INTRODUCTION AND GROWING OUT OF THE PANDEMIC

- 1.5 billion people travelled annually pre-pandemic, spending more than $9 trillion.
- In a crisis, make sure you use the best available people who can act fast.
- Even if your contracts do not allow renegotiation, in major crises it is in everyone's interest to find solutions.
- Analyse and challenge statistics carefully, many governmental bodies and international consultancies made much more pessimistic forecasts going into and coming out of the pandemic than was the reality.
- Ensure your competitors do not obtain benefits that you cannot have.
- Trade associations are very important organizations in crises for ensuring your industry sector is properly represented and receives appropriate legislative and financial assistance.

- There is a very strong demand for travel with great opportunities for retailers and hospitality. To really rejuvenate the sector requires businesses, financiers, local communities and politicians to work together.

- Airports and major landlords want innovation in the retail space with new products and services and to create new exciting experiences for customers.

- It is possible to negotiate property contracts where the landlord or airport is responsible for the number of people coming to the location; however, they expect this risk sharing to result in higher payments per customer.

References

Barton, L (2020) Travelex threatened with raid over £48m Congo bank bill, *Telegraph*, July, www.telegraph.co.uk/business/2020/07/04/travelex-threatened-collapse-48m-congo-bank-bill/ (archived at https://perma.cc/G6DP-AB3E)

BRC (2021) Card costs soar £150 million a year, *British Retail Consortium and CMSP*, brc.org.uk/news/corporate-affairs/card-costs-soar-150-million-a-year/ (archived at https://perma.cc/FE3G-8CDE)

Cohen, D (2020) Food for London now, *Evening Standard*, https://www.standard.co.uk/news/foodforlondon/7-million-raised-4-million-meals-delivered-a4473926.html (archived at https://perma.cc/FT5J-QR4X)

Davitt, D (2020), Lagardère travel retail targets variable-only rents for the rest of 2020, *The Moodie Davitt Report*, www.moodiedavittreport.com/lagardere-travel-retail-targets-variable-only-rents-for-rest-of-2020/ (archived at https://perma.cc/H3WS-XV8F)

El Norte de Castilla (2022) The CEO of Global Exchange clarifies that the support of the SEPI of 45 million is a loan with repayment, *El Norte de Castilla*, www.elnortedecastilla.es/salamanca/global-exchange-aclara-20220218191050-nt.html (archived at https://perma.cc/86ZH-7JVY)

Ibaraki, S (2021) YPO GIIN partnership – nearly $500 trillion global wealth prioritizing impact in 2021?, *Forbes*, www.forbes.com/sites/stephenibaraki/2021/08/05/ypo-giin-partnership---nearly-500-trillion-global-wealth-prioritizing-impact-in-2021/?sh=63a187701fce (archived at https://perma.cc/T4X5-85XY)

Ridley, K and Nicholls, P (2020) Private clubs in London cater to nurses and needy during pandemic, *Reuters*, https://www.reuters.com/article/us-health-coronavirus-london-clubs-idUSKBN22P1JY (archived at https://perma.cc/W9PX-DUAD)

2

Let's talk luxury

Luxury is in. Throughout the conversations I have had in recent years with leaders of major fashion labels and luxury hotels, there has been an unprecedented level of consumption of luxury brands' top products and, at the same time, a demonstrable increase in demand for suites and larger rooms in five-star hotels. So something is afoot, and it already started more than several years ago.

One of the undisputed leading influencers in retailing to international high-end tourist shoppers is the French multi-brand conglomerate LVMH. It owns brands such as Louis Vuitton, Dior, Moët & Chandon champagne, Tiffany & Co, Sephora retailing and many more (Davis, 2020). Here, LVMH Asia Group Chairman Ravi Thakran provides some fascinating insights.

CONVERSATION WITH
Ravi Thakran is Group Chairman of LVMH Asia, part of the family-owned LVMH Group with over 75 brands, revenues in 2021 of over €64 billion and 175,000 employees globally.

Sacha: LVMH is one of the great leaders in luxury retailing that also manages to sell some products in huge volumes. In your opinion, what are the best retail concepts you are seeing now, be that in Asia or elsewhere?

Ravi: Retailers are going through a major renaissance globally. If you look at the new Apple store in Singapore, I think it will be one of the best stores, selling technology products, in the world. As an example, there is Gentle Monster in Korea, which is a sunglass brand. I saw their store myself just recently. I've seen their stores in LA, New York and in other places. Incredibly cutting edge. It's something that we haven't seen much of. I would say that brands like

Louis Vuitton have been continuously transforming themselves, and that is why they are moving far faster than anyone else in luxury retail. But I would also say that in retail it doesn't have to be a leading brand. I was at Amazon Go in Seattle. It was absolutely revolutionary. I generally believe that soon we will start seeing stores without having a single person to manage them. All of this is certainly going to change quite a lot. Then at the other end of the spectrum there are stores that provide an experience. You can see it in beauty retail, people are a lot more excited about a mirror that can talk to the person and show them how they would look with a particular lipstick or make-up. In Beijing there are places that take all your body measurements through 60 cameras and within a minute, using artificial intelligence (AI), they show you which shirts or suits would be better for you, based on your body type and skin colour.

Sacha: Then what happens?

Ravi: You could order that outfit on the screen and then you can get a tailor-made suit delivered to you in only 72 hours. A lot has been talked about regarding this kind of technology but it has not seen much connection except in some of these places.

Sacha: How do you feel LVMH's approach to serving international travellers differs from how LVMH might serve local customers?

Ravi: Well, LVMH is going through the first three decades of its existence, so many people do not know that we are a very young holding company. We have always taken a very lead approach to retail, which is 'Keep it a little rare'. We always leave some demand out there for our products to keep up that desirability. So a lot of people see Louis Vuitton since we are present across all major cities of the world; however, we are the least distributed brand of all these brands. We have only 450 stores, whereas other luxury brands have presence in 10,000 points of distribution. Keep it rare. Second, the store has to be a place that provides an experience. If it only provides a product, e-commerce will eventually fairly easily replace that. But we are focusing on creating a complete brand experience and evolving very fast in that. Third, when it comes to e-commerce, everyone is looking for the next spot to jump on; we believe that providing a great customer experience on e-commerce is not so easy, so we have been slower at it. But we don't want just any e-commerce platform to represent our brand and experience; we are entering it using highly qualitative techniques, so we are getting into the world of the internet but in our own way, a unique way, and a very qualitative way.

Sacha: Who does LVMH consider its target customer? Is it purely the wealthy, or is it a mix?

Ravi: Our current customers are always a mix of people throughout, so our brands are for 'aspirational people', who might come in and buy a wallet or a belt but they really get recruited into the brand experience, and they aspire one day to have a bag or whatever. So our customers are a mix of aspirational people as well as successful people. They are all part of our brand journey. We do have a gamble, such as the TAG Heuer watch brand. It is considered a luxury brand, but it is a graduation watch in the United States and many other countries. When you graduate, your parents will typically buy you a serious watch and want to keep a price point for that purpose, although that is really our lowest price point watch.

Sacha: How many brands do you have within the LVMH portfolio?

Ravi: We have 72 brands. We have retail from Dior, FENTY, Loewe, Loro Piana, Bulgari, Sephora and Tiffany's – it's a fairly large plate.

Sacha: And you run the whole of the business for Asia?

Ravi: Yes, the bulk of Asia Pacific.

Sacha: That's really impressive. And what do you find most frustrating when dealing with landlords?

Ravi: Well, OK, for us, I can say that our brands are very powerful, and we typically have bargaining power. When a new mall comes up, mall owners always want to bring in the top brands first, so that they can attract everyone else to follow. What these top brands get in return is that they get the choice of location and much better terms for renting. So most of our locations around the world are, I think, in a privileged position. However, I think with landlords, the big issue sometimes is the complexity of terms. In Europe particularly, the whole practice of having to put in large 'key money' sums to buy out incumbent tenants, all these things can make it very complicated. In some countries it can be a phenomenal barrier for new brands to come up, which is not good for the industry. Industry needs a good penetration of innovation, but given the whole block that some developers have in major cities they can make it very difficult for younger brands to survive, never mind to thrive.

Sacha: How does LVMH attract international shoppers as opposed to locals? Is there a different strategy?

Ravi: There is a mix of strategies. First of all, as you can imagine, with 72 brands there is no one group strategy and we allow each brand to have its own strategy and at times two brands will have a very different rate of growth.

However, some broad messages on that are that we certainly serve travel customers, particularly in Asia, through airports, which have become a leading retail arena. In the past, airport retail basically meant tobacco, textiles and a bit of beauty, but now, particularly in Asian cities, the airport is often the number one retail location in that city. If we take Dubai, if we take Seoul or Bangkok, in all of these cities the airport is the number one mall, and every mall in the city is a shade of that. The Dubai Mall is the number one mall in the world, but still it is below the whole of Dubai airport, so travel retail – that's retail at airports – is huge in Asia. Western cities are very different. Particularly in the United States you can see there are few airports that have quality retail. And now, the second part is, of course, also in Europe. Asian people take advantage of better pricing there and also they can receive better perks when shopping there, which is a major attraction to shopping when they travel.

Second, even though our penetration levels in India, Indonesia, all over the Asian continent, Africa, Latin America, are very shallow, we do obviously serve those customers a lot in cities like London, Paris and Milan. Indians do travel a lot to Dubai; what Hong Kong used to be for China, Dubai is for India. Then for Latin Americans, Miami is a big hub; you'll find in Bal Harbour and Sawgrass outlet malls a lot of Latin American access, so I think we will always have these hubs from where we serve the market. In London, for example, or Paris, the tourist dollar is as important as the local currency and so that certainly will have an effect, so every advertising dollar has to be directed to the tourist as well.

Sacha: How do you train your staff in upselling, increasing the value or the amount?

Ravi: Again as we said earlier, each brand has its own way to achieve retail excellence; our way of doing business is sometimes contradictory to what you will learn in a business school. Never sell a product demand fully, never push your product, never go on sale, all these things; if Global Life and the streetwear brand Supreme were done like that, we could really sell a billion dollars of that particular collaboration. But we only did $250 million, we wanted to keep the market a bit exclusive. So overall in our business it's never about pushing, but always telling the customer about customization options, which mean not only putting your name on it but you can customize it by putting in some character that you love. It is always very subtle.

Sacha: What do you think is the future of retailing for LVMH? A lot of people talk about the death of retailing and the problems with it.

Ravi: In the past three years, I hear the talk of the death of retailers but we have grown at a very sound rate. So my guess is that good retail, whether it is offline or online, is thriving, and bad retail, whether it is offline or online, is dying. We have to provide the best customer experience – it is not about offline and online competing with each other, they are just two different channels of business, channels to approach the customer. In each of the channels you have to provide excellence. Those who are doing it are doing very well. If you look at Sephora, for example, in beauty, it is by far the number one beauty retailer both offline and online.

Categories of luxury products

Luxury products and services are seen as increasingly desirable by almost all consumer segments. As a result, it is having a dramatic impact on the travel and tourism retail industry. Silverstein and Fiske (2003) argue that today's consumers accept premiums of 20–200 per cent for the 'well-designed, well-engineered and well-crafted goods – often possessing the artisan touches of the traditional luxury goods' that were not found before in the mass middle market. These premium products can be subdivided into three categories, all making luxury accessible to a broader audience:

- **Accessible super premium** – pricing for these products is high for a given category of goods but still affordable for the middle classes. An example might be a premium vodka that costs 50 per cent more than Absolut Vodka.

- **Old-luxury brand extensions** – versions of products that the rich purchase but are much more affordable. Aston Martin made minor changes to the tiny Toyota iQ and sold it as an accessible low-environmental-impact Aston Martin badged model (Valdes-Dapena, 2009). Fashion houses do this all the time with diffusion ranges.

- **Mass prestige** – these are somewhere between mass-market and premium class, more expensive than conventional products but cheaper than luxury goods. So, for example, a hand cream from Kiehl's or L'Occitane at around $25 is still much more expensive than Vaseline but much cheaper than Crème de la Mer, Kaneibo, or Shiseido (Silverstein and Fiske, 2003).

Estimates for the size of the global luxury goods market exceed $247 billion (rising at over 10 per cent year on year) (Deloitte, 2019), and $1 trillion for the wider premium markets (Kastanakis, 2010), making it an increasingly vital target segment for retailers serving international shoppers.

Foreign tourist spending in the UK

The world is too large for me to cover all countries in this book. But perhaps a deep dive on what the UK inbound tourism market looks like would be useful as a guide. In 2018, the total expenditure by foreign visitors to the UK was £22 billion (Office for National Statistics, 2019). The top 10 countries contributed just 53 per cent of expenditure, which shows how important the wide number of other countries are. Visitors from the United States spent over £3.4 billion, while most of the larger European countries spent around £1 billion each. China and Canada both came in at around £0.7 billion each (Visit Britain, 2019). This, of course, disguises the fact that spending in retail is disproportionately higher among visitors from certain countries. According to *The Guardian* (Smithers, 2013), the average spend per customer is much higher among shoppers from the following countries and regions:

1 Middle East: Middle Eastern shoppers spend an average of £766 per transaction in the UK. They favour limited edition and luxury brands, including leather goods, watches and jewellery.

2 China: Chinese visitors spend a higher percentage of their holiday money on retail, with an average spend per transaction of £663. High tariffs and taxes on luxury goods sold in China mean they can save significantly more in the UK than in China. There are also fewer counterfeit goods in the UK and a better range of stock. European branded luxury goods are often 30 per cent more expensive in China than in the UK.

3 Thailand: Thai visitors are following Chinese trends of coming to the UK for shopping experiences, and there is a cachet in buying British. Like many Chinese shoppers, they like superbrands. Thai tourists have an average spend of £661.

4 Russia: Prior to the 2022 invasion of Ukraine, 60 per cent of Russians rated shopping as their top leisure pastime when coming to the UK, spending on average £597 per transaction. The top high-net-worth tourists were also coveted by British private banks and real-estate brokers.

5 Nigeria: As a result of the oil boom and emphasis by the British
   government on improving trade links, there is a growing, highly educated,
   wealthy Nigerian population in the UK, which is helping drive demand
   for flights for more and more Nigerian tourist visitors, with 30 per cent
   of visits being business related, which is higher than many other countries.
   Nigerians spend, on average, £573 per transaction (Smithers, 2013).

Many tourist shoppers, of course, are making purchases to give as gifts. In
gift giving, rarity and uniqueness confer an elite status that is attractive to
many people, and items bought abroad have many of those attributes, hence
one reason why tourists like to shop overseas.

Prada and Louis Vuitton will often have people queuing outside, even if
there are few customers inside. Why? Security is one reason, but it also
creates a buzz. Ostensibly they give the reason that they only want to have
as many customers inside as they have sales consultants, which makes good
sense in terms of the ability to focus on one customer at a time. However, for
some customers, the concept of queuing outside holds attraction, especially
among those who aspire to obtain something unique; sensing the buzz, similar to that of a new nightclub where you have to queue, becomes an
irresistible lure. People think something marvellous is going on in the shop.
They tweet about being in the queue, and a solitary shopping experience
suddenly becomes social as people chat with each other. I recently walked
past the Goyard shop in Mayfair, London. I was not really aware of the
brand's presence there, but could not help but notice the huge queue that
had formed outside the store due to their strict policy of one customer per
one salesperson at all times. In fact, the policy is part of their brand creation:
you, the shopper, will be part of something exclusive once you get in.

Most luxury brands are perceived as something mainly for the wealthy,
which the majority of consumers can only reach through occasional
purchases, such as luxury chocolates, special sunglasses or an eye-catching
limited-print scarf. Sometimes, a special bag must be ordered with a four-
month waiting list. We know that purchasing the clothes, accessories, cars
and other items that celebrities display on social media is financially unat-
tainable. Yet many tourists and local shoppers will buy some of these smaller
premium items. Many will try to buy them (or have a friend try to buy them
on their behalf) in the country where they originate since that is where they
will be the least expensive. For example, a US luxury brand, like Ralph
Lauren, is often much cheaper in the United States and so should ideally be
bought there, not in China. Generally, a French brand is slightly more

affordable in France than in other countries. Burberry is cheaper in London than in China, and so on. So if you as a retailer want to offer a premium brand, consider what your own country manufactures and promotes and try to stock that. There are many emerging luxury brands and products that may be interesting. Most countries will have trade associations that can help you tap into companies looking to get their products into the hands of foreign shoppers, even if that means limited-time pop-up promotions.

Myths about luxury

In researching this book, I found that a persistent myth associates purchasing luxury items with being elitist and uncaring. What is fascinating is that, often, relative to the industry's supply chain, nothing could be further from the truth. The luxury market might represent only a tiny percentage of goods sold. Still, its impact on premium mass-market products that do get purchased in volume, and on the lives of those who distribute and sell luxury items, is very important. Let's now look at some of the most prevalent myths.

Myth number one: luxury and premium items are environmentally unsound

Even more than the rest of us, anyone who can afford to purchase a $15,000 Birkin handbag does not want to be associated with or tainted by anything revolving around questionable ethics, such as poisoning towns and villages with waste from their leather tanneries or chopping down any more of the rain forest than a $100 handbag buyer would. In fact, for many who are actively involved in promoting luxury products, the social media implications could be severe – buyers of luxury and premium products who have significant social media standing tend to turn down any brand that could cost them followers. For example, Lululemon goes one step further, from 'do no harm' to using virtue as a selling point (Robertson, 2017). They are selling upscale exercise clothes. Their market research (which in turn is backed up by strong sales growth) shows that people are willing to pay a premium knowing that the Vancouver-based company has a very strong code of ethics and principles regarding waste management, water use, air emissions, and hazardous and non-hazardous waste. Premium and luxury buyers will pay for that kind of consciousness.

It is widely argued that, though the textile industry was forecasted to reach $1 trillion in manufacturing revenue by 2021 (this is much lower than the actual value of retail sales), it is also the world's second most polluting industry. Fast fashion (mass market) is responsible for a large part of this (Business Vibes, 2015).

Many fast-fashion manufacturers are forced into a downward spiral on pricing, whatever the environmental and human cost may be. Strong legislation in the West means that these polluting activities have often been outsourced to countries with low regulation and control, but it does not have to be this way. Many consumers, especially international travellers, do not want to feel that fast-fashion purchases are driving the use of toxic chemicals that are being dumped into rivers and pumped into the air. The last thing global travellers want is to think that the exotic countries they visit and take beautiful photos of might be harmed by their actions. Before, these nefarious manufacturing practices remained largely hidden. But with the rise of social media and local activism, the damage to people's health and their local environment is easy to see. If consumers are to be proud of their purchases, if they are to post them online, they need to feel ethically and morally safe, especially with luxury items.

To see the power of international activism, just look at the global backlash against the use of palm oil in food products, toiletries and cosmetics, led by a wide range of activists and Hollywood stars (Agence France Presse, 2017).

Myth number two: luxury and premium items are produced on the back of unacceptable labour prices

In fact, luxury goods have sufficient margins that they can be choosy and ensure they have an outstanding workforce committed to product excellence. This means increasing the skills of their labour force and ensuring the highest of standards. Therefore, the wages they offer are among the highest in their sector (Gupta, 2014). Maintaining quality is a critical factor here, and it is in their own best interest to attract and pay for the best skills and processes that money can buy. Many luxury and premium brands depend on the story of how their products are made in order to engage with their customers, hence visiting artisanal workshops, such as glassblowers in Venice, or modern manufacturing plants (in person or via exclusive video podcasts), such as Woolrich, is a major component of engaging customers with the brand. Nike had to undergo massive changes when it had to admit to the world that 'we blew it' on child labour and had to put a massive rescue plan in place to reverse the media storm (Baker, 2016).

Myth number three: luxury brands only care about the 1 per cent

While luxury items sell for a great deal of money, there are only a limited number of outstanding shops around the world that focus exclusively on servicing the needs of those customers. Much of the revenues of the large luxury brands such as LVMH, Burberry and Polo Ralph Lauren flow from the products targeted to mass markets, which connect to the higher-priced luxury brand. In fact, 70 per cent of Polo Ralph Lauren's revenues come from outlet malls (O'Connell, 2019).

Myth number four: luxury is a small market

The fact is that even the luxury segment for the so-called 1 per cent has expanded dramatically. This is born out of a dramatic increase in the consumption of all kinds of goods as the world becomes wealthier. In 2017, LVMH's fashion and leather segment grew by 14 per cent compared to the same time the year before, helping overall sales to grow by 11 per cent. Chinese shoppers, as mentioned, are important in the luxury sector, making up one-third of global sales of luxury products. For example, luxury fashion retail sales grew globally to €1.2 trillion in 2017, and much of this spending occurs in a travel setting (LVMH, 2018).

Attracting elite tourists

A lot of effort is being put again into attracting Chinese tourists. However, travel motivation for Chinese tourists is heavily status related, especially among their fast-growing middle class. Currently, many groups try visiting as many places as possible once they get their travel visas approved for a destination. There is also an increase in independent travel by Chinese tourists, who can be choosier and take more time. With its diversified tourism offer and image of prestige and glamour, Europe is at the top of the wish list of travel destinations, with the top three destinations being the UK, Germany and France (ForwardKeys, 2019). Eduardo Santander, Executive Director European Travel Commission, said: 'The 2018 EU–China Tourism Year initiative has been extremely successful. The growth in Chinese travellers has been solid, and the near future, judging by current bookings, will see the EU continuing to increase its share of this valuable market, not just to traditional destinations, but lesser-known and emerging ones as well' (ForwardKeys, 2019).

When offering accessible luxury and premium products for your customers, consider how you can utilize the same market philosophy to attract elite customers and those drawn to exclusive luxury products. Give the 1 per cent clients something they cannot get elsewhere. Arrange VIP experiences that go above and beyond what anyone else normally can expect to have. This could be private product collection viewings, private dinners with artists, curators, store buyers, artisans or designers, where, of course, guests are encouraged to wear items purchased from or gifted by you. Don't be afraid to train your staff to name-drop famous bloggers and celebrities who have purchased your products. Encourage VIPs to have their photographs taken with your products and post them online on your social media account.

At the Cadogan Estate's Retail Breakfast in May 2019, data from their tenants showed that the average top 1 per cent of retail transactions on Sloane Street was £22,000. I also learnt that 20 million visitors come to Sloane Street annually, and they have seen a 30 per cent growth in Chinese shoppers.

Many luxury products seem to exhibit a 'Veblen Effect', named after the US economist Thorstein Veblen, who first identified conspicuous consumption as a mode of status-seeking in *The Theory of the Leisure Class*, which was, remarkably, written in 1899. Veblen goods are types of luxury goods for which the quantity demand *increases* as the price increases (for fans of economics, this means a rather unexpected thing: an upward-sloping demand curve). Some goods become more desirable because of their high prices. This 'Effect' is tied to someone using a shortcut (price is quality) and the idea that you get what you pay for, meaning that a product's low price may be evidence of quality or viability problems. (Think how many people judge the quality of a wine just by looking at the price list.) It is also interesting to point out that the Veblen Effect is least likely to influence the very wealthy, as argued by Robert Frank of the *New York Times* (Frank, 2014).

The purchasing experience should also be luxurious

Opening a box of something delivered by post is not the same as stepping through the doors of a beautifully designed shop, being greeted by stylish salespeople, and trying on a wide range of creations in different sizes, colours and designs. The smells, the service, and the look and feel of the changing rooms create an occasion that adds to the luxuriousness of the item and turns it into a social event. At its core, the reason for someone making a luxury purchase is that you are creating in them a sense of privilege and status that the consumer can then express to their peer group (or to a peer group they aspire to enter into). This desire for social exclusivity extends beyond the big brand names we see in traditional department stores.

For example, a person who likes physical exercise might aspire not just to be fit but to be seen as part of a prestigious social niche within their chosen sport of cycling, horse riding, tennis, golf, etc. Just look at all the different hobbies people have, from fly fishing to skiing, and the media available, from magazines to online bloggers, conferences and trips that feed those interests. Everyone wants to feel and be part of something special, which often involves being part of a niche. So why would that be important to you as someone working in the retail industry? Because if you can attract those influencers within their niche, they will pull in more customers for your brand.

We all have so many groups we consciously and unconsciously consider ourselves to be a part of or influenced by. Therefore, for a retailer or any business selling a product or service, to appeal to all of them is impossible. So instead, consider how your physical setting and purchasing experience will enhance your customer's perceived value of the product.

Profiles of luxury shoppers

Minas Kastanakis has broken down the types of luxury buyers into three groups (Kastanakis, 2010): the hedonist consumer; perfectionist consumer and uniqueness consumer:

The hedonist consumer

This person seeks to derive physical pleasure from the activity of life, prioritizing beauty over practicality.

A hedonist wants aesthetic appreciation and sensual pleasure. This type of consumer values the perceived utility of a luxury product to arouse the senses or feelings or to evoke affective states. What does this mean to you as a retailer? My take on this is that you should make your shopping environment aesthetically appealing and physically pleasant, using opulent materials in products, wrappings and in the store design. Your salespeople should reflect this philosophy, be good at highlighting aesthetics, and have a keen sense of style. Using this product, your marketing techniques should draw the consumer into an emotional world of pleasure and happiness.

The perfectionist consumer

These people can make evaluative judgements on specific quality aspects, whereas most people would rely on and look for cues from the salesperson.

I have a little of this tendency in me, and I see it in many others who are, for example, interested in technical innovation in designing a clasp, a watch, or any products they look at. What should you offer them? Your products should use high-quality materials and processes in manufacturing, and the design should be more than just aesthetically pleasing but functional as well. You need to have salespeople who have deep knowledge and credibility when speaking about your products, ideally having even visited the manufacturer if possible. Your messaging has to be understated in order to be credible. Have your staff focus on the details of handmade production, state-of-the-art technological innovations, or the excellent delivery process you have. For these consumers, beauty is not the sell, but instead, functionality and quality standards are vitally important.

The uniqueness consumer

These consumers are usually creative, like choices and are counter-conformists. Such consumers are attracted to luxury products for their scarcity or uniqueness.

As discussed previously, the promotions you might use for this audience should portray exclusivity, whether real or perceived. For example, Veuve Cliquot Champagne offer a personalization service where their distinctive orange metal gift boxes can be printed with the customer's unique message. Likewise, Smythson Luxury Stationers has a service to emboss their customers' initials on their notebooks directly in their many retail stores around the world. Another popular way to offer exclusivity and uniqueness is by issuing limited special editions and creative design collaborations that are only available for a short while. In the tourist realm, many travelling shoppers might not have access to some of the goods available when they travel, and that alone can be a reason to buy: to bring back something everyone has been yearning for.

What makes premium retailers and brands successful?

They go all out. They invest a lot of money, time and effort in the small details, things that most regular shoppers would barely notice. For example, Harrods are comfortable spending hundreds of millions refurbishing their store to create a unique experience that their customers will keep coming back for (Smith, 2017). For luxury retailers, every detail is about world-class service, world-class design and putting on world-class events. They insist on hiring the best and even have floor managers and senior sales consultants who can earn tens of thousands of pounds in additional commissions annually (and in some cases over £100,000). These extraordinary staff members are able to tap into customers' aspirations and play a crucial role in the success of the companies they work in. They need to be rewarded and looked after.

Behind every successful large enterprise, someone started small and worked incredibly hard. Charles Henry Harrod started as a tea dealer in a one-room tea and grocery store in Knightsbridge in 1849. Today, the Harrods empire covers 1 million square feet of retail space (Griffiths, 2016), employs about 4,000 staff members and is the leader in luxury retail, with customers travelling to it from across the world (BBC, 2010). Now it is arguably the world's best department store.

Veuve Clicquot, the champagne house already mentioned earlier in this chapter, was started by Madame Clicquot, a widow ('veuve' means widow in French) whose husband had died suddenly. Despite there being no women in the very conservative wine industry, she set out to create a champagne brand (Geiling, 2013). She used her influence to ensure some of the most powerful people in the world at the time were given access to exclusive editions. By taking risks and really investing in her brand and distribution, she broke through so many barriers. In doing so, she created a champagne brand that is now one of the largest in the world. It shows that one must have a vision of where one wants to go, even if it changes over time, and it probably will. But achieving success does require stepping into that future and making it happen.

Any brand can enter into the premium market, even from a low base. In 2015, Aldi and Lidl, the giant German discount supermarket chains, began selling frozen whole lobsters for £5 ($7) (Armstrong, 2015). They used them to attract a whole new customer group with purchasing power into their stores. There is now a proliferation of restaurants selling upmarket burgers for many times the cost of McDonald's. They focus on the quality of the beef they use, and there are, of course, restaurants combining both options, such as the 'Burger & Lobster' chain, combining seemingly luxurious ingredients to appeal to a higher-spending customer.

In the 1970s and 1980s, airports and railway stations were dismal places, where food was confined to a limp prepacked sandwich. Today, many airports and railway stations have transformed their food and beverage options, often offering champagne bars, which help create a certain frame of mind to match the proliferation of good-quality retailers who are in the terminals and at the departure gates.

Interestingly, a luxurious environment that heightens the senses helps even other retailers in the surrounding area raise their prices for standard, everyday products. For example, why does a drink of Coca-Cola cost $1 in one venue, whereas in a nice hotel or a tourist café in Paris it is many times that price? It is the same product, yet local consumers and visiting tourists are paying for the added ambience or to take part in an experience.

In fact, almost every product can incorporate a premium element into it. From high-end vitamins to keychains, from olive oil to special editions of books – there is a rare characteristic that can be created in most products, and people will pay for that rarity. Once, my wife and I were looking at pashminas in a souk in Oman. The excellent salesman took me through all the different qualities of pashmina, and the more we learnt, the less attractive the normal pashminas seemed. We ended up buying an expensive pashmina, something we had not set out to do but did due to the rarity value the salesman was able to invoke. When you can go deeper into a product, when someone explains the story behind the production, the skilled people who dedicate themselves to making something special, your senses are alerted, you are pulled in, and you want the best. This is the skill that retail businesses, wholesalers and manufacturers need to learn.

As leaders, you have to train your staff to know the history of your company, the provenance of your products, and how to express it well to customers. Luxury sales are founded upon training and hiring staff with a discerning eye to know what quality looks like and how to make the buyer feel it is not about price but aspirational value. This not only moves people into spending more by buying the best you have to offer, but also helps increase sales of your other, less premium product lines that people can afford more easily. It used to be that luxury buying was most common among middle-aged or older people who had amassed wealth, knowledge and status. But today, younger generations are fully aware of most luxury brands and aspire to own them. In fact, according to Bain's Insight Market Study on Luxury Goods Worldwide in 2017, the main growth engine of the luxury market is a generational shift, with 85 per cent of luxury growth in 2017 fuelled by generations Y and Z. A broader 'millennial state of mind' is also permeating the luxury industry and changing how all generations make purchases.

Shoes, jewellery and handbags are ranked as the three fastest-growing product categories, increasing by 10, 10 and 7 per cent annually, respectively, at current exchange rates. Apparel, beauty and handbags still make up the bulk of global luxury purchases, amounting to £61 billion, £54 billion and £48 billion respectively – collectively representing 62 per cent of the personal luxury goods market (D'Arpizio et al, 2017).

Marketing to the younger generations is all about 'experience' and photo-ops and creating a sensual, artistic, 'wow' atmosphere that they consider part of the purchase experience. If you are willing to put the effort in, you will be rewarded with lots of luxury- and premium-segment customer sales.

China and the luxury marketplace

The 2019 McKinsey report 'China Luxury Report 2019: How young Chinese consumers are reshaping global luxury' re-emphasizes the importance of luxury and premium brands reaching younger generations (Lan et al, 2019).

The report states that, firstly, Chinese consumers are set to contribute almost two-thirds of global growth in luxury spending. You already know this. Their outlay is set to almost double to 1.2 trillion RMB by the middle of the decade when they estimate that Chinese consumers will spend 40 per cent of the world's spending on luxury goods. It is not that China does not have luxury brands in Shanghai and other cities, but that the majority of them, about 70 per cent, in fact, will be doing their luxury spending overseas. This is because of an increasing affinity for outbound travel, the price differential resulting from China's import tax regime, and the brands' pricing policies.

Second, McKinsey and Company are projecting that it will be the post-1980s and 1990s generation, many new to luxury, who will power the Chinese market. This generation Y, consisting of 10.2 million luxury consumers, accounted for more than half the total spending on luxury by Chinese consumers in 2018.

The post-1990s consumers are the vanguard of China's urban middle class, a dynamic and digitally engrossed cohort that, as 'the single child generation', are the recipients of an outsize level of familial support.

Now here is where it gets interesting. Big brands are important, but relatively less so among young consumers than the older generation. The young generation consumes media and the luxury lifestyle it portrays, so they are more heavily social and trend dependent – which means new brands and styles need to market themselves creatively. This generation wants 'the new' not the old.

This opens doors for niche brands – from those that are unique to those rarely seen on the street or unavailable in mainland China. In fact, McKinsey reports that the post-65s/70s consumers have no interest in Chinese luxury brands, but this could change too. They might begin to opt for a high-end Chinese brand as these brands gain prominence.

Now, with all the focus on social media, you would think social media and key opinion leaders would be the key to success. But McKinsey's studies show that among all engagement channels the most impactful is in-person and in-store. Celebrities get the stores known on social media. LV, for example, works closely with a core group of brand ambassadors with global reach, such as Chinese Canadian star Kris Wu, but hires others on an ad hoc basis according to the needs of individual elements or product launches.

That said, pioneers are pushing into new media, such as video-sharing apps like TikTok. For example, US fashion brand Michael Kors partnered with key opinion leaders to create a series of catwalk videos on various city streets. The company generated 200 million views for the more than 30,000 user-generated videos submitted (Dragon Social Limited, 2019).

Offline is still expected to be the preferred luxury sales channel in the near future, but it is expected that post-90s consumers will shop across different types of brick-and-mortar stores and no longer focus only on premium department stores. That said, they are not averse to taking the purchasing plunge after being offered premium desserts, champagne or other beverages, or being otherwise entertained in-store.

But, similarly to everything else we are seeing, young consumers are more likely to make a purchase if a great personalization service or product uniqueness is created. This can be delivered in futuristic ways. Virtual try-on services and matching suggestions curated by AI both increase the likelihood that consumers will purchase online or in-store.

Let's now take a look at how one of the world's most famous retailers develops its relationships with international tourist shoppers.

CONVERSATION WITH
Michael Ward, Managing Director since 2006 of Harrods, London, has grown it dramatically to over £2 billion in annual revenues, making it one of the most iconic department stores in the world. Previously owned by the Egyptian Mohammed Al Fayed, the Qatari Investment Fund now owns it.

Sacha: Harrods' name is now considered the height of luxury and one of the first names an international traveller associates with London. That is quite a coup to achieve.

Michael: Customers value Harrods' values and its brand. We trade on Britain's soft power, cultural and creative heritage. It serves us more than anything else. It is indeed part of our identity.

Sacha: What are Harrods' annual sales, and what percentage is from foreign visitors?

Michael: Our last reported annual sales were £2.1 billion. It is very difficult to tell who is an overseas visitor among our purchasers since most of the international people who spend here have a UK address or have an office.

Sacha: What actions does Harrods take to attract new international customers each year – both those who are in London and others before they arrive?

Michael: Our customers are very high-net-worth individuals. We spend a lot of time in China holding events, twice before Christmas, talking about our products and what is currently in vogue. We hold business events for individuals who introduce us to their top-tier clients in China or the Middle East who resonate with our brands. These people become our customers. They will then go on to tell their friends about what we are offering and making available to our customers.

Sacha: So you focus on a smaller number of people rather than a large number?

Michael: Yes, and it makes an extraordinary difference to be targeted in who you are selling to and to know what those customers want.

Sacha: In what ways do foreigners buy different things compared to local shoppers?

Michael: Those with high net worth want the unusual. Our biggest seller in our butchery department is Kobe beef. We also sell exotic fruits. We focus on the high-value customer who might spend £3,800 in one shopping trip.

Sacha: What trends do you see happening with your foreign customers?

Michael: In the luxury high-net-worth market, they are looking for products curated especially for them. There are many luxury items out there, but we offer personalized services. A tea tailor, for example, will curate a tea that is personalized for our customer. We have a master perfumer who will create a perfume for the customer. This kind of personalized shopping creates emotional bonds. In addition, we have a wellness centre, where our dieticians and personal trainers will give you a vitamin infusion that is exactly what your body needs, or a dietician can help you drop two dress sizes with a certain programme. This kind of experience is what high-net-worth foreign customers come for.

Sacha: How do you know what brands to promote at what time?

Michael: We are aware of what is going on in the world and what we can offer to our overseas visitors who cannot gain the same range in other luxury stores. Let's say someone wants to buy a pink diamond ring, but pink diamonds are as rare as hen's teeth. It's really difficult going round to lots of different jewellery stores. But we arrange with our major jewellers, Winston and Bulgari, for five pink diamond rings to be here when the customer is next in London. We also have a concierge service to ensure we can meet all of our customer needs.

Sacha: Are you helping brands that are not well known?

Michael: We actually invest in the brands of tomorrow. I am on the board of a group where we develop local brands. Through them, as an example, we have developed over 1,000 brands, which have been enormously successful.

Sacha: In the case of luxury brands, is it the price that identifies it as a luxury sale, or different elements?

Michael: It is the perceived value that makes someone buy or not.

Sacha: What type of techniques are you training your people to use to bond with customers?

Michael: We have an internal learning and development centre where our staff are constantly learning about brands and what goes into the products so that they can interact with customers and explain product attributes. Most of our sales are not internet based, but instead through personal relations. Customers like to talk to our people and trust them.

Sacha: Why do you think your customers like to shop in the store versus ordering the product online?

Michael: I think it is wholly about the experience. I think customers may wait for many months for a particular bag and when it finally arrives they want to open it in the department, experience the feeling and share the kind of glow.

Sacha: Do you use rewards cards as part of your customer relationship management (CRM) strategy?

Michael: Yes, and they are a huge motivation. Our customers bring their Harrods Rewards cards into the store.

Sacha: It has been said that it is hugely important for corporate brands to incorporate care of the environment into their products and that the supply chain is ethically grounded. Is this something Harrods factors into its strategy?

Michael: Well, luxury brands have long-term relationships with quality. Most of these luxury brands source suppliers who use the best environmentally conscious techniques and materials. In addition, our store itself, by providing the world's best luxury goods, also helps the economy of London. International travellers spend billions while here, in hotels and other tourist ventures, which keep many people in business earning high incomes.

Sacha: Do you think the government could do more?

Michael: The UK government sadly does not treat us as essential to the economy. They have done little to help people get visas to visit. The government has been punitive to the bricks-and-mortar retail business with high business rates.

Sacha: Are you using much artificial intelligence (AI) in your business?

Michael: AI, of course, is monitoring the last websites our customers visited to suggest new purchases in line with their searches. Merchandisers are now 'data scientists' and they can predict trends. But it has been my experience that great merchandise buyers for Harrods buy by instinct and take risks. As the saying goes, 'People do not know what they want until we have created it'. Creativity is a huge part of this business, and we look to showcase and curate in ways that one cannot find anywhere else. That is, in a phrase, our brand.

Sacha: Why has Harrods Rewards cards worked for your tourist customers?

Michael: Our success is that we don't really have tourists. We have 'international visitors' who are regular shoppers and therefore value the card and the status it gives.

LET'S TALK LUXURY

- Luxury is a huge market, growing over €1.2 trillion and much of this spending occurs in a travel setting (LVMH, 2018).

- 'Keep it a little rare', as LVMH tries to. Luxury is not about the mass market, but aspects of luxury can be attainable to many more 'aspirational' people than before.

- Airports are a vital part of luxury retailing and branding in many cities, especially in Europe and Asia.

- Some of luxury and travel retailing is contradictory to what is taught in business schools. For example, never sell entirely to a maximum product demand level, never push your product, and never go on sale.

- Look at your brands and products and seek what new premium ranges could be created as 'accessible super-premium', 'old luxury brand extensions' or 'mass prestige' lines.

- The successful premium retailer goes all-out, obsessing about the details. Staff are taught regularly about new products, their qualities and provenance, and how to improve their international cultural communication skills.

References

Agence France Presse (2017) Harrison Ford's environment documentary questions 'shocked' Indonesian forestry minister, *HuffPost*, www.huffpost.com/entry/harrison-ford-environment-indonesia_n_3899141?guce referrer=aHR0cHM6Ly93d3cuYmluZy5jb20vc2VhcmNoP3E9aGFycmlzb24rRm9yZCtwYWxtK29pbCZxcz1uJnNwPS0xJnBxPWhhcnJpc29uK2ZvcmQrcGFsbVoWmc2M9MS0yMiZzaz0mY3ZpZD0yNkI3QjJBMkIzNDU0Qzx (archived at https://perma.cc/Y2QX-NXQ3)

Armstrong, A (2015) Tesco takes on Aldi and Lidl with £6 lobster, *The Telegraph*, www.telegraph.co.uk/finance/newsbysector/retailandconsumer/12007372/Tesco-takes-on-Aldi-and-Lidl-with-6-lobster.html (archived at https://perma.cc/55ME-45YL)

Baker, M (2016) Nike and child labour – how it went from laggard to leader, *Mallen Baker*, http://mallenbaker.net/article/clear-reflection/nike-and-child-labour-how-it-went-from-laggard-to-leader (archived at https://perma.cc/7HAF-9TXK)

BBC (2010) History of Harrods department store, *BBC News*, 8 May, www.bbc.co.uk/news/10103783 (archived at https://perma.cc/N5Y2-URNL)

Business Vibes (2015) 30 shocking figures and facts in global textile and apparel industry, *Business 2 Community*, www.business2community.com/fashion-beauty/30-shocking-figures-facts-global-textile-apparel-industry-01222057 (archived at https://perma.cc/NP9H-YLDE)

D'Arpizio, C et al (2017) Luxury goods worldwide market study, fall–winter 2017, *Bain & Company*, www.bain.com/insights/luxury-goods-worldwide-market-study-fall-winter-2017/ (archived at https://perma.cc/KVP3-9KCB)

Davis, D-M (2020), 'LVMH Chairman Bernard Arnault is worth $113 billion. Here are 17 of his luxury conglomerate's iconic brands', *Business Insider*, https://www.businessinsider.com/lvmh-brands-iconic-luxury-goods-bernard-arnault-2019-10 (archived at https://perma.cc/JS4V-KLPP)

Deloitte (2019) *Global Powers of Luxury Goods 2019*, Deloitte, London

Dragon Social Limited (2019) TikTok: a look at China's #1 up-and-coming social media, *Top Digital Agency*, https://topdigital.agency/tik-tok-a-look-at-chinas-1-up-and-coming-social-media/ (archived at https://perma.cc/89TR-P7SY)

ForwardKeys (2019) Chinese tourists flock to Europe, *ForwardKeys*, https://forwardkeys.com/chinese-tourists-flock-europe/ (archived at https://perma.cc/G2W3-F6D4)

Frank, R H (2014) Conspicuous consumption? Yes, but it's not crazy, *New York Times*, www.nytimes.com/2014/11/23/upshot/conspicuous-consumption-yes-but-its-not-crazy.html (archived at https://perma.cc/QE8D-MFSH)

Geiling, N (2013) The widow who created the champagne industry, *Smithsonian.com*, www.smithsonianmag.com/arts-culture/the-widow-who-created-the-champagne-industry-180947570/ (archived at https://perma.cc/X53M-K9WQ)

Griffiths, E (2016) The history of Harrods in 1 minute, *Culture Trip*, 17 June, https://theculturetrip.com/europe/united-kingdom/england/london/articles/the-history-of-harrods-in-1-minute/ (archived at https://perma.cc/B5X3-X7QH)

Gupta, S (2014) What to expect when working in luxury retail, *CareerAddict*, www.careeraddict.com/what-to-expect-when-working-in-luxury-retail (archived at https://perma.cc/K2WM-T78U)

Kastanakis, M (2010) *Explaining variation in luxury consumption*, City University, London (unpublished)

Lan, L et al (2019) China Luxury Report 2019, *McKinsey & Company*, https://www.mckinsey.com/~/media/mckinsey/featured%20insights/china/how%20young%20chinese%20consumers%20are%20reshaping%20global%20luxury/mckinsey-china-luxury-report-2019-how-young-chinese-consumers-are-reshaping-global-luxury.ashx (archived at https://perma.cc/99DK-6Q79)

LVMH (2018) Excellent first half for LVMH, *LVMH*, www.lvmh.com/news-documents/press-releases/excellent-first-half-for-lvmh-3/ (archived at https://perma.cc/WZ2Z-4ZG9)

O'Connell, L (2019) Revenue of Polo Ralph Lauren worldwide from 2002 to 2019, *Statista*, www.statista.com/statistics/263880/polo-ralph-laurens-revenue-worldwide/ (archived at https://perma.cc/25KG-KV28)

Office for National Statistics (2019) Travel trends: 2018, *Office for National Statistics*, www.ons.gov.uk/peoplepopulationandcommunity/leisureandtourism/articles/traveltrends/2018 (archived at https://perma.cc/QU68-ABKS)

Robertson, S K (2017) Lululemon kicks off first global advertising campaign, *The Globe and Mail*, 15 May, www.theglobeandmail.com/report-on-business/lululemon-kicks-off-first-global-advertising-campaign/article34983686/ (archived at https://perma.cc/Q2QH-BFFG)

Silverstein, M J and Fiske, N (2003) Luxury for the masses, *Harvard Business Review*, https://hbr.org/2003/04/luxury-for-the-masses (archived at https://perma.cc/ZL68-A65H)

Smith, S (2017) Harrods begins £200m refurbishment – the biggest in the department store's 170-year history, *The Telegraph*, www.telegraph.co.uk/business/2017/11/24/harrods-begins-200m-refurbishment-biggest-department-stores/ (archived at https://perma.cc/2XB7-ZYZ4)

Smithers, R (2013) Overseas shoppers: who spends what in the UK, *The Guardian*, www.theguardian.com/money/2013/oct/14/uk-retailers-relaxed-visas-chinese-visitors (archived at https://perma.cc/MK6N-QGFC)

Valdes-Dapena, P (2009) A tiny Aston Martin for James Bond types: Toyota teams up with Aston Martin to create an ultra-mini luxury car, *CNN Money*, https://money.cnn.com/2009/06/29/autos/aston-martin_iq/ (archived at https://perma.cc/3GP8-SA87)

Visit Britain (2019) 2018 Snapshot, *Visit Britain*, www.visitbritain.org/2018-snapshot (archived at https://perma.cc/J2ES-CKWG)

3

Why travel and tourism retail has become so big

The end of Covid-19 lockdowns has spurred people to travel far and wide again, seeking new experiences and escaping the confines of their daily lives. As a result, the opportunities to increase the profitability of your business from the hundreds of millions of affluent consumers among the more than 1.5 billion people travelling the world are varied and vast (UNWTO, 2020). One way to do so is to provide tax refunds to international customers on their purchases. Global Blue is the largest provider of this service, so I thought you might like to hear what their CEO has to say on international shopping.

CONVERSATION WITH
Jacques Stern, CEO of Global Blue, the world's largest tax refund company, based in Switzerland. He is also Vice Chairman of the supervisory board of the shopping mall giant Unibail-Rodamco-Westfield.

Sacha: Please could you explain what tax refund companies such as Global Blue do.

Jacques: Global Blue is the leader in the world of what we call tax-free shopping, which is a value proposal to merchants and especially luxury merchants to help them to manage the process of VAT refunds. So in simple words, when a Chinese traveller is going to Madrid and buys a handbag in a boutique, we provide the technology to the boutique to issue a tax-free form and enable the traveller to get their refund after having received a proof of the export by Customs at the airport. We therefore manage all the processes, from issuing in-store, validation and refund. We refund the tourist either in cash or to their credit/debit card or mobile wallet, either in town with our partners, for example at a branch of ChangeGroup, or at the airport after validation.

Sacha: How many countries provide tax refunds on purchases made by international shoppers?

Jacques: In the world 59 and we are presently in 52 countries. So Global Blue every year refunds $2 billion of VAT. We have 70 per cent market share in the countries where we are present. This does not account for some countries like Australia or Thailand, where the government has in-sourced the management of the VAT refund process. So I would probably think that the market could exceed $3.5 billion of VAT refund in the world.

Sacha: About how many international shoppers are taking up the tax-free refund?

Jacques: The number of people who are eligible who are issued the tax-free form is only 50 per cent so a lot of people miss out.

Sacha: How much of an economic advantage has tax refund services brought the countries that enable tax refund schemes?

Jacques: It's definitely a very strong argument to attract tourism. For example, Russia, where VAT has existed for more than 10 years, recently introduced tax-free shopping there. UAE did so too in 2018. The Indian Ministry of Finance is testing goods and services tax (GST) refund for international shoppers. So it means that almost all the countries that have VAT or GST have a system of tax refund.

Sacha: How do you feel shopping is different abroad from shopping at home?

Jacques: Well, I think there are a few things to consider. You have two components: one that is price related and one that is experience related. So price related, we know that the large luxury brands have a policy whereby you give the best price in the home country and then increase the price elsewhere.

Sacha: For example, Tiffany's home prices would be in the United States, and Tiffany's Europe prices would be 10 per cent more than in the United States.

Jacques: Second is the consumer buying for the experience of being at the destination, which is often enhanced.

Sacha: What trends have you seen in international shoppers' habits over the past decade, and how do you think they will change in the coming 10 years?

Jacques: Well, the past 10 years have been the decade of the Chinese. You see the middle-class formation creating wealth in China and people eager to travel and to have experiences abroad, including shopping. Shopping represents more than 40 per cent of the budget of a Chinese person on holiday. So I think what we have seen in the past 10 years is more and more Chinese people coming here [to Paris] and flooding the world, not only Europe but also Asia. What can we expect for the next 10 years? Today there are 100 million Chinese people travelling per year. Obviously the expectation is to reach up to 250 million in 10 years.

Sacha: How has the rise of Asian shoppers changed the services offered in Western markets?

Jacques: Quite strongly with a difference by definition. I think one of the companies that understood the wave sooner was Galleries Lafayette Department Store in Paris. Fifteen years ago they started to have teams going to the Asian market to advertise Paris/Galleries Lafayette. They then started to have staff coming from Asia, particularly China. Today, without going too much into the detail, more than 50 per cent of their business is coming from international travellers. This shows it is important for the traveller to know about your business before they arrive. So marketing can be done traditionally but it can be done more and more through social media, especially with the Chinese. Obviously when they arrive at the destination, you have a range of marketing initiatives in order to make your brand known. Global Blue provides a couple of ways to do that for the brand, such as what we call the 'drive to store'. For example, a tourist receives a message when they land saying, '10 per cent or more refund if you shop at XYZ in the next two days, and spend over £5,000'.

Sacha: What about for smaller, more independent retailers?

Jacques: We can connect them to our global shopper database of more than 13 million people to whom we can communicate directly or through our partners. Boutique customers have the same shopping tax-refund opportunities as our department store customers.

Personally I never like to pay full retail price. From negotiating discounts for paying in cash (so retailers get paid instantly and have no card fees), to obtaining additional small gifts and benefits, I find international travel a great opportunity to flex my negotiation skills, be that a high-end store in New York or a luxury hotel in Madrid.

Fortunately, for those more timid shoppers, most countries offer an easy discount for international visitors – VAT refunds. For decades, international visitors to the UK could get their VAT back on all their shopping. However, as a part of Brexit, the UK government decided to eliminate this convenient process. Tax-free shopping is now only available for goods purchased in the UK and sent by post directly to overseas addresses, including the EU. This means that the customers' own government will immediately impose taxes on everything purchased, negating many financial incentives to visit. Instead, shoppers have significant incentives to go to Milan, Paris or Madrid instead, where they not only buy the things they want tax-free but also spend significant sums in restaurants, hotels and other venues. I am hopeful that the UK government will bring back cash refunds for international shoppers soon, so that the whole UK tourism economy has a level playing field with other countries around the world, particularly in Europe.

What are some of the drivers for travel growth?

As incomes continue to rise around the world (despite intermittent disruptions) and travel costs continue to reduce, the number of people travelling internationally is growing. This makes the sector a truly global force for economic development, driving the creation of more and better jobs and serving as a catalyst for innovation and entrepreneurship. The Secretary General of the UN World Tourism Organization, Zurab Pololikashvili, stated, 'In short, tourism is helping build better lives for millions of individuals and transforming whole communities' (World Tourism Organization, 2019).

As an example, Roger Dow, CEO of the US Travel Association, writes that travel in the United States is an industry that generates $2.5 trillion in economic output and supports 15.7 million jobs (Dow, nd). For one, travel prices by air, sea or land have become dramatically more affordable in recent years. Improvements in aviation technology, improving fuel efficiency, and enabling the more rapid turnaround of aircraft to raise utilization levels have driven down prices. Although rarely spoken of, innovations in finance through loans and leasing have enabled a dramatic growth in airline manufacturing and hotel construction, expanding competition. Business model disruptors, such as Airbnb and Uber, have also increased the availability of services to travellers. When you combine this with a wide range of price comparison websites and the deregulation of the airline and ground transportation sectors, travel costs have lowered drastically. As a result, more than 1.5 billion people now travel internationally every year, where previously, it was the preserve of the few.

The UN World Tourism Organization (2019) reports that tourism is the world's third-largest export category after chemicals and fuels, and ahead of automotive products and food. China is the largest spender, constituting one-fifth of international tourism spending, followed by the United States. Were it not for the Covid-19 pandemic, it was estimated that 50 million Indian tourists would have travelled internationally in 2020. As discussed by Jacques Stern earlier, Chinese consumers allocate 40 per cent of their vacation budget to shopping. Pre-Covid, around 10 per cent of China's 1.4 billion inhabitants travelled internationally; by 2027, this number is expected to have doubled to 20 per cent as the middle classes expand there.

This is all ideal for retailers wishing to earn more money. It's that simple. Given consumers' changing behaviours, with travel accounting for an increasingly large amount of their annual budgets, your business has a huge opportunity to attract more international customers. I define the travel and tourism retail industry very much as serving both pre-trip outbound customers who are locals and in-trip inbound foreign tourists.

The location of the retail experience might be in a shopping mall, on the high street, or in a travel gateway such as an airport, cruise terminal or railway station. It might be a single-brand store or a multi-brand mini-department store. It may be omnichannel such as Nike, or purely physical, like Primark. There is a myriad of potential customers for you to market to since international shoppers come in all varieties: weekend getaway types, overseas students, families on budget holidays, families on luxury holidays, honeymooners, and those looking for adventure, a new culture, a spiritual or love connection, or an experience that they can tell others about. Notice that the majority on this list are leisure travellers. Yes, business people do shop, but typically far less so than people on leisure trips. Why that is the case, is a subject we will discuss later.

Then divide these groups again into people travelling from varying countries of origin, ages, health conditions, sizes, economic powers, languages and religions. It becomes clear that they all have different needs and wants. If you can find a way of serving them according to their needs, wants, aspirations and values, then you will have a winning formula.

Today's travellers are diverse in thousands of ways, which opens unlimited opportunities to service them and create a unique business model. Most importantly, travellers behave 90 per cent of their time in the usual way that standard behavioural scientists expect them to as they go about their daily lives. Yet suddenly, when they start to go into travel mode and decide to go on a trip, they behave differently; their desires and aspirations change. They go from being certain about what they will be doing and what they will need to purchase for their daily lives to being uncertain about what they will be doing abroad, what the cultural norms will be in their destination, and what they will need to purchase for their travels. This change of mental state, this excitement and uncertainty, even in some people this nervous volatility, is a golden opportunity for you and your teams – if they can remain open to it and serve these travellers the right way.

The products and services the travelling public need are very different from what they usually purchase. Travel is a period of time, a state of mind, when something special, something different, is happening. But how to capitalize on this, you might ask?

Well, imagine if you listened to your local customers and understood their needs, not just as your regular customers, but also at the moment they experienced levels of greater uncertainty – just before an international trip, as outbound travellers. How would that affect your relationship with them? If they felt heard and understood, if they felt they could buy from you extra items 'just in case'. If you had return policies that allowed them to buy with confidence and come back if they didn't use those extra clothes, bags or toiletries. Would they feel even closer to your business and want to shop with you, and trust you even more in their normal day-to-day lives?

How helpful would it be if your sales consultants regularly asked customers about their upcoming travels, checked weather reports, and looked at social media on a phone or tablet with them? And then, these sales consultants helped them make purchases that would enhance their feelings of safety, well-being and connectedness to those places and people they are embarking on the trip to. Imagine how these customers would want to come back to your store or link back to your store's social media account just to tell about their experiences. How would that impact your future sales?

Now think beyond your local customers travelling outbound. Imagine reaching customers who are inbound from exotic places around the world, coming to your store with excitement and joy just for being here in this moment, on this trip. How great would it be for your brand to be seen as a go-to place by people worldwide who fly in and post about you on social media? Would those interactions and transactions help your retail brand and grow your sales?

What impact would all this have on your teams? Would they gain more skills, feel more useful to customers, feel happier, more successful, and have higher job satisfaction? Would that, in turn, attract better-skilled staff, reduce staff turnover, improve your relationship with your suppliers and your bankers and potentially boost your profits?

If the answer is yes, then keep reading…

Core international shopping drivers

First is the '**purpose-driven**' shopping visitor. Whether the goal is a new coat, a new camera, a wedding gown, the latest designer handbag or a vintage evening purse, the idea of travelling on a shopping trip can be traced back to ancient Roman or Babylonian times and probably even before then. It can mark a rite of passage, a coming-of-age trip, or a regular seasonal activity. But this shopper means to set aside time for choosing locations and particular stores. They will have researched their trip, spoken to friends, and see shopping as a core reason for travelling. They will have avoided purchasing items in their home country because they will be travelling abroad. They are embarking on this dedicated journey through the city's streets and neighbourhoods. They will embark on shopping for the experience of it. This shopper often accounts for the most significant economic impact, with more dollars spent on more things, in more places, by more people than ever before. Indeed in today's social media world, these shopping moments by social media influencers and regular members of the public alike are often snapped and broadcasted for all the world to see.

Second, the '**serendipity shopper or impulse shopper**'. These are the visitors for whom the destination is the activity. They were not planning anything but happened to simply chance upon something that caught their eye that inspired them. They act on impulse and are only really interested in a retailer if it feels relevant to the experience of the trip. Otherwise, they don't necessarily want to shop. Of course, if the right item or opportunity comes along, they might unexpectedly spend a lot on something they didn't even think they wanted.

Third is the '**souvenir shopper**', the person who feels they need to bring home or give as a gift a record of their time spent wherever they were travelling. Typically, this shopper has other, more important activities than serious shopping to occupy their travel time. Consequently, their purchases are targeted to a few convenient locations stocked with the items they are most likely to buy. The object may be inexpensive, but almost always it is symbolic of the destination. Souvenir shops from the Orchard Road in Singapore to the Drottninggatan Street in Stockholm sell essentially similar 'made in China' merchandise with different logos and colours – bags, scarves, hats, coffee mugs, glasses, t-shirts and more.

Finally, there is the **'distressed or last-minute shopper'** who will pick up the essentials they need for their trip, often at the departing airport. They are less price sensitive and are receptive to convenient offerings. Hence, many of the latest duty-free stores have created meandering walkways where you are never more than 5 metres away from their varied offerings.

Now clearly, all visitors can exhibit some of the attributes described previously at various times throughout their trip. While clearly most shopping occurs on leisure visits rather than business trips, thinking about customer types can assist you and your teams in designing products and services around their needs.

People travel and often spend for emotional reasons

If we understand this, we are already ahead of the game. I break it down this way: people travel for love and to feel love, to buy things, to see and experience new things, to meet new people, and to deepen the connection they have with others and, hence, themselves. This also applies to business trips – people travel for business, especially internationally, to establish deeper connections with people than they can by telephone or video call. They are excited by it because of the sense of adventure it gives, the opportunity for learning, deepening relationships and returning home with stories to tell their loved ones. That makes our job clear for those of us in the retail industry. Our job of marketing to the traveller is to enhance these experiences and provide creative, emotional vehicles for them to gain the experiences they want and for us to grow our business in doing so.

As an example, people undertake travel for many emotional reasons, among them the fear of missing out (so-called FOMO). Today's desire to be everywhere at once is heightened by social media and increasing awareness of all the available activities, business opportunities and choices. There are three types of FOMO:

- not seeing, doing or experiencing all the things at that destination that are relevant to them personally

- not liking a chosen destination and seeing another destination online that looks better

- not participating in things that their friends, colleagues, competitors and relations are doing back at home, which they are seeing on their social networks

As businesses that cater to travellers, we cannot do much about the third type in the above list, but we can strongly influence the FOMO of the first two types. If we help people to have great experiences, we are able to make them feel at ease that their chosen destination is the right one. We can also help guide them to experience what they truly want to experience. If we do this, we ensure their trip is a great one, they will post online about it, and we will get new business from doing so.

Naturally, too much of anything is just too much. Hence we can also celebrate JOMO, the joy of missing out. This means going to regions of the world or to restaurants and places with limited or no connectivity. JOMO is about re-creating a sense of peace, enabling access to calmness and higher senses that one doesn't get to reach daily.

This doesn't stop people from returning rapidly to FOMO mode afterwards, but businesses that can help international and domestic customers seeking JOMO moments will attract more customers. We may see this trend growing as devices get more and more addictive, and more than ever, people feel the need to detach from the 24-hour digital world.

These are some tangible reasons why travellers will spend with you. Perhaps your product is not available in the traveller's home country, or it is cheaper at their destination. Perhaps there has been a shift in exchange rates, or maybe there are tax advantages with the VAT refund. Perhaps the customer is in a different frame of mind and will take the time to visit your store, whereas, at home, they have no time. We all enjoy the buzz that comes from seeing what is new, exciting and different in a foreign country. Though I must confess, that means sometimes I have had the experience of buying a piece of clothing on a trip that seems just right in that country, and then I come home only to feel a bit silly in that eccentric Austrian shirt or Moroccan caftan! When away, people also shop for something that appeals to their higher senses, something they do not have time to look for at home, such as a painting or piece of art. This is perhaps why on the Spanish island of Mallorca, there are hundreds of artist galleries selling all kinds of art to the millions of tourists on holiday. The visitors have a more relaxed state of mind, and many seem to want to use that time to buy a small or larger piece of art, whether they are yacht owners or regular tourists. When subject to stress, our brains go into a reptilian mode, affecting the outer and higher-functioning brain activities. Hence on a relaxed trip abroad, the colours, sounds, textures, and the concept of aesthetic beauty and luxury, become much more appealing. Then, we are more predisposed to shop for it. Hence, providing environments for shoppers to relax, sit down and have background music to change their state can be very important (Psychologist World, nd). Consumers, in general, tend to prefer to shop where they can enjoy an 'experience'. For example, pâtissier Pierre Hermé and beauty brand L'Occitane have collaborated on a 10,000 foot lifestyle store in Paris that offers well-being products, a terrace restaurant, in-store perfumery, coffee and cocktail bar, and macarons (Isaac-Goizé, 2018).

International pricing differentials

One of the major reasons consumers choose to make purchases internationally is to save money. The prices might vary because a product is manufactured locally or because recent currency changes make that country particularly cheap in that particular season. For example, after the Brexit vote, the British pound devalued substantially, and suddenly people flocked to London for shopping, tourism went through the roof and, indeed for a while, England had the cheapest luxury watches (in dollar terms) anywhere in the world. 'According to the global market research company GfK, sales of watches priced at more than £10,000, or $12,320, were up 67 per cent in the British capital in September, compared with the same period last year. The figure was almost as high outside London, up 56 per cent' (Swithinbank, 2016). These local benefits can be increased further through tax-refund services from Global Blue or Planet. The local sales tax in many countries can be returned to the traveller either at the airport or, now, at some city locations before departure. For example, we at ChangeGroup provide instant cash refunds for customers in Paris, London and many other cities. This means that the traveller has essentially 'received extra money' and will be inclined to spend this extra cash we give them.

Some countries are experimenting with digital refunds to customer credit cards, but this is often resisted by customers who have travelled on long-haul flights. They are concerned about long delays and errors and alerting authorities to their spending and activities back home. If they were simply to get it loaded on their card or bank account, it is far less likely they would spend it – having cash in their wallet encourages them to spend it in surrounding shops immediately. The lesson here is to ensure all your sales staff offer foreign shoppers a tax-refund form, and help them fill it out. So many customers do not realize they can claim their tax back, which is leaving spending power going to waste. Many tourists are hesitant to obtain a reclaim.

Know your desired customer

Data shows that when a domestic and a foreign customer are offered the same retail environment, it can be anticipated that the foreign customer will purchase more items while also spending more per item. Interestingly, the time of day and the day of the week that purchases occur tends to be different for domestic customers versus international ones (World Tourism Organization, 2014). Knowing your customer base enables you to analyse your customer spending power compared with how much you need to invest in the services you provide. For example, our company, ChangeGroup, offers different shop solutions for different areas. Our location on the Champs-Élysées in Paris is very different in its design and product selection to the shops that we have at local shopping malls. This is because it attracts mainly foreign tourists and thus has different average transaction values (ATVs) from other branches. This then affects the way we look at the customer journey, the optimal customer service experience, how our central overhead costs are allocated, and many other factors. These shops service very different customers, and we adjust accordingly. We also try to analyse very clearly whether our customer base is inbound (coming from elsewhere) or outbound (going elsewhere). Lately, we have noticed a lot of business emerging from customers who are about to travel longer outbound distances. Because of that, we are studying their needs and habits. One advantage, of course, is that because they often live or work locally, they can return to us repeatedly, so providing excellent pricing and servicing is to our advantage. They are still effectively tourists, just outbound ones needing to prepare before they travel.

How do we conduct our surveys? Well, sometimes we work with great strategic management consultants such as Boston Consulting Group, LEK or Deloitte. However, a lot of the work can be done much more simply. For example, we recently did 23,000 customer surveys over a three-day period by simply having a series of multiple-choice questions appear at the end of each transaction on our point-of-sale (POS) system, which our sales consultants asked our customers to fill in. When we need to find out very detailed information, what we found effective is to offer a small financial incentive, such as $10 to every customer who is willing to spend 10 minutes with one of our team members, answering a more detailed set of questions on an iPad (it is essential that you have the questions translated into 10 or so languages so you can get international shoppers to respond). Have the questionnaire professionally designed and structured so that you can get meaningful reports from it that can drive real decision making. Getting things like net promoter scores (NPSs) can be a good health check on your store, but first, consider how that will drive your decision making.

Identifying outbound tourists

Outbound tourists (i.e. local people preparing for their trip abroad) may need gifts, luggage, sports goods, entertainment systems, suntan lotion and special medicines for their trip abroad. In addition, many people buy special clothing for their trips, as they want to feel attractive and confident while travelling. These different items can be very profitable and open up many significant retail opportunities.

Airport shops have this down to a science, with many airports becoming mini shopping malls selling far more than just duty-free perfume, cosmetics, spirits and tobacco. Today, airports are full of premium brands selling clothing, shoes, lingerie (such as Victoria's Secret with their iconic shops now rolling out at major airports), watches, jewellery, iPhones, tablets and even homewares. What is interesting is how the pricing is adapted according to the product. Clearly, duty-free items tend to be much cheaper than at local shopping malls, but the clothing and homewares tend to be priced almost the same as regular retail, although often with the tax deducted. Lastly, since people will pay a significant premium for last-minute distressed purchases such as food and beverages to take on the aircraft, these tend to be more expensive at the same outlets or convenience stores than in local shopping malls.

Applying the 4Ps to tourism

This is a great time to talk about how the four Ps of market strategy (many readers will be familiar with them) now need re-examination in the world of tourism. My experience is that too few leading MBA university courses and too few academic books cover the impact of tourism on Product, Price, Place, and Promotion in the vastly important travel sector. We will address this later in the book. Still, briefly, in an airport, the 'Products' are geared towards outbound tourists, and the 'Place' is found after airport security, where last-minute purchasing can occur in so-called 'dwell zones' when travellers happen to have time on their hands and are in a positive frame of mind while waiting to go somewhere exciting. Years ago, the 'Promotion' mechanism used to be geared around signage focusing on the fourth P, the Price, due to tax-free discounts. But now, increasingly, it is the exciting, aspirational aspect of what is on offer that airport promotion must address. For example, showing how a new outfit might look great on the beach or on the ski slopes or emphasizing the joy that loved ones will feel as you present them with a gift.

Catering to inbound tourists

Contrast this departure behaviour with inbound tourists in the first moments of their arrival. If airports could make lots of money from them, they would. Airports are expensive places to operate, with all their immigration facilities, security processing, aircraft infrastructure and wellness needs of passengers. Airports subsidize those costs by operating mini shopping malls and renting out the spaces. So believe me, if they could, they would try to sell more products to arriving passengers. The inbound tourist has just come off a flight. They are not thinking of what they might be able to buy in this country; they are probably tired and thirsty and just want to get to their hotel or business meeting. This is not the right time to sell them very much at all, except for some takeaway drinks/snacks (not at a sit-down restaurant) and some currency exchange for helping them buy things locally with their foreign cash. Yes, millions of people prefer to travel with their foreign cash rather than use credit cards. In fact, according to the European Central Bank, the Federal Reserve and the Bank of England public websites, cash in circulation is growing in absolute terms and as a percentage of GDP. Occasionally, though, inbound tourists arriving at an airport can be open to buying some duty-free items if they see a bargain or a small gift to give to people they know (for example, I often bring my office co-workers some chocolates when I return home – which sometimes means buying something on arrival). Inbound and returning tourists are in a different mental state when they arrive. They only truly start to relax when they finally reach their destination and can start to enjoy themselves. If your place of business is not at an airport (as is the case for most businesses), then how you access those inbound tourists is absolutely key. Your location in a city, the ease of access for tourists from their hotel or where they are spending time in the city, enjoying meals, visiting the sites or going out for entertainment, will be vital. Over the years, I have seen how moving a retail store just 30 steps towards or away from a prime area where tourists are walking can dramatically impact sales. Tourists can be hard to attract. They often have other things on their mind, and you have to put your products and services directly under their noses. This is, of course, unless you happen to be a destination store that is so special and unusual and so well promoted that tourists will flock to you regardless of your location. I am a big believer in investing in your business and in your retail location to get it right and adapt to your customer needs.

Vicki Stern, MD at Barclays Investment Bank, covering equity research in the tourism sector, said to me in 2019: 'The emergence of disruptors in recent years has been interesting. Fifteen years ago we didn't have Airbnb, delivery apps, OTAs (online travel agencies). The internet has for sure created new challenges. Companies need to keep challenging their business models and adapt accordingly.' As an aside, going back to that discussion on airports, South Korea has created innovative duty-free stores in downtown city locations like Lotte Myeongdong and Shinsegae Myeongdong. Now tourists can show their passport and flight ticket to the store when making a purchase, and the duty-free goods are sent directly to the airport. If other countries were to allow it, it could be an international trend to help downtown retailers have the same benefits that airport retailers have today, going beyond tax-free to being duty-free as well.

Technologies to analyse what you are selling and to whom

The point of sale (POS) system that cashiers use at the till can only tell which stock-keeping units (SKUs) are selling (SKUs are individual product items in a particular size or colour). However, digital video recorders driven by AI can connect to your security CCTV cameras. They will analyse your customers' age, sex, ethnicity, frame of mind (happy, stressed or sad), and, most importantly, show virtual heatmaps of which parts of your store are most frequented and which are less so. You can thus determine – without breaching GDPR and other privacy regulations – your total universe of potential customers walking inside or outside your location and what type of people are then purchasing at the tills.

Where external videos are not allowed for regulatory reasons (even though new systems do not record actual images but only the outline of people and make their images fuzzy), you can use census data from local authorities or landlords instead. This will enable you to compare the hit rate of the number of customers you serve at your tills versus the given volume of people coming in through your doors or walking around outside.

Once you know all this, you can tell if you want to make changes to your product lines, or you can adjust your signage and visual merchandizing to attract your target market better. You can use many different key performance indicators (KPIs), and invariably these can be linked to staff bonuses and other incentive schemes. Over the years, I have tried many different systems. My belief in incentive schemes is to keep things as simple as possible and as rapidly rewarding as possible. Specifically, decide what an individual can truly have an impact on, and focus their rewards on that. The fact is you can often find out what sells in your store, who is buying and when, what are your peak sales times, and what salespeople do the best – all by using your store systems. Don't guess these answers but use the systems you have in place. If you have staff, get them to do surveys; if you have a POS system that can ask questions, use it. If you have CCTV, use it in fast-forward mode, and you will get something similar to a heatmap of where customers spend the most time in your location. A guessed answer is often quite wrong. It can be what you want to believe rather than what is really going on in your store. Do actual research. If you know who is buying and when, you will know where to place your focus and where to look for unrealized opportunities.

Is there a better, more profitable group to go after?

You will need to compare the likely customer acquisition cost of attracting more tourists to your current customer mix (analysing whether you have to change the location of your premises and what that means in CapEx, rent and other real-estate costs) or changing your advertising (type of media, frequency, messaging and so on) and assess whether that would be a good investment.

Analysing the cost of customer acquisition, based on the type of customer, is something that internet shopping sites do very well. I learnt a lot from a failed investment I made in an internet insurance comparison website in Italy. The monthly data they presented opened my eyes to the costs associated with attracting different types of customers and how the revenues changed depending on who was buying from us. On the internet, you can quickly see how different AdWords spending on Google, social media ads, or hiring more social influencers and even running offline media adverts can impact the number of people visiting your site and the number that then go on to make a purchase, using their credit card data to gain customer insights. This can also be done in a retail environment by analysing your sales and who spends the most and when. MasterCard (represented by your payment processor), as well as Planet Tax Refund and Global Blue, have vital data on which nationalities spend in your part of the city and in the region as a whole, which includes demographic data to help you know to whom you should market and how; so reach out to them to see which tourist shoppers you are missing out on! Once you can identify a new group of people to target, you can adjust your actual storefront to attract this clientele (new signage), what hours you should be open, and what types of salespeople (speaking which languages) you need. You can be more cost-effective and attract a more profitable customer base productively. If you see things are not working, it may not mean you have to move retail location. Sometimes it's a question of changing your offering. There was a wonderful new Italian restaurant in the heart of tourist-busy Mayfair in London – the restaurant was in a great location and was operated by two well-known restaurateurs (Arjun and Peter Waney), but despite the glamorously designed refit, it did not take off. It might have been because of competition, or because there were too many customers from countries less interested in Italian food, or even because of its name, or it might have been any number of factors from price to product mix. Anyway, the owners decided to change things since they were obviously committed to the rental contract. They redeveloped the premises into a Japanese restaurant called Roka, which was so successful and attracted so many more customers that they have now opened many more Roka restaurants internationally. They didn't let an initial setback deter them; they went for the opportunity to capture foreign and local customers in the area and turned around what was not working. So, as the saying goes, failure is often an opportunity in disguise.

Make sure you are not re-enacting the sidewinder missile problem

What is that? When the British military was testing semi-active radar homing (SARH) air missiles for combat against single targets, their missiles worked well. But then, in real life, when there were multiple aircraft in formation, the missile could become confused as to which target was its intended one and so just flew through the formation (Ramsay, 2016). In other words, the sidewinder missile cannot decide which target to hit when there are too many equally attractive ones! A business going after the tourist market can suffer from the same problem. There are all kinds of tourists with very different needs, as we know, and it's possible to get paralysed thinking about it. The secret is to determine your perfect target market, deliver to it, and see what happens. Then repeat the exercise and go after another target. Millions of outbound and inbound tourists spend vast amounts of money; you just need to get some of them into your location to be successful. You don't need all of them!

Finding the right brands to stock is one thing, but for manufacturers and brand owners, developing those products sought after by international consumers is just as, if not even more difficult. You can now read from one of the leaders building her own luxury brand empire within an existing giant multinational group.

CONVERSATION WITH
Vasiliki Petrou is CEO of Unilever Prestige (which includes brands such as Ren and Dermalogica), with $2 billion in annual sales. She is the former Global MD of Max Factor Cosmetics and a Fulbright Scholar.

Sacha: Unilever is known for a wide range of products that people consume domestically. How important are retail sales to international travellers for you (i.e. pre-trip, at the airport, while on vacation)?

Vasiliki: International travellers are important to us. In terms of pre-trip our travel sizes for core items do very well, there are certain essentials in the regimen that our consumer cannot go without, so having this option is convenient for travel – as well as trial. We have always been selective about our distribution and that means many new consumers discover our brands while visiting our retail partners, for example if in London they might visit Harrods or Selfridges. These selective locations are important because it can be a new consumer's first experience of the brand and we put a lot of thought into maximizing that brand experience.

Sacha: How have your consumers changed their behaviours post-Covid?

Vasiliki: During Covid-19 everyone talked about how the high street would change forever but that is not what we're seeing. There is still such an important role in our bricks-and-mortar stores and retailers, if anything I think consumers crave it more. It's about meeting the needs of consumers in that physical space – what are they going there for? To be educated, to connect, to explore or to be entertained. Post-Covid I think the perception of skincare has changed as well – it's healthcare now.

Sacha: What trends do you think you will see in international consumers over the next five years?

Vasiliki: As we know, Covid-19 disrupted travel and it is true that things are starting to recover, including travel retail. However, I've heard recently that even though things are improving quickly in the UK they don't expect footfall driven by tourism back to pre-Covid levels until 2025. I don't believe the international consumer is any different to our usual consumer. Trends are transient. I think what we can offer the international consumer, who perhaps doesn't know our brand, is an exciting opportunity to explore. If they visit us in London, for example, they will get to experience full brand immersions in some of our flagship retail partners.

Sacha: As one of the largest fast-moving consumer goods (FMCG) and beauty product manufacturers, how has Brexit affected the supply chain and costs?

Vasiliki: Like others in the industry, we are also seeing double digit inflation on our input costs across raw materials, packaging and manufacturing costs. We are offsetting this through savings programmes where we are optimizing our network but also using our collective group scale to negotiate better pricing on transportation as well as manufacturing items across our geographies.

Sacha: It is great to see women are coming into senior positions. How do you ensure a level playing field, and what benefits does that mean for companies?

Vasiliki: I'm a huge advocate for women in business. It's why I took on the role as chairwoman of the CEW UK who actively encourage and mentor emerging female talents in the beauty industry. For me it's also about having diversity of thought at the board table – if you have the same people time and time again you will always create the same output. I want diverse faces, backgrounds and genders, but also having representation from creatives as well. Having creative minds in positions of leadership really helps unlock new spaces and ideas.

Sacha: What trends do you see for M&A in consumer brands serving international customers in the coming years?

Vasiliki: Talking specifically from a beauty perspective I think we'll see the convergence of spaces. Beauty and skincare has become healthcare to consumers, so we'll see more medi-brands and tele-health brands coming into the mainstream. Wellness is also going to keep merging into beauty – our mental well-being is as important as physical well-being so those brands that make a positive impact on how we feel will definitely be desirable.

WHY TRAVEL AND TOURISM RETAIL HAS BECOME SO BIG

- More and more consumers are now travelling due to lower-cost airfares, a wide variety of places to stay, and a desire to have meaningful experiences they can tell stories about.

- Retailers now have a wider range of travellers to cater to: young, old, varying religions, various languages, business, honeymooners, families, and the list goes on.

- There is much money to be made from inbound travellers, but also outbound – as they prepare for their trip.

- Three different shopping needs for travellers include shopping for souvenirs, purpose-driven items such as a coat or bag, and the lure of entertainment and taking part in what the city has to offer.

- People often travel for FOMO (fear of missing out on experiences) and for JOMO (joy of missing out and needing a break from the rat race).

- People spend on 'experiences', in other words, doing something they would not do at home, or because they have the time to spend selecting a handbag, a piece of jewellery, or another decision that requires thought, which they wouldn't have time for at home.

- Variations in prices are set internationally by manufacturers. Currency fluctuations and tax refunds can have a big impact on the end price to international shoppers and hence their purchasing behaviour.

- Use AI video systems to identify what types of people you are selling to currently versus who is walking outside your location. Use it to determine where the hot and cold areas are inside your shop as well.
- Use surveys to find out why people are buying, specifically, are they from abroad or if they live locally, do they intend to use their purchase abroad? If so, what can you stock to assist them further?
- Consider the 4Ps in relation to tourism: Products, Pricing, Place and Promotion.
- Is there a better customer for you to target? A more lucrative client type?
- If something is not working, be open and proactive about changing it.
- Don't think about going after every tourist – just a specific market segment that you can serve well.

References

Dow, R (nd) U.S. Travel Association, www.ustravel.org/profile/roger-dow (archived at https://perma.cc/59D6-WD97)

Isaac-Goizé, T (2018) Pierre Hermé and L'Occitane create an experience on the Champs-Élysées, *New York Times*, www.nytimes.com/2018/01/26/style/paris-champs-elysees-pierre-herme-loccitane.html (archived at https://perma.cc/2VD8-9MRZ)

Psychologist World (nd) The subliminal influence of ambient music on shoppers, *Psychologist World*, www.psychologistworld.com/behavior/ambient-music-retail-psychological-arousal-customers#references (archived at https://perma.cc/BMW5-UD4H)

Ramsay, S (2016) *Tools of War: History of weapons in modern times*, Alpha Editions, New Delhi

Swithinbank, R (2016) Watches see a 'Brexit' boom, *New York Times*, www.nytimes.com/2016/11/02/fashion/watches-brexit-sales.html (archived at https://perma.cc/SSS2-9AAT)

UNWTO (2020) International tourism growth continues to outpace the global economy, *UNWTO*, www.unwto.org/international-tourism-growth-continues-to-outpace-the-economy (archived at https://perma.cc/Z2ND-TVG3)

World Tourism Organization (2014) *Global Report on Shopping Tourism*, vol 8, UNWTO, Madrid
World Tourism Organization (2019) *International Tourism Highlights*, UNWTO, Madrid

4

Combat your competitors with ESG differentiators

In today's world, many consumers are asking themselves how they can alter their actions to protect the countries and communities they live in and visit. Environmental, social and governance factors are key issues that are often legally required to be reviewed at board level today. In 2006 my parents and I received the Queen's Award for Export at Buckingham Palace. At the time, environmental matters were on the periphery. That all changed later that same year when Al Gore came out with his groundbreaking film *An Inconvenient Truth*. Today King Charles III sits on the throne, and his decades-long environmental activism is well known. How can we use this important movement of popular opinion and make money from this? How can the concept of reduce–reuse–recycle be applied in our businesses and supply chains? In my view, any differentiator is an opportunity to stand out from your competitors. The luxury giant Chanel believes it can use this to its advantage.

CONVERSATION WITH
Andrea d'Avack, President of the Chanel Foundation and Global Head of Corporate Social Responsibility, former President of Chanel Perfumes & Beauty

Sacha: International tourism receipts exceed $1.4 trillion a year. How does Chanel attract customers when they travel internationally?

Andrea: Retailing at airports is very different than retailing in downtown. At airports, there are lots of people for a short period of time so the offer must be much more rapidly readable and understandable. Each of our boutiques in city centres displays a range of goods targeting the customers that are most relevant to them. There is no central stocking or buying requirements. We have lots of customers from different countries, so we have sales assistants who speak those languages. We need to appeal to foreign shoppers in all we do, while of course trying to preserve sufficient space for local customers and not be overcrowded by tourists.

Sacha: The fashion and cosmetics industry is the second-biggest freshwater polluter in the world, and low-cost, fast fashion is often linked to worker exploitation across its supply chain. How are Chanel products different?

Andrea: Fast fashion is one of the most polluting industries; it is cheap fashion that is thrown away. Luxury products are much more controlled throughout the production cycle and those garments have a much longer life. They are even sold second-hand and also passed on from one generation to another. Almost 100 per cent of our cosmetics and fashion garments are made in France and Italy, so that means better laws and internal control, from human rights to environmental impacts. We also have better control because as a business we are vertically integrated and own much of the supply chain.

Sacha: How do you communicate to consumers Chanel's approach to corporate social responsibility (CSR), and is this part of your brand equity and unique selling proposition (USP) to consumers?

Andrea: As a privately owned company we have always sought the long-term value of the brand, not short-term profit. Once you understand that you cannot do short-term things, it is about understanding the social and environmental impact of the business.

Sacha: The Organization for Economic Co-operation and Development (OECD) says that the global trade in counterfeit goods is worth $0.5 trillion annually, with Chanel being one of the top targets. How do you combat this?

Andrea: That is a lifelong fight. We use our legal teams in each country, we train local Customs authorities in finding and identifying counterfeit goods, we invest consistently in trying to control this as much as we can. Counterfeit goods do not have the same quality standards, nor environmental standards, nor provide the same factory working conditions, and that hurts everyone. Counterfeit goods can even be dangerous, with materials and chemicals that are hazardous, especially when it comes to cosmetics.

Sacha: Western luxury brands have been very successful in selling their products to Chinese customers. Do you see the Chinese developing their own international luxury brands in the future to sell to the West, and will they embrace CSR?

Andrea: The notion of luxury is often linked to a strong sense of foreign appeal, and particularly French origination, and this remains very important. This is more so of fashion as opposed to cosmetics. There are very powerful Korean and Japanese cosmetic brands. Perfumes are not very big in Asia; there is less demand. We have to show we are responsible brands, and so will Chinese brands adopt CSR? They have no choice, as the environmental and social impacts are too large.

Andrea invites readers to look at these important links:

www.lse.ac.uk/GranthamInstitute/investing-in-a-just-transition-global-project/
https://sciencebasedtargets.org/
www.vogue.com/article/fashion-pact-sustainability-g7-summit-emmanuel-macron

---

Like many organizations, our company ChangeGroup has always felt that it needs to give back to the communities it operates in, with 3 per cent of our profits going annually to charities worldwide. This includes our own one that we created in 1996 called Tree Foundation and which was run for more than 25 years by the very dedicated Dr Yehiya. We have hired special advisers on environmental matters, install low-energy LED lighting in all branches, use recycled and recyclable materials in as many of our fit-outs as possible, only use heating and cooling in areas that specifically need it and not allow it to escape outside through open doorways. In addition, we have replaced millions of plastic customer wallets with self-composting plastic. This means that even if there is no recycling at the destination of the customer, it will simply decompose on its own. This plastic is more expensive but very worthwhile. We place pressure on our suppliers to take action on their own to reduce climate change impacts but also ensure the inks and dyes used in manufacturing processes do not pollute villages, forests, rivers and oceans.

Of course, none of these things are useful as competitive advantages unless you communicate these advantages to the people you want to influence – regulators, prospective new employees, prospective landlords, and of course, consumers.

It is not always easy to do, but you have to analyse your current competitors. Then, you will have to foresee who will be your future competitors. Your investors – be they your corporate head office, banks, or existing or future shareholders will also require this information and need to feel you are aware of your surroundings as you carefully target more tourist shoppers. They – and you – should make a point of regularly asking yourself who might try to steal your current and future customers, and how might environmental, social and governance (ESG) be used as a differentiator.

Other businesses may copy your business model, and you are going to have to figure out a way to protect yourself. This means looking at those 4Ps (Product, Price, Place and Promotion) and seeing what you can do to create barriers that are difficult for your competitors to overcome:

- Can your products be unique or have unique attributes?
- Can your pricing be different, e.g. because of special supplier arrangements?
- Can your promotion be superior by reaching more target customers with messaging that truly engages them?
- Can your place(s) of business be more unique or superior to your competitors?
- Look at those who can influence your success. For example, can you work out a deal with your suppliers – supply exclusives or a different product line with ESG benefits that are clearly put on the label?
- Can you become a wholesaler and thus control which stores get access to the best products first that you sell already, but you are still transforming the industry with ESG? For example, can you position a regular product differently?

Here is an example of innovative product positioning. Cheese fondue is not a traditional Swiss dish; it was a marketing creation of the Swiss Cheese Union (Schweizerische Käseunion) to sell more cheese from 1919 onwards (Ronan, 2016). They took excess production going to waste and made it into a sharing experience, dramatically increasing demand. In other words, can you create a unique brand that consumers will have positive associations with that does good?

Suppose your products can have unique attributes in ESG. Can you get regulatory protection for your products, as many wines, spirits and other items do, concerning the quality of production and ingredients used? If you cannot control the product, can you control your competition? For example, pharmacies are heavily regulated in many countries and competition is severely restricted, which is great for their business model. This even applies to bakery licences in France, preventing large supermarkets from selling fresh bread. In England, bars, banks and real-estate brokers and casinos can only open in certain permitted locations, restricting competition. All of this can protect your margins.

Protect yourself from unethical or illegal competition. Our company has encountered operators who have tried to pass themselves off as us. For example, we have had former employees set up in competition against us, using very similar colours and shop designs. We even saw a photo of a currency exchange bureau in *The Times* (of London) with our exact logo in Baghdad, in a photo of an anti-Western riot. It actually showed a mob burning the British flag in front of 'our' shop! We joked about who would have to travel to Baghdad (at the time, a war zone) to deal with this copyright infringement. Joking aside, copying is almost to be expected if you are successful at what you do; it is, after all, the sincerest form of flattery.

Products like perfumes, designer bags, clothes, cigarettes, and even KitKat chocolates compete against knock-off products. This type of competition erodes profits but becomes even more dangerous when they involve money laundering (in the case of financial products or smuggled items using organized crime) or dangerous products, such as illegal cheap alcohol containing petrol, or medicines and cosmetics using inferior or poisonous ingredients. How do you protect yourself against the unethical competition? An important step is to figure out what your target customer actually wants. Then change your product, pricing, distribution or quality accordingly, and the customer will follow. Point out the differences between your product quality and those that are inferior or illegal.

As an example, your competition may offer lower prices because they are not paying pensions or staff payroll taxes, or not heeding health and safety regulations. I have to combat this daily around the world with unscrupulous competitors who can undercut our prices by ignoring local and international laws. You must know how to get government agencies involved to defend your position. In 2015, Nick Squires wrote in the *Telegraph* that '70 per cent of extra virgin olive oil is actually adulterated, cut with inferior oils. In the United States, olive oil is a market worth $1.5 billion per year. Police carried out Operation Golden Oil in Italy, which led to the arrest of 23 people and the confiscation of 85 farms for passing off Italian olive oil that had been produced in other Mediterranean countries' (Squires, 2015).

When you see illegal activities going on in supply chains, report them. It will work in your favour to maintain the reputation of your industry. Quality standards must be maintained if tourists and local consumers are to have faith that they can safely buy from you and others representing your sector.

Sometimes you can work with competitors

I generally don't believe in price undercutting as a business strategy because then everyone is in a race to the bottom. Pricing should be fair but ultimately maximize your long-term profitability. The fact is that anyone can sell a good-quality product cheaply. That is not talent; that is sheer laziness. It also does not result in customer loyalty. A good product deserves to be adequately paid for with a margin that allows everyone in the supply chain to make money and maintain quality standards. There is fair trade cocoa and fair trade coffee, yet why has the race for fast fashion resulted in the poisoning of rivers and indentured labour practices? Why should environmental laws apply in the West but not to supply chains abroad? Moving factories abroad may reduce the environmental damage to Western countries and reduce their local carbon footprints. Still, all the while, the industry's overall impact can get much worse by allowing terrible standards to exist in the supply chain abroad, and the amount of carbon released into the earth's atmosphere remains the same, if not worse.

Personally, I think responsible brands who maintain good environmental standards and fair labour practices have not always communicated these qualities effectively enough. They simply have under-promoted their unique selling propositions (USPs). Imagine if Nike paid millions for celebrity endorsements and then did not tell consumers about them. Or if an artisanal chocolate maker did not mention that all their products are organic. If the consumer is not made aware of these important differences in attributes between a responsible clothing or leather goods manufacturer and an irresponsible low-cost item, then don't blame consumers for buying the lowest-priced items. Those low-cost items are made without regard to environmental or ethical labour standards. Companies need to work hard to link these positive attributes of their supply chains to the minds of consumers. Whole Foods sells many responsibly made products in their US and UK stores and ensures consumers know about it. Anita Roddick created a global phenomenon in her retail and cosmetics empire, the Body Shop, before selling it to L'Oréal. You must link your brand to its ethical standards in the minds of the consumer, which can lead to phenomenal success, enabling charging a higher price point for the additional value. You just have to make sure consumers know about those value adds!

Fortunately, things are improving, even where sloppy marketing has failed. The G7 countries and major fashion houses are waking up to the challenge and joining forces to make clothes more sustainable. More than

20 fashion retailers and brands, including the owners of Gucci, Kering, H&M and Zara's parent company, Inditex, have worked together with G7 leaders to make a global pact to fight the climate crisis and protect biodiversity and the oceans (Butler, 2019).

According to the UN Environmental Agency, 'Without action, the industry could account for a quarter of the world's carbon budget by 2050' (United Nations Environment Programme, 2018). Growing numbers of young people are turning away from fast fashion towards reuse and resale sites such as Depop in the UK, ThredUp, and the RealReal in the United States, and YCloset in China. There is a boom in second-hand stores, and tourists flock to vintage markets and surrounding retailers in London, Paris and New York, looking for things they cannot purchase at home. This fulfils two needs of younger generations. The first is to be constantly seen in trendy new clothes, and the second is to be seen as a sustainably conscious consumer. According to *Forbes* magazine, the second-hand market is expected to overtake fast fashion in the next few years and be 50 per cent bigger than it by 2028 (Stein, 2019).

There is a tremendous change of mindset occurring as regards reusable goods around the world, not just for clothing and accessories, but for homeware and electronic appliances too. Some savvy retailers already sell antiques, used goods or upcycled goods alongside newly manufactured items.

People are making travel choices based on values and societal impact

According to my conversations with Nik Gowing, the former BBC anchor who has travelled the world reporting on and investigating social conflict, 'populism' can be incorrect and belittling. The anger people feel on the streets against corporations, institutions and governments about income inequality, the destruction of communities and the environment can be summed up not as populism but as 'push-backism'. If we are to thrive in this changing world, we need to be prepared to think outside the orthodoxies that enabled us as leaders to rise up the ladders of our organizations (Gowing, 2018).

Many airlines are stepping up and renewing their fleets and aiming to be carbon-neutral in the coming decades. However, the difference between the best- and worst-performing airlines is as much as a 50 per cent increase in carbon footprint (Nunez, 2015). This is huge, not only on the environment but also on price competitiveness, since the most efficient newer aircraft can consume much less fuel, so tickets can cost less. In 2019, the concept of 'flight shame' or '*flygskam*' (in the original Swedish) was launched, which had a negative impact on the number of people flying in some countries. Yet some well-meaning initiatives have limited impact on carbon footprints and can severely impact the economies of people and countries around the world (Wynes and Nicholas, 2017).

Many travel companies have fortunately embraced travellers' desires to do something about the plight of those less fortunate and the environmental crisis. The travel industry has a great role to play as a powerful force for change. In his book *Factfulness: 10 reasons we are wrong about the world – and why things are better than you think* (Rosling, Ronnlund and Rosling, 2018), Hans Rosling states that while, currently, the majority of the world's level-four citizens (those with sufficient disposable income to travel) reside in the West, by 2027, half of all level-four income people will be in non-Western countries (not because of falling incomes in the West, but because of rising prosperity, particularly in Asia).

Twenty years ago, 29 per cent of the world lived in extreme poverty. Now that number is 9 per cent, with China now having only 0.7 per cent of its population under the Chinese official poverty line, which is a wonderful testament to the power of international trade. Following a similar trend, since 1997, Latin America has gone from 14 per cent to 4 per cent, and India has dropped from 42 per cent to 12 per cent under the poverty line. These are wonderful trends in themselves that need to be supported for the good of humanity (Rosling, Ronnlund and Rosling, 2018).

The travel and tourism industry has a huge ability to create countless jobs and opportunities for countries and people around the world. Indeed, in the coming decade, it is estimated that 100 million new jobs will be created worldwide in the travel and tourism sector (World Travel and Tourism Council, 2019). This is why I truly believe in growing international travel responsibly and sustainably. I truly applaud this improvement in human quality of life. But for it to be sustainable for the long term, the resources of the planet need to be kept clean and protected. Otherwise these improvements in human quality of life will go backwards very rapidly.

The travel industry is making small steps, but needs to accelerate this. I have noticed how many hotels from Marriott to Four Seasons have started to place high-quality large refillable containers in bedrooms, as opposed to small disposable shampoos, body lotions, conditioners and soaps. This is a start, and people should applaud this more in their online reviews. But what of energy use?

My own home uses solar power for electricity, air-sourced heat pumps and geothermal for heating and cooling. The investment in the technology will all pay for itself in less than five years. Hotels should state the percentage of energy they use that comes from non-GHG (greenhouse gas) emitting sources, and travel aggregators (such as Expedia and Booking.com) should enable consumers to filter search results by this. It will have to happen because consumers want this choice, and if the current travel comparison sites will not give it to them, then competitive forces will mean new aggregators will – just like Google lets you already select airline flights based on carbon emissions.

Restaurants and hotels can do more to tackle food waste. Buffets save customers time, but how much of the food gets donated to local charities? One-third of all food goes to waste in the United States, with similar amounts in most western countries. The carbon footprint of food waste globally is greater than that of the airline industry (Kaplan, 2021) and there are hungry people in almost all societies. So why not challenge hotels on this the next time you stay in one?

Retailers are using more sustainable packaging, but plastic still dominates. There are many things that can be done to improve supply chains – and luxury brands are a major driving force in this.

Useful ESG auditing

Make CSR (corporate social responsibility) and ESG (environmental, social and governance) meaningful to your organization. Try to align your CSR/ESG policies with the broader strategy of your company. Don't just give money away; make sure you work holistically and effectively and that your staff and customers can participate. Look at applying this in all you do. For example, is there really a need to use plastic in packaging? Can your manufacturing supply chains clean effluent water better before discharging it into rivers? Can they use solar panels for electricity and use ingredients that don't involve cutting down rainforests? How can you make sustainability a priority? How can we protect the planet so people can continue exploring it for generations to come and have consumers still come to our brands?

Because of the legal requirement for many large companies to report officially on their ESG actions, there is a huge movement to provide ESG audits by accounting firms and management consultancies. These processes can often be expensive and yet lead to poor-quality data that only provides a basic rubber-stamping exercise to fulfil basic levels of regulations. It does little to really assess where ESG weaknesses and easy opportunities might be.

I decided to ask Tina Beattie, former Global Head of Debt and Equity Research at ABN Amro Bank, who is now co-founder of ESG:One. She said: 'At ESG:One we feel the best way to achieve this is to link your reporting and regulatory requirements to your existing operational data and risk management system. This ensures you achieve a very quick baseline gap analysis on missing information and, more importantly, with a simple questionnaire-based approach you can automatically update missing information. Granular data direct from your operations ensures continuous assessment and, more importantly, the ability to measure your improvements. This makes ESG real and alive and part of your everyday strategic decision-making process, rather than a backward-looking auditing approach.'

An excellent example of the connection between ESG and business success is the two organizations founded by Douglas Miller to take the best of venture capital know-how and apply it to transform the world of business (Asian Venture Philanthropy Network and European Venture Philanthropy Association). I reached out to Doug to understand how he has switched his activities to encourage others to improve the world.

Based on his experiences of fighting in the US special forces in Vietnam, Doug applied his skills to investment banking and venture capitalism, becoming a highly successful managing director, first at Continental Bank from Chicago. He then created and owned International Private Equity Limited (IPEL) in London, which raised more than $7 billion. His focus then became social enterprises. In the many years I have known Doug, he has always espoused the idea that you should always be looking ahead and have not just a plan B but plans C and D. In life, you always need multiple contingencies. You need to be the best prepared as possible, and ESG is no different. It is complex and requires real work. He believes companies need to fight competitors asymmetrically, not just head-on.

ESG is an example of an asymmetrical competitive advantage. Doug received an honorary doctorate for creating scholarships for under-represented ethnic groups to go to university in the UK and the United States. He seed-funded the charitable programme and then got companies to pay millions into it as it gave them access to the talent they needed. Furthermore, he insisted universities work with donor companies to mentor the students, giving those who had few of the advantages of their fellow classmates the opportunity to study part of the course abroad and even arranging for corporate executives to provide them with experiences in fine restaurants and theatres to understand how to interact in society and business. In other words, give students the social skills that enable them to work in luxurious environments, whether in high-end retail, five-star hospitality or presenting a strategic vision to an important board meeting. Walmart and other retail groups greatly valued these programmes. They hired many of the graduates as they understood that they need minorities who come from diverse ethnic communities to fully reflect and understand their customers (personal interview, 2019). This is an example of CSR/ESG totally aligning with an organization's purpose and creating value by attracting and developing talent.

Something else about ESG is the need to consider factors other than cost when sourcing products from your supply chains. For example, in many countries there is the need to consider the director's personal liability when it comes to environmental responsibilities, health and safety, anti-child worker audits, and modern anti-slavery protections. Beyond that, suppliers also need to have healthy-enough margins to have a reasonably strong balance sheet and agility in production.

During the pandemic, as in previous crises, ESG and supplier relationships became fraught worldwide. Many companies quietly watered down or ignored difficult aspects of their internal standards in procurement relationships, and many suffered as a result. I interviewed one of the world's largest apparel suppliers, whose international group is listed on the Indian stock exchange, to find out what happened.

CONVERSATION WITH
Pallak Seth is the CEO of PDS Ltd, listed on the Bombay Stock Exchange in India and headquartered in Hong Kong with a presence in 22 countries. It is a powerhouse producing 1 million fashion apparel garments daily for about 200 of the world's leading retailers and international brands.

Sacha: How did Covid-19 affect your global fashion manufacturing group?

Pallak: Owing to Covid-19 we had to reduce output by 40 per cent from 1 million items a day. Like all suppliers, we were dealing with a wide range of risks, including the issue of the financial health of our global retail customers. They would traditionally take goods and sell them with 90-day payment terms secured with receivable coverable insurance. This credit insurance was temporarily withdrawn by the insurance companies due to the risk of so many retailers becoming insolvent. Retailers need a big supply of garments to survive and continue to serve members of the public. However, many in the supply chain would not give retailers stock without them paying for it upfront. Fortunately the large supermarket chains selling apparel saw a big increase in numbers of customers and they seemed creditworthy and are paying suppliers like us on time, so it just meant adjusting our product lines.

Sacha: How do you feel retailers and their relationship with suppliers will evolve?

Pallak: I feel that for the standard department-store chain, the business model is dead. Strong retail concepts are effectively subsidizing weak traders and this cannot continue forever. It is well documented that many retail conglomerates are EBITDA positive (earnings before interest, taxes, depreciation and amortization), but their profit after tax (PAT) is negative because the owners have taken most of the equity out and levered them up with lots of debt. Frankly, I sometimes feel that I have become a banker now, funding their operations by effectively lending out stock to retailers and waiting to collect money from them. Of course this will affect what terms they can get from us. If some of the retailers cannot buy the best products at the best prices, they will not survive against their competitors. The private equity owners of many of these retailers need to reinvest back into their retail companies.

Sacha: What has been the impact on suppliers of the financial weakness of many retail groups?

Pallak: So many medium-sized suppliers in Bangladesh and other countries are too small to properly conduct and then update checks on the creditworthiness of the retailers they do business with (internationally). As of July 2020, $7 billion was owed, in the form of overdue payments, cancelled stock, pushed-back stock, to factories just in Bangladesh and might never be recovered. Factories in Sri Lanka, India and Vietnam have similar issues. With retailers holding back payment for orders they have received, or cancelling orders they made already, the impact on the supply chain and the workforce is terrible. My company PDS is big enough to weather this, but so many others are not. Some of the toughest retailers to deal with have been the middle-market US companies and this is causing many small and medium-sized suppliers to go bankrupt.

Sacha: Turning for a moment to issues of diversity in the workforce, which is such a hot topic with the Black Lives Matter movement, how does PDS handle this?

Pallak: Actually I feel our sector is rather good at this. We recruit and promote the best person for the job, regardless of their age, sex, race or caste, or other factors that are not merit based. We have factories in more than 20 countries and have a wide range of people in senior leadership positions. Also the apparel industry has a large proportion of women in senior positions, and if you take a look at our customers, the retailers, the buyers from these international brands tend to be women.

Looking at this interview with Pallak highlights an interesting issue retailers are faced with, whether to behave badly with suppliers or treat them fairly. In an area where there is little governmemt regulation, there is a great deal of pressure from competitive forces to lean on small suppliers to lend you money for free. Clearly this is not in society's best interest, it makes for poor governance practice too. I once worked for a very large company whose standard payment terms were 90 days + end of month (EOM). Only the largest suppliers had power enough to negotiate a change to those terms. Smaller suppliers could be forced to stop growing or potentially go bankrupt while waiting for their money, and factoring/payment finance was often not available to them. Late payment of local agricultural suppliers is legislated against in places like Estonia. This ensures no one in the supply chain is abused. This is so important for small companies who find it harder than large companies to raise debt and capital. More countries need to bring in payment legislation with automatic interest penalties that levels the playing field for everyone, especially start-up and smaller companies, because this creates financially stronger entrepreneurial enterprises that can keep growing.

COMBAT YOUR COMPETITORS WITH ESG DIFFERENTIATORS

- Find out about your competition, who they are and how they work. Get to know what you are up against so you can plan your USP accordingly.
- Report any illegal or unethical business practices you see from your competitors. They are downgrading your business sector, and you have every right to stop it. You do not want the tourist to distrust your particular USP.

- Work with your competitors. Are there areas where you can promote your locations as a centre of excellence? Are there ways to advertise together? Are there ways you can recommend each other while still keeping your own business's financial integrity?
- Use targeted CSR to fight your competition asymmetrically.
- If you have ethical supply chains, promote that to the consumer, and help them understand the difference between your products and unethical products; consumers value the unseen, so help them!
- Trust in quality as your USP. You cannot stop competition and innovation, but if you have a quality product, excellent delivery, and helpful and effective salespeople, your business will be known as a place people want to come to.
- You might not be able to ask your suppliers, hotels and hospitality venues to place solar panels on their roofs, but can they at least purchase electricity from 100 per cent renewable sources? How can you use this on your product labels?
- Make sure your ESG audits are meaningful if you want to improve your organization and use it as a differentiator.
- If you want the best products and services that comply with ESG from your suppliers, treat them well and pay on time.

References

Butler, S (2019) G7 and fashion houses join forces to make clothes more sustainable, *The Guardian*, www.theguardian.com/world/2019/aug/21/fashion-g7-summit-sustainability-kering-inditex-macron (archived at https://perma.cc/CZQ4-6CSS)

Gowing, N (2018) *Thinking the Unthinkable: A new imperative for leadership in the digital age*, John Catt Educational, Woodbridge

Kaplan, S (2021) A third of all food in the US gets wasted: fixing that could help fight climate change, *Washington Post*, www.washingtonpost.com/climate-solutions/2021/02/25/climate-curious-food-waste/ (archived at https://perma.cc/5M6K-KEE7)

Nunez, C (2015) Why some airlines pollute more: 20 ranked on fuel efficiency, *National Geographic*, www.nationalgeographic.com/news/energy/2015/11/151117-icct-transatlantic-airline-fuel-efficiency-ranking/ (archived at https://perma.cc/6JMP-H4JT)

Ronan (2016) The story of the Swiss cheese mafia, *Smith Journal*, www. smithjournal.com.au/blogs/history/2423-the-story-of-the-swiss-cheese-mafia (archived at https://perma.cc/KQQ5-MG4E)

Rosling, H, Ronnlund, A R and Rosling, O (2018) *Factfulness: Ten reasons we're wrong about the world – and why things are better than you think*, Sceptre, London

Squires, N (2015) Italian olive oil scandal: seven top brands 'sold fake extra-virgin', *The Telegraph*, www.telegraph.co.uk/news/worldnews/europe/ Italy/11988947/Italian-companies-investigated-for-passing-off-ordinary-olive-oil-as-extra-virgin.html (archived at https://perma.cc/7M6T-RU9K)

Stein, S (2019) Secondhand could supplant fast fashion in a decade: ThredUp and The RealReal are leading the way, *Forbes*, www.forbes.com/sites/sanfordstein/ 2019/03/26/resale-revamp-thanks-to-thredup-and-the-realreal/#52836d441f3e (archived at https://perma.cc/4MEQ-H436)

United Nations Environment Programme (2018) Putting the brakes on fast fashion, *UN Environment Programme*, www.unenvironment.org/news-and-stories/story/ putting-brakes-fast-fashion (archived at https://perma.cc/JK6Z-PNLW)

World Travel and Tourism Council (2019) *Travel and Tourism Economic Impact 2019*, World Travel and Tourism Council, Madrid

Wynes, S and Nicholas, K A (2017) The climate mitigation gap: education and government recommendations miss the most effective individual actions, *Environmental Research Letters*, **12** (7)

5

Encouraging tourists to spend money

As we have seen in earlier chapters, your team must first analyse the investments and ongoing costs to attract and serve the travelling consumer. Next, you will have to identify your unique selling proposition (USP). You will have to understand how to train staff on servicing a diverse customer base who need instant gratification. You will also have to know how to ramp up your technology to both service and attract these customers. Finally, you will have to analyse the economies of scale and scope in terms of having more products available for this potential market. It's a lot to focus on but well worth it.

Let's now hear from leading travel retailer WHSmith on how they managed to do it incredibly successfully and took a 200-year-old business that was focused only on the UK to become a global business in just 10 years.

CONVERSATION WITH
Louis de Bourgoing, International Chairman of WHSmith plc, founded in 1792, and which now operates more than 1,700 stores at travel and high-street locations for news, books, convenience, electronics and gifts.

Sacha: WHSmith Travel is growing rapidly outside the UK, from one airport store 10 years ago to 316 stores in 58 airports today. How does serving travellers in airports differ from serving local customers in other retail settings?

Louis: We have much less competition from e-commerce; customers can compare prices, but they cannot buy. It's very convenient to buy at an airport.

Today, airports are much less about duty free. As airport rents go up, you are seeing pricing of perfumes and cosmetics being not that different from the large city-centre stores such as Sephora. It is much more about convenience and quality of marketing. Yes, you see international brands, but increasingly there are more local brands available, which is a great opportunity. We are creating concepts such as souvenir stores. For example, in Oman we use local artisans, sourcing quality local products, because when you are travelling in a country you might be unsure about quality, so instead you might buy at an airport because, even though you know prices might be higher, the quality will be better.

Sacha: What can retail companies do to win airport tenders?

Louis: There are two types of competitor in airport retailing. First, the really big players like Dufry or Lagadère offering a wide range of well-known retail brands that they own or franchise and put into airport settings globally. They do not alter the franchise concept; they just operate it. Their know-how is to create a good mix of retail in a section of an airport and manage and operate the concepts well. Then there are companies like us that own one or two concepts, and use our knowledge to adjust, to tailor it to the specific travel retail environment. People look at our stores around the world and think they are all the same, but this is not true. The product we are selling is dedicated to that place. Of our products 80 per cent are sourced locally, be that in Oman, the Philippines, Australia, Germany, China, India or the Middle East. To build the supply chain is really specific. Some airports like Amsterdam, Atlanta or Heathrow are international hubs, others like Dusseldorf in Germany are huge, but have mainly local people travelling. Each time, you have to adapt to what travellers need. We have joint ventures (50:50), franchises and directly operated stores. Our franchise model is in 17 countries, and we have a strong dedicated franchise support team, helping with tenders, design and construction, sales optimization, supply and so on. This is particularly important for some countries like India where you cannot just own your own operations.

Sacha: How much customization do you do?

Louis: We have 25 people in Hong Kong sourcing product in Asia, and we also have designers in the UK designing our own branded products, which is really important in terms of uniqueness, pricing and quality. Landlords want the store design to be adapted uniquely for them, but the more we do that, the more we have to spend on capex. We have to be careful to stay competitive in terms of retail pricing, so we can customize a bit, but we explain to landlords that there is a trade-off. We also need to ensure that our brand can be recognized internationally, and our layout needs to be quick and efficient in serving customers.

Sacha: How important is location selection to the success of a store?

Louis: It is crucial, but the best locations at an airport are often given to duty free because their margins and sales per square metre are the highest [Sacha's comment: alongside currency exchange!]. We can have 10 stores at an airport as it is a convenience offering that varies somewhat from landside arrivals, where we also serve people working in and around the airport as well as meeters and greeters, to airside, where it is mainly outbound customers. The trend is moving more and more sales airside, where there is greater dwell time. We have a team in London with internal architects, doing 2D and 3D plans to help landlords at the start of their development. We try to exchange ideas and help them design the retail portfolio early on. We also constantly evolve our retail concept designs based on the feedback we receive from the field.

Sacha: You just purchased InMotion travel stores for $198 million. Could you tell us more about this chain?

Louis: Yes, they have 117 airport stores across the United States selling electronic accessories. Our InMotion stores are growing rapidly and our main competitors in this space are Capi and Dixons in Europe, but we are fairly unique in the United States. We purchased this to gain access to a new market [the United States]. We are going to develop in North America, and we are also adapting InMotion and expanding it to Europe and Australia. The training of staff there is key, because in five minutes customers have to feel safe and secure buying something for $300 or $400. You cannot use a self-service checkout for that, like we can have in some low-priced retail concepts.

So let's look at some scenarios. You may already be servicing travellers, and nothing in your business needs to change. Let's say you have a large pharmacy retail store and sell other things, such as suntan lotion, cosmetics, travel accessories (inflatable cushions, umbrellas, locks and travel adapters), bottled drinks, non-prescription travel medicines like quinine tablets and tablets for airsickness. Your challenge will be in training your staff to be helpful and interested. They will need to be extroverted enough to engage the customer in a conversation and find out if they are going on a trip or have just arrived from somewhere. Then your staff may make suggestions, 'Do you need some sunglasses for your trip to Argentina?' and so on. Once you study this and know what type of person is coming into your place of business, you can adjust your stock, pricing model and customer service. Suppose you have more outbound customers (i.e. locals travelling abroad) – in that case, you need to price your products sensitively so that these customers feel you are reasonably priced and still want to return. If your customers are mainly inbound tourists, you can go to a wider price point as they are probably coming to you because of other factors to do with location and speed of service, and hence the price is less of a factor in their decision making.

Perceived uncertainty in travel retail can be a goldmine. Travellers often feel uncertainty in a new place, so they overbuy. 'I may need a hat, an umbrella, extra jeans, and three books because there may not be a bookstore in my language', and so on. Uncertainty is a salesperson's open window to go from a single sale to a multi-sale.

Wherever you place information about your business, you must make your USP extremely clear, front and centre. That way, you will attract more qualified buyers who are serious about purchasing a product or a service from you.

Educate your employees about what influences people to buy

There are six principles of influence that are shortcuts to universal behaviour, according to psychologist and author Steve Martin (not the comedian!). He has advised large corporations and even the British government on how to nudge people's behaviours. His work draws on that of Dr Robert Cialdini. The principles are reciprocity, scarcity, authority, consistency, liking and consensus (Cialdini and Martin, 2017). Here's how I like to think of them:

Reciprocity

If you are looking for a Turkish carpet and the salesperson gives you a cup of tea, a glass of wine or champagne, you feel honour bound to buy a carpet. Likewise, when beauty salons give you make-up demonstrations, you are inclined to want to buy some products in response. That's reciprocity.

Scarcity

We used to sell Beanie Bears from Ty in our accessory shops. These bears sold for around $12. As a retailer, we had to buy boxes of assorted beanies that would include one or two rare ones that are collectable. Because these were unique, we regularly received calls from around the world offering 20 times more for the rare ones. Similarly, Neuhaus and Godiva chocolates put out special editions, and people want to be the select few who have access to them to give them as gifts. Zara and H&M create products only available in limited quantities from famous designers, and customers come in specifically for those. The products, to them, are rare and thus desirable.

Authority

People pay attention to those they think are in command. Some retailers dress their sales staff in lab coats or smart suits. People trust people in uniform, especially uniformed staff in crowded places, such as door greeters. It is in our nature to follow someone in a position of authority, including a salesperson who shows expertise. Certificates and awards on the walls can help display authority. Endorsements by famous people in advertising campaigns are also a type of authority.

Consistency

Consistency means if a customer already has a particular branded pair of sunglasses or a particular brand of shoes, upgrading to the same or similar brand of luxury handbag is consistent with who they are as a person. A clever sales consultant pointing this out can do wonders for upselling. In retail, it can also mean that you can be relied upon to deliver the same high-quality product, service or experience, time and time again. This is one reason brands such as LVMH or WHSmith receive repeat customers. Delivering consistency means that you can be trusted; you deliver. Consistency also shows itself in the brands of toothpaste, make-up and other consumables people buy. People want brands they recognize that are of a reliable quality, price or experience.

Liking

Yes, tourists will purchase your product or service, of course, if they simply like your brand or your place of business's display or if the product reflects how they see themselves. But what is meant here is something else. They have a higher probability of buying if they like your sales team and how you treat them because the customer, in turn, wants to be liked by your salespeople! Salespeople who ask customers questions, take a deeper interest in where they have come from and what they plan to do, and perhaps discuss a shared experience are far more likely to be liked and advance in a sales career. Empathy displayed through tone of voice, body language, and words used, all help liking, and the top salespeople I know use these to their advantage.

Consensus

When people are uncertain, they look to others to decide what to do. If many of your friends are buying selfie sticks, you probably feel more inclined to do the same. If a card in your hotel says, '75 per cent of people who have stayed in this room have reused their towel', you are probably going to do the same. If everyone in your group on holiday goes into Burberry to buy gifts to take back home, then you likely will too.

These six principles can be applied to many situations, from the design of packaging and celebrity endorsements to staff uniforms and signage. Use them wisely, and they can nudge your sales up significantly.

Cash payments are key

So let's talk about accepting the highest possible number of customer sales and not paying other companies for the privilege.

A friend of mine was recently in Italy, made a large purchase and was horrified to find that her credit card company charged her a £290 'overseas card usage fee' on top of a very unfavourable exchange rate. Or how about our experience in our tourism shops where we can pay several per cent in charges from the bank for each transaction, pay terminal fees, wait for three to ten days to get the money and have the risk of chargeback from a customer at any time within half a year!

As a business, you should naturally also be able to take cash. It is safe and secure, you get the money instantly, and there are no chargebacks!

Moreover, many inbound tourists prefer to pay in cash (see Figure 5.1) – research that LEK strategy consultants conducted for our company on hundreds of international customers in multiple countries in 2019 showed that most international travellers preferred to travel with cash for various reasons, including the need for security and cultural habits. There may be poor payment infrastructure in their home or destination country, or they may prefer the anonymity of cash. Using cash also lessens the chances of credit cards being cloned and the danger of identity theft. Many also prefer to hold cash to make quick purchases and for tipping. Most interestingly, many people – for many reasons – opt to buy travel money before they travel internationally, even if they use cards or Google Pay and Apple Pay at home.

In Berlin, as in many parts of Germany, many restaurants and shops refuse to accept any credit card payments, insisting on cash so that they don't have to pay expensive card-processing fees and wait several days to be paid. Cash provides a degree of certainty in unsettling times; it works even if there is a power cut or cyber hack, which is reassuring for travellers,

FIGURE 5.1 Travellers prefer cash

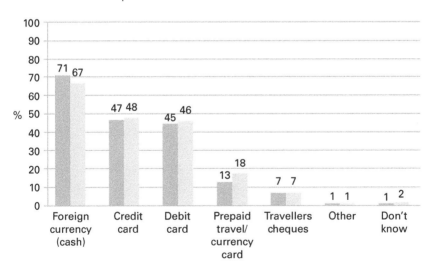

SOURCE UK Travel Money Report (by Mintel), February 2022

especially those going to more exotic locations. Additionally, in many countries, people are used to receiving discounts for not using credit cards. Find out where your nearest currency exchange is located so that you can direct your inbound customers who prefer to pay in cash. In fact, being next to a bureau de change can reap rewards for you as a retailer. A store manager in Sydney told our staff that his sales had increased 25 per cent because tourists had started coming to him once they got their cash from our bureau de change located near his store. If a foreign customer is travelling with foreign cash in their pocket, then unless they can easily change it nearby into the currency you accept, you have missed out on a customer with purchasing power that they might use in a competitor's store instead. (Here's a tip: make a deal with your local currency exchange bureau to offer special promotions for your customers.)

Let's now hear from a global leader in this space.

CONVERSATION WITH

Jose-Antonio Lasanta Luri: CEO of Prosegur Cash (listed on the Madrid stock exchange, with 45,000 employees in 20 countries, providing cash services to retailers, banks and ATM providers), formerly with McKinsey strategy consultants and Rothschilds & Co investment bank.

> **Sacha**: Cash usage dramatically increased after the Covid-19 pandemic, particularly among international travellers. So why is the value of cash transactions increasing?
>
> **Jose-Antonio**: Thank you, I understand this is a great question since we have seen a great increase recently of forex currencies being managed by us. I believe there are several reasons that we should acknowledge:
>
> - The first one is the recovery after the pandemic situation. People are returning to normal and back to travel.
> - The second one is that inflation and devaluation of currencies are creating opportunities for travellers in different parts of the world.
> - Also, there was some travelling demand that was contained during the pandemic period and that has been exploited recently.
> - The last point is that insecurity in digital payments is increasing exponentially in exotic destinations.
>
> The great question here is how many of these conditions are here to remain in the long term.

Sacha: For retailers, what are the benefits of continuing to accept cash when so much media talks of companies experimenting with going cashless at the tills?

Jose-Antonio: I believe that there is no discussion on the advantages of cash versus other methods of payments for the retailer; other participants in the value chain could have other benefits but not the retailers. In order to focus on only the two most important reasons, I would mention cost and data value.

Cost is the main difference of cash versus digital payments but also credit card payment systems are almost entirely paid for by retailers. In a study carried out by Bangor University in the UK, the cost of the credit card systems for retailers was 1.3 per cent as a global average versus 0.2 per cent of the cash systems for retailers – a difference that seriously affects the retailer's margin.

We are currently in a world in which the value of data is increasing. Why are credit card companies getting richer at retailers' expense? I still do not understand that all this data is being given for free and without any minimum controls.

Sacha: Why do more than 80 per cent of international travellers (particularly on leisure trips) carry cash with them, but at home, they might not carry any cash at all?

Jose-Antonio: I reckon that travellers prefer to carry cash for several reasons. As explained before, the first one is better control on spending. It is clear that you can manage your personal money better with cash than with credit cards.

Also, there is a big business of credit card fees with international travellers that many travellers try to avoid. The most striking case has been Brexit; credit card companies have increased their fees after Brexit when there is no clear justification for it.

The last reason is the rising fraud happening in digital payment systems, mainly in international trips, since the card user could be unaware of the fraud until they get home.

Sacha: Where do foreign shoppers typically obtain their spending cash, and is it beneficial for a retailer to be located near those locations?

Jose-Antonio: As statistics say, only 5 per cent of the cash is exchanged at the airport and 15 per cent at forex branches directly or through forex ATMs. Still, 80 per cent is done at different locations. I understand that digitalization should help forex experts to capture a larger part of the market. I believe there is a symbiosis between businesses, retailers and forex businesses. Retailers benefit from having forex businesses close, and forex businesses benefit from having good retailers nearby. It is a win–win combination.

Sacha: Thank you Jose-Antonio for your insights.

Using loans rather than discounts

Travel is expensive, and attracting outbound tourists to your retail location can be based on factors such as the location, shopping experience or range of products. But what if some of these items are not unique to you? What if you and several of your competitors are selling the same products in similar locations? One mechanism to encourage sales is to offer discounts, e.g. on major luggage brands or travel accessories. But discounting can tarnish a brand's image and can be a race to the bottom, with your competitors launching successive waves of discounts in response.

But there is, of course, another way to make it possible to attract customers who are hesitant to purchase for financial reasons – offer on-the-spot loans through a third party. This could be a bank or a specialist company that arranges on-the-spot consumer finance. You can find companies that will work with you to provide low or even zero interest rates (for an initial period) for the consumer, though you may have to give up a little bit of your margin to do so.

Alternatively, some companies offer costly interest rates and give the retailer a big introductory fee. So – personally, I think that mechanism will ultimately hurt you as a retailer as those customers will be spending more money on paying back their previous purchases than buying new things from you in-store.

Clearly, this only works for local residents, not foreign customers. It's very quick to get a credit check nowadays. For example, Thiele, one of Denmark's biggest eyewear companies with a Royal Warrant from the Danish Royal Court, provides in-store iPads to apply for an on-the-spot purchase loan for prescription sunglasses.

Going one step further, companies like Svea in Sweden and Finland can analyse the data on a debit card in real time and offer local consumers instant in-store credit based on national databases (Svea, 2019). As a result, responsible consumer loans can boost sales of products and services to outbound tourists, from camping gear to designer clothing.

Bank transfers for expensive items

One point to remember is that many luxury retailers, e.g. fine jewellery or antiques – who do not want to pay credit card fees, wait for the money to be deposited into their account or risk customer chargebacks – not only accept cash but also accept bank-to-bank money transfers. This enables people to pay in advance and ensures you are protected as a retailer. However, it requires your sales staff to be properly informed on how to explain the process to customers and ensure they have the correct bank details easily available for the customer.

This is particularly good where the product needs some preparation or customization, and the customer has to return anyway. An initial partial cash or credit card payment can be taken, with the rest to follow.

Let's talk about plastic

No, not the environmentally hazardous material… I mean electronic payments. These things are often spoken of in the media because so much is spent on public relations and advertising by fintechs and banks.

The world of plastic card payments (be that physically or on a phone or other device) is dominated by the US-based Visa and Mastercard. Yet, in addition to the usual credit cards, make sure your payment terminals accept cards from Asia, such as Japan's JCB, AliPay or China's Union Pay.

There is a move for retailers to accept various other forms of quasi-money, such as Bitcoin, Ethereum or Dogecoin, which all have a wide range of issues in themselves, particularly around price stability.

WeChat is huge in China and operates like a Facebook payment platform that bypasses the credit card and banking platforms, so people top up their online accounts and spend it using QR codes on their smartphones. Moreover, WeChat keeps track of all its customer purchase data and makes suitable suggestions for similar products, along with broadcasting your purchases to your friends, family and the authorities. This provides both benefits and privacy and reliability of access concerns to some users, especially when shopping abroad.

Thierry Lebeaux, Secretary General of European Security Transport Association (ESTA) in Brussels, is particularly concerned that shops and hospitality venues that deny local and international shoppers the opportunity to pay in cash are losing out on customers. He believes that we are sleepily giving away our data to large corporations to use as they will, paying the card-processing companies too much money, and exposing our national economies to dangers when electronic payment systems are either disrupted or manipulated. He had this to say when I asked him about electronic money of all kinds:

> Cash is the only form of central bank money (i.e. guaranteed by the central bank) and therefore the only form of public money. In contrast, all forms of e-money are commercial, i.e. private forms of money. Therefore, each per cent of payment in e-money lost to cash is contributing to the privatization of money. Cash is a volume-driven business, and a critical mass is necessary to its sustainability. It is a fallacy to think that cash could only be a fallback to e-payments when they are disrupted or fail for whatever reason: in order to work at times of crisis, cash has to work smoothly every day.

ENCOURAGING TOURISTS TO SPEND MONEY

- Make sure you are on Google My Business maps and that the information is accurate.
- If you are marketing to the Chinese, make sure your search engine optimization (SEO) works on Baidu and WeChat in addition to Google.
- Ensure your site is easily found using voice searches such as Siri, Alexa and Google Assistant.
- Have a mechanism in place to get customers to leave positive online reviews, as these are key for search engine rankings.
- Train your teams on the six principles of influence: reciprocity, scarcity, authority, consistency, liking and consensus.
- Accept cash. First, make sure you accept cash no matter what the banks or card-processing companies want you to do.
- Encourage ATMs and currency exchange companies to open near your locations so you benefit from having customers with disposable cash in their pockets to use on impulse purchases.
- Consider offering loans via third parties rather than discounting.
- Have a transfer of bank funds ability so they can avoid the cost of credit-card conversions for costly items such as fine jewellery.
- For Chinese tourists, take Union Pay, Ali Pay and WeChat.

References

Cialdini, R and Martin, S (2017) *Yes!: 60 secrets from the science of persuasion*, Profile Books, London

Svea (2019) More than just payment methods: simple payments for your customers, easy business for you, *Svea*, www.sveapayments.fi/en/ (archived at https://perma.cc/7TD3-S25A)

6

Excellence in customer service

Disney is famous for its attention to detail in its eye-catching and engaging retail stores and theme parks worldwide. I have sent senior managers on training courses at Disney and found the insights they have learnt to be transformative. I recommend you pay attention to this next interview.

CONVERSATION WITH
Dan Cockerell, former Vice President of Disney's Magic Kingdom, United States.

Sacha: Disney is known as the brand to aspire to in terms of customer entertainment and operational excellence. Tell me about your background at Disney.

Dan: I worked at Disney for 26 years, starting on the Walt Disney World College Programme. I spent five years as a frontline manager at Disneyland Paris, and 21 years at Walt Disney World, Florida. My last role was Vice President of the Magic Kingdom, leading 12,000 employees. I have now left Disney to start my own consulting company, imparting the knowledge I gained at Disney and sharing that with other companies to help them be more successful in their operations and retail activities.

Sacha: How many retail outlets does Disney operate itself in parks and outside parks?

Dan: In Florida, Disney has approximately 150 retail locations in theme parks and around 170 in waterparks and hotels. Then separately we have about 200 Disney stores around the United States, 40 in Japan and 70 worldwide.

Sacha: How does Disney maximize the profits from its retail locations?

Dan: We source and manufacture our products to be distributed across all the parks, such as Mickey Mouse ears and other mainstream, high-volume items, through the same factories to get pricing advantages through volume. A Mickey in France looks the same as a Mickey in California. We have to be nimble in our different product development since we are always creating experiences for our guests, sourcing retail items that strengthen the emotional attachment to our brand. We also need items that are right for our lower-price-end guests, as well as high-ticket items. We often look to where the movies are going to put the big dollars, and source and create products accordingly, for example products to go with the Mary Poppins franchise. We did not foresee how popular *Frozen* would be, did not source enough, and played catch-up for 18 months. We are also very conscious of product placement. As an example, when *The Last Jedi* came out, they did not use any light sabres in the film, and we saw light sabre sales stay flat. In the next film, light sabres appeared again, and our sales followed accordingly. Universal was very smart to feature magic wands in their sales locations since they played such a big role in the movies. We think strategically about where we place characters or products that Disney represents.

Sacha: How do you train your staff?

Dan: We train them to be teams and specifically to be friendly. Studies have shown that when a sales employee greets a guest, sales go up, just because of the fact that the guest was recognized. This approach also mitigates loss. We encourage open-ended conversations, such as 'How is your day?', 'What are you doing during your vacation?', 'Who are you shopping for?' Then the guests help you know what they are looking to shop for. Our cast members (sales staff) provide service and thus make sales. They have to understand the product lines and, since we keep adding new items all the time, we have team role-playing all the time on how to sell, creating situations with guests and the cast member where the cast member gets to know the features of a coffee mug, the stitching and the pockets, for instance, all the standard retail benefits of a product. Something else we do with our trainees is focus on their technical skills of being able to pair-up products. These create additional sales. But we never forget to encourage our staff to smile, engage with the guest and make eye contact. Of our income 35–40 per cent is from retail sales. We study this very carefully. We have a unique environment of 40,000– 60,000 people coming through. We had to learn a lot about conversion in the stores, for example. We have technology sensors on the door that show how many people come into the shop and we make our operators accountable to convert these guests to sales. Using metrics, we can tell how we are doing and help cast members change behaviours. We consider the retail aspect of the business part of the show, with costumes and an immersive environment.

Another aspect is that they know their job is to make sure the guests are having a great vacation. If a guest's flipflops break, we give them a pair as a gift. Our purpose is great vacations and the cast members have their role to play in this.

Sacha: How does Disney select its frontline staff? What skills and attitudes do you seek?

Dan: These people do not work on commission. They are people who like to serve and perform. They like to work in teams, have big personalities, are extroverts and show stamina. They are active in their community, school, that kind of thing. It takes a lot of energy to operate in the Disney environment and success becomes its own reward. We know the questions to ask to see if the applicant has the type of personality for this job.

Sacha: How does Disney check that its staff are doing the right thing?

Dan: We isolate which members are better selling, who proactively engages with people, talks to children. We offer team incentives, and give each location its goals. We are 100 per cent result oriented. We collect continuous feedback from our guests and this guides us and we review monthly. We require that our team leaders be accessible and approachable. Twenty years ago we gave performance reviews, but we found they created more issues than value. Now we give feedback in real time, right then and there, and correct errors and give kudos where deserved.

Sacha: How does Disney motivate its staff?

Dan: Cast members are nominated, and become legacy award winners; 1 per cent of the staff receive that award. We also hand out smaller things like movie tickets, non-monetary incentives.

Sacha: Other things our readers might be interested to know?

Dan: We like to think of how we work as turning transactions into interactions. Add to that the right pricing. But we are all about the connection with the customer. We make sure we have six different language capabilities at a given time. Of course, there is the whole social networking piece. We sold 1,000 rosebowl Mickey ears with a social media campaign that said that's all we had. Scarcity works. We create events. We need to always keep up the Disney quality, enhance the brand and not take advantage of it. All our campaigns have to hold up to that standard.

Body language with customers is key

International tourists often feel disoriented, jet-lagged, and may be unable to read the local script on signs, especially when coming from the Middle East or certain parts of Asia. Disney has learnt to engage these people and change their state of mind into being curious, engaged, and eventually even delighted. Now, your teams need to do this too, but in their own unique way – no one can expect to or even want to mirror Disney exactly. It simply isn't suitable or appropriate. However, we must be able to improve the shopper's state of mind, or else what is the point?

Forging a personal relationship with a salesperson engenders trust, and the visitor will more willingly take their advice. People behave differently abroad, and local advertising mechanisms for foreign shoppers will not work. People unfamiliar with an environment will feel safer with one-on-one contact and want to listen to suggestions. There are many ways to communicate your products or services to those who do not know the language and want to engage with you.

Longstanding research first described in Albert Mehrabian's (1972) book *Silent Messages: Implicit communication of emotions and attitudes* showed that even if you speak the same language as the person you are talking to, 55 per cent of communication is non-verbal, 38 per cent is the tone of voice, and just 7 per cent of data received is what you say. Recent researchers have questioned these ratios, and indeed great speeches and the use of persuasive language can be compelling. My take on this is that non-verbal communication helps persuade people of the validity of what you are saying. Here are some important ideas from researchers that can be applied to retail:

Mimic movements

Mirroring another person's gestures and actions indicates that you are synchronized with them and can boost their sense that you are persuasive and honest. Moves like this can be beneficial to both of you feeling in sync. It can also help you feel their feelings, which is another way of imagining that you are standing in their shoes. This technique from Dr Catherine Shainberg enables you to see things from the other person's perspective, which can be useful for dealing with staff issues and customers (Shainberg, 2005).

Watch for body leaning

According to Peter Barron Stark's management consulting firm, if you notice that the other person is leaning away, change your sales pitch or ask them questions to understand where their disinterest may be coming from. Also, lean forward and show interest in their words, indicating that you like them as a customer (Stark, nd).

Smile genuinely

Researchers Stouten and De Cremer have shown that genuine smiles at the appropriate time in a conversation foster feelings of trustworthiness in people seeing them. But beware, as non-genuine smiles at an ill-timed point can appear to indicate that the person is trying to cut them off and terminate the discussion (PON Staff, 2019).

Strong and relaxed posture

Andres Lares, a managing partner for corporate consultants Shapiro Negotiations, says that the larger you can make your body presence with posture and a wide stance, the more authoritative and confident you look. This authoritative air gives strength to your words because it will be perceived that you have confidence in what you are saying and that you appear as an authority on the products you sell (Tariq, 2019).

Be alert and present

This is vital! All the above can only occur if your team is ready for the customer. I emphasize to our hundreds of sales consultants around the world that they need to be at the front, visible and present, paying attention to people as they walk into or near our stores, so people can easily chat with you. You can engage them in a conversation, asking questions about their plans and, from there, start selling. We audit this, mystery shop it, and tell managers about any branches where staff need to improve.

Demonstrations as non-verbal sales

As mentioned, non-verbal communication becomes increasingly important with foreign people (and people from one country may not interpret your body language in the same way as people from another country or culture). As an example of using non-verbal selling, if you are selling a pasta maker or a powerful liquidizer, a person in your place of business can show the machines in action and hand out samples of what they make (yes, I have even bought kitchen machines and gadgets across the world because of techniques like this!). Other examples that come to mind are seeing a masterclass in Venice for glass works. Tourists of different nationalities are taken to a factory for free to watch the glass blowing being demonstrated. Then, of course, they tour the factory retail outlet and often buy all kinds of unusual glassware. There is a little unspoken social pressure in this environment as the salesperson has given them something (in this case, a tour and demonstration) and the visitors now feel compelled to reciprocate by buying something. This product training and demonstration technique can also be used to sell many different things, such as sports equipment.

Overcoming customer objections

A customer may be in love with the idea of buying a product you have shown them but, especially with more complex products, will they buy them? One big mental hurdle is that of product warranties and rights to return, which are often useless internationally due to language barriers and the cost of shipping. In my experience, even many big brands, such as Adidas or Sony, do not have a global returns policy. If you buy a pair of sneakers on holiday, you cannot necessarily return them or get them repaired for free in your own country. This information must be made very clear without dampening the customer's desire to purchase the product. The best way to do this is by being honest when making the sale. This also will be much appreciated. There is nothing worse than the customer feeling that they were tricked. All of this translates to managing an expert staff, people who know how to use what you are selling and who have a passion for and expertise in the product. This knowledge will transcend language and facilitate sales because it will create certainty for the customer.

If your sales staff are not passionate, it can work against you. I once was in a five-star hotel restaurant in Wales and asked the waitress which two choices she would recommend. She answered, 'I'm really sorry, they don't let us taste the food here.' It told me that the management did not care about staff training, and if they can't do that at the front of house, what is happening in the kitchen? You cannot expect new retail sales staff, who might have never experienced five-star treatment or experienced what it is like to buy something in an expensive luxury shop, to be able to give a luxury service. Training should bring the staff into the luxury experience, to see it through the eyes of discerning travel and tourist shoppers. If budgets allow, why not take new recruits to celebrate the end of their probation period with a high tea in an expensive hotel or some other luxury environment to experience being a guest themselves, and all the subtle things that make up premium service techniques?

Another major objection can be time pressures. If a tourist buys an article of clothing on a trip and it needs altering, that can become a business opportunity rather than an obstacle. Bicester Village, a high-end shopping village near London focused on premium international shoppers, has a four-hour turnaround for an onsite tailor, thereby servicing locals and tourists who have little time to wait.

In Hong Kong, you can arrive for a few days on a business or leisure trip and go to one of the many famous yet reasonably priced tailors. The buyer gets measured on day one. On day two, they try on a partially completed product, and on day three they have fully bespoke tailored suits and shirts to match. There is a huge industry in Hong Kong geared towards the international traveller. Similar reasonably priced bespoke tailoring industries exist in Thailand and many other South East Asian tourist hubs.

By contrast, London's famous Savile Row retail shops have not caught on to this and half of the great tailors (many of whom had been there for hundreds of years) have closed down in recent years (Norton, 2006). Even today, they have not yet moved much from their three to six months-long waiting times and are sadly under-serving international customer demand from time-poor people who cannot just come back months later. Moreover, local Londoners cannot afford their prices in the same volume as before, so these businesses need to adapt and seize international shoppers instead by responding much quicker.

Shipping services are essential

Restricted baggage allowances and expensive airline baggage charges have dramatically impacted travel and tourism retail. We have seen dramatic drops in the sale of larger items to tourists in our group's giftware and souvenir shops. Today, tourists often come in and want to remove all packaging and try to squash items into their carry-on luggage on our shop floors! Many smaller retailers do not think of the power of offering shipping or stocking smaller products.

Sprüngli, a bakery and confectionery chain in Switzerland, started shipping their mini macarons a few years ago and now have an international client base (Sprüngli, 2019). Shipping logistics involve many moving parts, which must be managed well. Your staff will need to have a basic understanding of customs in each country you ship to; for example, there may be restrictions on sending champagne or other alcohol to Middle Eastern countries. I suggest partnering with professional couriers with specialist cross-border knowledge. Many shops selling antiques are used to this, from Cambodia to China, but surprisingly few shops selling new products offer international shipping. Apart from the leading courier companies like DHL, FedEx and UPS, there are specialist companies that are very good at moving luggage around the world at a much lower cost, such as sendmybag.com or mybaggage.com. I don't suggest making money from shipping – make money on your products but remove the obstacle of international shipping.

Return policies and repairs

If possible, offer easy and accessible return policies and repairs. Most likely, people will not want to ship to you for repairs since it will be time and cost inefficient for them. But they will make returns if you either cover the costs of shipping or alternatively agree to pay for local repairs to be made if needed. This will help drive your international sales. For example, I bought a set of 12 chairs in Belgium once, and rather than ship them back, the shop agreed to pay the costs for a local upholsterer to make a few repairs that were needed. The hallmark of retail success is making all these processes easy for your customer and cost-efficient.

Use reciprocity and scarcity to entice customers

I walked into a Hotel Chocolat retail store in London, which is part of an upmarket chocolate company. The first thing I heard was, 'Try our latest chocolate of the week.' This tiny gift, of course, made me feel I should spend more time in their shop and possibly buy something. (Remember 'Reciprocity' – one of the key influencers I wrote about in Chapter 5?) So I did taste and, of course, started to notice the attractive seasonal products made for Easter and Valentine's Day on their shelves. And I did feel the social pressure to make a purchase in return for this gift of delicious chocolate I had just eaten. This chain of chocolate shops, co-founded by CEO Angus Thirlwell, has built a powerful business in the UK and Japan based on time-limited seasonal items. By creating a product that is time-limited, they have also created a sense of urgency, which helps drive demand. In fact, in that store, every season is a chocolate season, and one is drawn in by its creativity. They also offer a subscription service to send the buyer a different box of chocolates monthly, using their 170 retail stores to drive online sales very successfully, with over 200,000 online customers (Gooding, 2018).

Another example of a supplier creating uniqueness and scarcity around a luxury item happened to me while I was in Sri Lanka. I wanted to get something special for my wife as a memento. The salesman in the jewellery shop could see I liked their quality, but not the designs. To overcome my objections and create scarcity, he said, 'We will create a design based on what you like and have it ready before you leave.' I was leaving in a week, so I was sceptical. But the salesman got right down to work with me to create the design I wanted, and the new necklace was ready for pickup before I left. We now have a souvenir from Sri Lanka that comes with a story and individuality: this is what luxury means.

Responding to complaints

We had a bad customer experience at one of our airport branches, and the customer wrote about it on social media. We were particularly worried about their post, as this influencer had a lot of followers. However, our managers were able to resolve the customer's problems so speedily and effectively that this customer now praises us from time to time in their posts. The same is true for smart handling of complaints in one-on-one situations. Do not attack; listen, empathize with the customer and, if possible, empower your staff to ask this question and be able to fulfil it: 'How can I make you feel great again about using our shop?' This gives your team real authority to take action and protect your brand. Frontline staff sometimes have to face angry and abusive customers, who might be having a bad day for reasons that have nothing to do with the customer service they have received. It is vital that you teach your teams that not everything is personal. Give them training and specific tools to handle these situations. A helpful trick is to use the same descriptive words as the customer. For example, if they say, 'I am angry that it has taken so long to be served', it is not a good idea to reply by saying, 'I am sorry you are feeling frustrated.' The customer will feel that they have not been properly heard. They are not frustrated; they are angry! So say, 'I am sorry you are angry, and here is what I am offering to make you feel better...'

I spoke with Frederik Schreve, the founder and Managing Director of Oktave, a leading agency in customer service education and branding for retailers. He describes offering excellent service in prestige retail as translating authentic intentions into distinct and concrete client-driven caring behaviours.

To make a memorable impact, Frederik says there is a very simple formula: EMPATHY + SURPRISE + EFFORT. When I interviewed him for this book, he said, 'Did you know that clients who feel delighted and authentically engaged are willing to spend 46 per cent more than clients who feel just satisfied?' He feels that for some brands, the evolution of client expectations will require a reclarification of their purpose as well as a profound transformation of behaviours at different layers of the organization, which is an area that requires detailed planning and dedicated work. The great news is that when this is done in a structured and methodical way, sales growth is exponential and sustainable.

Train staff to overcome bias

I tell my staff in our corporate welcome video: 'I don't care what you have seen or learnt from your friends, your parents or society in general; everyone is a unique individual and deserves your best service, irrespective of their nationality, race, age, gender, religion, education level, or any other way you categorize them.'

Our customers come from around the world, so there is no room for people's biases. I also do this because we need to hire and promote the best people. We employ 80 nationalities, and this diversity helps us serve our international customers better. Unfortunately, most humans display a bias against so-called 'out-groups' – people who are different from them. Interestingly enough, this type of subconscious bias can even exist between two members of the same outgroup, suggesting the transfer of biases are not race-neutral. Still, maybe we're moving in that direction. (Sexton, 2015). Biases hurt not just your ability to hire the person best suited for a job role but also affect the service that customers, especially foreign ones, receive.

Promote more women

As a leader and human being reading this book, if you believe in creating a successful business and a world we are proud to live in, you need to fight unconscious bias in yourself and your teams. Make sure that the processes in your organization are geared to fair recruitment and towards promoting the well-being of all your employees and clients each day. When serving international tourist shoppers, this will be a key component in your success. Fortunately, there are some good organizations you can partner with to ensure biases are overcome, and issues don't just become a set of boring statistics. Here I sought out the help of a leading author on the subject.

CONVERSATION WITH
Tine Arentsen Willumsen, CEO of Above & Beyond Group, founder of The Diversity Council based in Denmark and author of Womenomics: Gender diversity and the rise of female-driven growth potential.

Sacha: Why is diversity and inclusion important in the workplace?

Tine: As we look to the future of the workforce, with the goal of improving and encouraging gender diversity and inclusion, especially at the highest levels of organizations, we recognize the importance of a holistic approach. Managers need to be trained in leadership that emphasizes the advantages and benefits of a diverse and inclusive environment and encourages people to bring 'all of themselves' to work – their uniqueness and differences.

Sacha: Many people might not think in terms of gender-related spending power. What data is out there available on this?

Tine: According to figures from *Forbes*, global spending by women reached $18 trillion already in 2018. Think about the magnitude of this figure for a moment. The female economy is now estimated to be as high as $28 trillion, and women represent a growth market that is more than twice the size of China and India combined (King, 2017).

Sacha: How are women affecting business?

Tine: Well, I would even go as far as to call women a disruptive market force, and one that you should prepare well for. Global research by De Beers estimates that by 2025, 50 per cent or more of households in the United States will have a woman as the main provider. What is interesting about these figures is that women are not just reaching a par with men due to more equal pay and opportunity, but many are actually overtaking their partners in terms of income.

Sacha: What about female spending power in other countries?

Tine: Well, despite the fact that women's purchasing power constitutes the vast majority of consumer spending many businesses continue to overlook this fact. Chinese women have long been renowned for managing the family finances, with women also being key investors in shares, real estate and even Bitcoin. In 2019, China ranked as one of the highest in the world for female labour-force participation, with 61 per cent of Chinese women over the age of 15 working (International Labour Organization, 2019). When it comes to personal wealth, Chinese women also lead the way. Of the 88 self-made female billionaires in the world, 56 of them are Chinese (International Labour Organization, 2019), with the World Economic Forum declaring that China is the best place in the world to be a female entrepreneur. They attribute this to the economic boom, the work ethic, the high interest in tech, and the norms of grandparents caring for newborns that enable women to aspire to move beyond the traditional maternal role.

Sacha: I understand that Scandinavia is leading the way in terms of gender equality?

Tine: Well, Sacha, let me tell you a story then. I have a girlfriend who is a very successful lawyer with her own law firm in Denmark. As a single woman, she went shopping one day and walked into a boutique and tried on fur coats. The man in the shop helped her try on several coats, but when she asked for the price he said to her, 'Why don't you come back on Saturday with your husband, then we can talk about the prices!' No surprise, she left the shop and never returned. Meanwhile, she has also told her entire circle of friends to never ever shop in this boutique again.

Sacha: I guess this is why we need to fight discrimination globally in retail as well as in all other parts of the economy.

Tine: Yes, even in advanced countries. I always tell my team never to make assumptions about people.

EXCELLENCE IN CUSTOMER SERVICE

- Know that customers will value one-on-one interaction since they can be disoriented due to language barriers, different cultures, or jetlag.

- Demonstrate your products for customers to help overcome language issues, so they can see how your product works and feels.

- Demonstrations also promote feelings of reciprocity in customers when they try free samples or enjoy a product demonstration.

- Teach your employees to be passionate and use honest smiling, leaning in and other positive body language, including, most importantly, being present at the front of the store.

- Provide same-day services and, if anything needs altering or designing or special considerations, make sure you are prepared to have the product ready by the time the tourist leaves.

- Be sure to have shipping services for those who cannot carry what they buy. There are many shipping outsourcing businesses to choose from. Actively promote this option to international customers considering a purchase.

- Offer time-limited special products. This will motivate customers to act.

- Respond patiently, politely and openly to complaints. Empower your staff to ask and fulfil the question, 'How can I make you feel great again about our service or product?'

- Teach your staff not to make assumptions about customers or people who are applying for job positions.

- Train your teams to overcome their unconscious biases. For example, being open and welcoming to all customers is key to success in international tourism.

- Educate your staff about the six factors influencing people to change their behaviour and nudge them into buying.

References

Arentsen Willumsen, T (2018) *Womenomics: Gender diversity and the rise of female driven growth potential*, Above & Beyond, Copenhagen

Gooding, M (2018) Hotel Chocolat tastes success with 200,000 new online customers, Cambridgeshire Live, www.cambridge-news.co.uk/business/business-news/hotel-chocolat-tastes-success-200000-14921311 (archived at https://perma.cc/N5P7-E2ZM)

International Labour Organization (2019) Labor force participation rate, female (% of female population ages 15+) (modelled ILO estimate), *The World Bank*, https://data.worldbank.org/indicator/SL.TLF.CACT.FE.ZS?locations=CN (archived at https://perma.cc/3VZ6-AL82)

King, M (2017) Want a piece of the 18 trillion dollar female economy? Start with gender bias, *Forbes Media*, www.forbes.com/sites/michelleking/2017/05/24/want-a-piece-of-the-18-trillion-dollar-female-economy-start-with-gender-bias/#84ea71d61237 (archived at https://perma.cc/KGF8-DEM2)

Mehrabian, A (1972) *Silent Messages: Implicit communication of emotions and attitudes*, 2nd edn, Wadsworth, London

Norton, K (2006) Savile Row never goes out of style, *Bloomberg*, www.bloomberg.com/news/articles/2006-10-31/savile-row-never-goes-out-of-stylebusinessweek-business-news-stock-market-and-financial-advice (archived at https://perma.cc/Y3B7-WBAU)

PON Staff (2019) Program on negotation, www.pon.harvard.edu/about/welcome/ (archived at https://perma.cc/MY95-G9FZ)

Sexton, N K (2015) Study reveals Americans' subconscious racial biases, *NBC News*, www.nbcnews.com/news/asian-america/new-study-exposes-racial-preferences-americans-n413371 (archived at https://perma.cc/6U79-Z9U9)

Shainberg, C (2005) *Kabbalah and the Power of Dreaming: Awakening the visionary life*, Inner Traditions, Rochester, VT

Sprüngli (2019) Dessert: the dessert is the crowning glory of any fine meal, *Sprüngli*, www.spruengli.ch/en/shop/dessert/ (archived at https://perma.cc/ALT9-ZX9E)

Stark, P B (nd) Nonverbal negotiation skills, *PeterBarronStark Companies*, http://peterstark.com/nonverbal-negotiation-skills/ (archived at https://perma.cc/FEW5-ZYPC)

Tariq, I (2019) 4 ways to close sales with non-verbal communication, *Entrepreneur Europe*, www.entrepreneur.com/article/341492 (archived at https://perma.cc/3828-CREX)

7

Experiences are the new product

Today's businesses catering to the tourist sector have to first and foremost ask themselves, 'What gives meaning to our customers' visit?' Not only why the tourist is taking the journey here, but what is it that will stay with them long afterwards? Inevitably that means the feeling and emotions they experience. Great retail can and must change people's state of mind, but there is one group of people who spend their careers focusing on just that – music, sports and entertainment artists. Many international shoppers expect to spend time not only in great retailers, great restaurants and hotels but also experience outstanding live events. Let's hear now about this gigantic multi-billion-dollar business and what it means for international travel and retail partnership opportunities.

CONVERSATION WITH
Paul Samuels (Executive Vice President) and Hugo Brady (Vice President), AEG Entertainment Group, providing concerts and sporting events globally to over 100 million visitors annually.

Sacha: Many readers will have travelled to your spectacular events worldwide to feel energized and experience something unique. However, many people will not know AEG itself. Tell us about it.

Hugo: AEG is a global entertainment company. We own our own venues, like the Staple Centre in Los Angeles, the O2 in London and the Mercedes Benz Arena in Berlin. We own the hardware, so to speak, of entertainment venues worldwide, but we also put on our own events, such as the AEG music festivals and touring sporting events, as well as domestic events such as the Barclaycard British Summer Time festival in Hyde Park, for which people travel from all around the world to make a weekend of it. Since we are aware that people come from all over the world to see our shows we have, for example, at the O2 built a five-star Intercontinental Hotel, an iconic retail mall called Icon, cinemas and a trampoline park, right next to the arena. This offers something for everyone: shopping, shows in the evening – and makes more people come in and spend money.

Sacha: How big is the global events industry?

Hugo: We have many business areas including running festivals and sports events. For example, we take a football team, soccer team or hockey team, which are owned by us as well, and take them on tour. Globally we hosted in the region of 22,000 events pre-pandemic, plus we operate 150 entertainment venues. Our records show that we cater to around 100 million guests a year. We have certain core locations, such as Los Angeles, London and Berlin, although we do have venues in 100 other locations. We completed a recent piece of work with Deloitte in relation to our London business. We particularly looked at the wider economic impact of our London business and how much it touched on many points for inbound tourism, especially the iconic locations. Content is key in certain situations; as an example, Wimbledon is one of the only places you can go to in London to ensure seeing tennis champion Federer win, and so on. The Staples Centre in Los Angeles attracts big names in music such as Adele. The Rolling Stones will be at our London Stadium. So we find that about one-quarter of our customers for the arena events come from outside the UK, since that is the only place most tourists can see superstars like Beyoncé.

Sacha: How do you attract foreign visitors to these events?

Paul: We work with the artists to attract as many tourists as possible. We message our international customers through our large database. Let's say we are running a global tour of the Rolling Stones or Justin Bieber; we will work with their promoters to let their base know where they are playing. We also bring in unique content, for example Country 2 Country, our country music festival that sells out every year.

Sacha: How do you partner with local businesses?

Hugo: In our 100 locations, we have successful venues in London, Glasgow, Stockholm, Paris, New York and, of course, many other places. Cities are attracted to our venues because when travellers come to see our events they spend significantly more on accommodation, retail and bars, and this is an economic boon to the area. The cities know we will promote our events domestically and internationally. Most businesses that are servicing the tourists coming to our events are happy to collaborate with us on marketing.

Paul: We work with brands and partners to establish themselves within a market. We help them to raise their profile in relation to their services. We partner with hotel groups like Marriott and retailers and airlines in the United States and Europe to attract international tourists. Live entertainment has a certain cachet and our partners have been very successful with these partnerships and people coming to see the content we offer.

Sacha: How do you handle security in these venues?

Paul: We have always been front and centre with security. We are a privately owned company and have always been a leader in security, even before the recent tragic attacks in Manchester took place. We were – and still are – using airport-style security for all those attending our events and thankfully we have not had problems.

Sacha: What trends do you see in the events industry over the next 5 to 10 years?

Hugo: Stepping back into history, one of the key reasons live entertainment is so big is that, with the death of physical CDs, artists have to perform to make money and be known as a brand. This trend is continuing. There is a rich crop of young artists doing very large global tours, such as Taylor Swift. Sports franchises also are looking to increase their footprint and sell more merchandise globally. As an example, we work closely with the National Basketball Association (NBA) as they have grown into different markets – London and Europe. China, of course, is huge as a new market for both sports and entertainment. We don't see this diminishing. We operate a number of venues in China – we own one in Shanghai. So we take the teams we work with and create tours across Asia. It's a huge market and it has its challenges. On the other hand, according to Forbes, Bangkok has the most international overnight visitors of anywhere in the world and their government sees it as a benefit for the country. We are working with a local partner and building two arenas. South America is also a big market for tours. The fact that we have 10,000+ people coming to these venues shows that the market is growing. Even Asian artists, like K-Pop groups, from South Korea, have people queueing up in London and Europe. It is truly one world.

Paul: Also there is Indian content like the Indian T20 fast-paced cricket matches that are being exported as content around the world. British rugby has exported to the United States. And then there are the international games such as New Zealand playing Ireland in the United States! Our AEG Sports division is on the move both growth-wise and literally!

Sacha: How are foreign tourists interacting with your events?

Hugo: Online, naturally. Concierge sales are less relevant, although we have ramped up our own hospitality at the events. People will pay for a good experience, so we have our own VIP services. We have multiple products; you can buy on a subscription basis, with a contract, or have VIP licences. We work with partners on this. The O2 in London really invented priority ticketing. We work doing this with Amex and their card holders, offering their customers special access. In addition, there is a dramatic increase in having to create experiential events, where people can take selfies and share that experience. We have to have high-powered Wi-Fi to keep Instagram fed! Our events are big occasions for our customers. They buy their tickets a year in advance and save up for the experience, ready to have a great time, travel, be entertained and have true emotional experiences.

What is fascinating about this interview with Paul and Hugo is the passion they have for ensuring customers have access to the best performers possible and that this acts as a strong pull for international visitors to come to a particular country. So let's look at some other experiences and how they are important in retail.

Building retail around children's desires

Many people travel with children, so it is important to factor in their experiences and retail opportunities, too. After all, a parent or guardian is always close to where the child goes. Many luxury brands have built mini versions of their most popular products, which adults find adorable, even if they are sometimes less meaningful for the children themselves. This, of course, changes rapidly for pre-teens and teenagers who are very brand knowledgeable and have a heightened sense of what is in and what even their parents should be buying. This is largely due to the multiple ways in which brands engage with social media influencers and mass media, which teenagers consume avidly.

A way to ensure children engage with your retail outlets so that they pull in the adults who actually have the spending power is to look at how you can create attractive points. This can range from store design and treats to video gaming equipment and break-out areas. It is also about having 'in' brands that they like, in sizes that suit them. These should be included in all of your marketing materials as otherwise foreign shoppers may not know about what you have to offer.

Let's be clear, many international visitors will not want to leave their children behind at the hotel while they go out shopping. Having a bored teenager or pre-teen who just wants to leave your shop means they are pulling away a potentially high-spending adult from your store!

Remember the hero factor. Adults want opportunities to be a hero to their children and to have bragging rights with other parents. So create something where adults and children can be involved together. This does not mean having a boisterous, fun time, but it can involve things that parents want to teach their older kids. For example, an interactive demonstration of the historical, scientific, safety or nutritional components of your products or services could be very attractive.

Many millennials are focused on value add, so whatever your business is, get the message out about what special attributes you add to your product to make it special. This can transform into a mini experience that they can post and talk about, thus justifying in their minds that they are getting something special, worthy of their time and money. People travel for a wide range of reasons and seek a broad range of corresponding experiences. Given below are some examples.

Photo opportunities

In 1909, Selfridges famously displayed in its London department store the first aeroplane to cross the English Channel, so that tourists and locals could be photographed inside it.

Some hotels now are investing in brightly coloured, unusually designed bathrobes so that people take photos of themselves in them and post them online.

More recently, Range Rover daubed one of its latest cars with shocking graffiti text and parked it on London's famous Knightsbridge Road to be seen and photographed by tens of thousands of international luxury shoppers who shared the shock images on social media. It was so successful in going viral that it even made it to the evening news.

This is clever marketing. Your product needs to be positioned so that it tells a story that people want to share. Show your product in different situations and offer photo opportunities with it. It is good marketing for your business and rewarding for the traveller.

Cultural experiences

Many people seek cultural experiences when they travel. These can be as varied as learning to make sushi in Japan (as I once did!) or going to a traditional afternoon high tea in England. In addition, people go on classical music tours or visits to architectural sites.

Whatever your country's most iconic cultural offerings, you can offer 'retail experiences' around them. Find products that fit with those experiences and cross-sell with the people who provide these experiences using online and in-store promotional messaging. For example, you could link to music walks centred around the lives of famous music artists in your town, or literary or film walks that start or end in your store. Dublin has a Joyce Bloomsday walk, London has Sherlock Holmes, Vienna has Sissy and the Third Man, and New York and LA have countless organized walks drawing on famous scenes from movies and TV. However, the powerful global fan base of Indian Bollywood films and TV take the adoration and engagement of stars to a whole new level. Bollywood productions are less famous in the West but are very popular with vast numbers of Russian and Chinese people. Indeed Bollywood stars are instantly recognized in many former communist countries because of longstanding exports of Indian film and TV shows.

Tourists love seeing renowned buildings, but a rest and a free drink in a retail store that sells products similar to ones used in scenes of the film or in parts of a book will be very welcome too. Link yourself to non-profit organizations already doing this or even companies specializing in tours.

Educational business opportunities

Some people like holiday trips that provide educational or skills-building opportunities. People like to learn. If you sell cooking equipment or sports goods, team up with travel companies or distributors that could offer special excursions for cooking or sports activities. Language schools run cultural appreciation courses where students shop, interact with locals and learn to go deeper into a society. Tie a learning opportunity to your products or services. Some people like to explore residential investment opportunities while on holiday. Many others like to attend business conferences, and in the post-pandemic world, many like to work remotely and use the opportunity to explore business opportunities.

Medical tourism

Medical tourism is another growing area where people go to particular cities for their medical speciality or to address their medical issues at a lower price than in their own country. For example, Boston in the United States has world-class hospitals that people from all over the world travel to. Singapore and Dubai are also becoming medical centres known for the best doctors with the best technology (Amondson, 2014). A friend of mine flew his mother to Singapore for medical treatment and even flew his dog to Singapore for top veterinary treatment. Many choose to travel to Brazil and Thailand for more affordable facelifts and plastic surgery (Said, 2013). This book is about retailers, but many types of businesses can make significant additional profits by promoting themselves to international travellers. Countries market themselves as a place to come for low-cost surgery and for being a warm place with a view (such as Greece), in order to help you recover. England is now a destination for dentistry, as are some Eastern European countries. There is a particular dentist on Harley Street who markets by providing a Bentley to pick up his foreign customers at the airport for free, arranges a variety of pleasant activities for them to do while in London, gets them into the Ritz casino and takes them on a private shopping trip, has them ferried around in the Bentley – all while going through major reconstructive dentistry.

Charities and fundraising experiences

Charities, school trips and fundraising experiences reflecting tourism with a heart are of enormous interest to many people these days. Volunteerism is big, where people want to give back while on holiday. People go to build housing in underdeveloped locations, making new friends and feeling good about helping the world. Consider all the equipment that living in rougher conditions involves. Remember that local customers travelling abroad are a key market segment you may not be focusing on enough. Travel retail is not just glamorous; it can be very targeted and needs-based. Again, well-informed salespeople are key. Once I was going on a trek to Machu Picchu in Peru, but the salesperson of a speciality store did not know the climate there well enough and sold me the wrong type of sleeping bag, leaving me freezing cold at 9,000 feet. Needless to say, I wouldn't return to that shop.

Art, concert, festival, theatre and music tourism

Concert, festival and music tourism is something that our previous interview with AEG talked about as immensely popular. People take jazz cruises and go to concerts and music festivals, which is a huge income-producing area, attractive to both domestic and international travellers. The opportunities to tie yourself in with venues and sell relevant products and services are huge.

Art Basel, Frieze and major exhibitions pull in hundreds of thousands of wealthy consumers from across the world each year. For example, the 2015 Art Basel in Switzerland attracted 98,000 visitors from 33 countries, 77,000 visitors from 32 countries in Miami Beach, and 70,000 visitors from 35 countries in Hong Kong (Blake, nd). To access these kinds of vast tourist numbers, try to find ways to link with organizers of major events in your area.

When I was in Las Vegas, my wife and I visited amazing shows like Cirque du Soleil and live concerts in between dining at fabulous Michelin-starred restaurants night after night. These venues had formed interesting joint promotion schemes with various shopping and casino locations around the city. Personally I don't like to gamble (I take enough risks professionally not to need to get a buzz from it), so our interests were on all the other amazing things available.

As a retailer, you would be wise to consider forming such partnerships with hotels, event companies, theatres, or whatever would suit your customer base. In our New York branches, where we offer currency exchange and ATM services, we also have offerings through our partners for Broadway theatre shows, concerts and tour bus tickets. We felt that people would come and exchange money and then buy tickets, so we worked with the owner of Broadway Pass, Teodor Panterov, to create spaces where his team could be. They help tourists to get into *Hamilton* (the much sought-after theatre musical) or other in-demand events and advise them where to go shopping before they go out for the evening.

Creating relevant in-store experiences

Making your shop an experience in itself is, of course, a brilliant strategy. Lego shops worldwide have huge queues waiting to get in to see their latest creations of giant sculptures, which have been adapted to local environments. For example, in Leicester Square, part of the heart of London's tourism, their shop has the latest Lego models on display in all kinds of designs. They provide a space where children and adults can play with Legos. There are London landmarks in Lego shapes, which is especially fun for tourists. The whole store has a Disneyland type of experience, with Lego being the interactive treat rather than cartoon characters.

Patch and American Girl shops create stories around their dolls (which come in a broader range of sizes, skin and hair colour than, say, Barbie, which many children around the world have trouble identifying themselves with). The company finds all sorts of ancillary products to sell around that story. Children and parents gravitate to these displays in droves.

If you are in the food industry, show a chef cooking in the window and give out samples. Every product can be interactive. For example, a luxury leather goods shop, like Dunhill, shows how craftspeople work on leather bags, takes the tourist through the shop, smelling the leather and so on. The key is heightening the product experience, making your store beautiful with a wow factor that makes tourists want to be there, and linking to their personal journey, be it for adventure, education, business or something else. An example of this is how Vienna has capitalized on the fact that visitors are often able to do their shopping in historic buildings and against the background of a rich imperial heritage. This ensures that they get an unforgettable and unique shopping experience.

Selling to millennials

There has been much speculation about what drives and motivates the different generations of consumers. A report by CB Insights Research (CB Insights, 2019) explores key consumer areas (from raisins to motorbikes!) that millennials have been accused of deserting – and digs into the real story behind the clickbait headlines.

Department stores

Traditional department stores are often pricey and have a limited selection, but 50 per cent of millennials say they still prefer going to physical store locations; 70 per cent of millennials say that they shop at off-price retailers like TK Maxx and Marshalls. In fact, in the last decade, off-price retail sales went from $18 billion to $35 billion – a jump of 94 per cent (CB Insights,

2019). Millennials also seem to favour fast-fashion outlets like H&M and Zara over higher-priced brands. However, these brands have increasingly become scrutinized due to their controversial environmental standards and labour practices. Suppose department stores can tap into the current desire for 'experience' in a store, such as meeting designers and even listening to live music as they shop, while also addressing their concerns about cost and ethical consumption. In that case, they could still draw younger shoppers back in.

Premium products

Millennials do like luxury, but the concept of what luxury is has been evolving for them. Vintage trainers costing thousands of dollars are now a luxury item. LVMH has been evolving their product lines to enable them to offer luxury products for less money. Tapestry, the owner of Coach Bags, has boosted its revenues by 31 per cent following the acquisition of Kate Spade, a favourite among millennials. Gucci is increasingly successful with millennials, with sales rising by 86 per cent in 2017 after their 'geek chic' campaign (CB Insights, 2019). As millennials earn more, they are likely to have more disposable income to spend on luxury, which, as many social media posts clearly show, they aspire to do.

Sports

The tastes of younger generations for sports are clearly changing. Soccer is rising in popularity, with people following teams far away from their own homes. This has driven a demand for branded clothing, bags and accessories from teams as diverse as Real Madrid in Spain or Manchester City in the UK. This has driven soccer teams to create speciality stores in their home-towns, which are places where the fans can travel to experience the energy and passion they want to associate themselves with by buying unique, branded merchandise.

A good example of changing tastes is golf. In the mid-1990s, 9 million 18–34 year olds in the US were playing golf, compared to just 6 million today (CB Insights, 2019). Overall, the sport has lost 5 million participants in the United States since 2008, according to the US National Golf Foundation. Golf, of course, is often associated with beautiful surroundings and an exclusive sport that Baby Boomers and generation Xers have flocked to. While in Japan and other parts of Asia the sport has a very strong follow-ing, millennials in the United States have not taken to the sport in the same way, potentially because the sport requires regular longer time commitments and elicits fewer feelings of inclusiveness and accessibility. In addition, coun-try club activities may have too many rules and restrictions around them, often including banning the use of mobile phones.

Nevertheless, when I interviewed Stephen Bebis, former CEO of Golf Town based out of Canada, and one of the largest golfing product retailers in the world, he said the following about people who are going on a holiday or international work-related event: 'Buying golf products for a golf-related trip is a pre-planned purchase, well in advance of a golf trip. Rarely do we see impulse purchases before a scheduled trip. Golfers who are travelling are prepared and think through what they will need in advance of their golf trip, and invest in good equipment so when they arrive at their destination they are ready to play. On arrival at a golf resort or golf course, you see mainly sales in balls and gloves and items that may have been forgotten, for example, rain gear.'

Traditional gyms with lots of solo equipment, such as Gold's, LA Fitness, and 24 Hour Fitness, are facing investor concerns. Millennials and genera-tion Z make up only 35 per cent of members, even though, on average, these generations view fitness generally as a higher priority than older generations. In fact, the spend on fitness is much higher ($40/month versus $25/month for generation X and just $15/month for the Baby Boomer generation) (CB Insights, 2019). Millennials are paying for group classes and gyms that offer equipment with strong social interaction. This has big implications for the types of fitness products and garments that millennials are buying. Interactive on-demand equipment that links to apps with real people doing virtual coaching is also a new trend from companies like Peloton Bikes and Echelon Fitness. However, some of these business models have yet to break into prof-itability (Arthurs-Brennan, 2019). During Covid-19 a lot of solo equipment was sold, but it will be interesting to see what happens in the future. It is clear that when people travel they are often interested in purchasing clothing and accessories that complement their workout passions.

Video gaming

Online gaming is also getting in on the branded product experience. Increasingly they let users create lifelike avatars that they can then clothe, accessorize and photograph. Brands such as Prada, Chloe, Missoni, Saint Laurent, Christian Louboutin and Burberry have all signed up to various platforms, including the ADA Project in China. Users pay a fraction of the cost of the real items yet can feel they are part of the brand journey and upload images to Instagram and other social media platforms. This enables customers to obtain many of the self-expression benefits online without owning anything in reality. How does this relate to physical retail? Well, now, younger generations are getting exposed earlier to brands and seeking retailers who can supply them with variations on the themes they see in virtual worlds. Gaming is a huge business, and retailers who can tap into gaming culture through what they offer can be very attractive to international consumers.

Changing tastes in drinks

In a demonstration of changing tastes and habits, millennials drink less beer. Bucking the trend is craft beer, which is on the rise, and there is a real sense of community that has grown up around them. Craft beer consumption has grown by 500 per cent in the past decade (CB Insights, 2019). However, the Japanese Tax Department is so worried about the longer-term impact of decreased alcohol consumption affecting their tax revenues that in 2022 they launched a competition to find ways to increase alcohol consumption by young people. The National Tax Agency's 'Sake Viva!' idea competition, seeking business plans from young people or groups to help 'revitalize' the nation's liquor industry, was launched in July 2022 but immediately faced a social media backlash: 'Japan tax agency's pro-drinking campaign sparks backlash' (*Japan Times*, 18 August 2022). But young people's interest in all the new non-alcoholic and health drinks also presents many opportunities for innovation. Molson Coors and many other food and beverage manufacturers are experimenting with non-narcotic marijuana-infused beverages and other botanicals. It is vital to stay awake to consumers' continually evolving tastes and adapt accordingly.

Watch the generations

Before going out and changing all you do to cater to the tastes of the younger generations, let's not forget that Baby Boomers and generation X are still the ones with the most disposable cash and the time to shop. They actually have billions more than the younger generation. The parents and grandparents of millennials account for 53 per cent of airfare, and 59 per cent of accommodation spent. But this will change in time. Millennials are making international travel more of a priority than previous generations did. In the United States, they plan on taking five trips in the year, three of which are international. That's more international trips than generation X and more than Baby Boomers. However, at present, their budgets are more constrained, with millennials spending, on average, $4,400 on travel in 2019, compared with $5,400 for generation X and $6,600 for Baby Boomers (Geldfeld, 2018).

Create your own branded product lines

As I travel the world, I am impressed by the range of goods that get branded by the retail outlets selling them and that people will purchase for their uniqueness – a Ritz Hotel teddy bear, Harrods' toiletries, confectionery, chocolate or jam rebranded with a retailer's name like Fortnum's, or umbrellas carrying slogans unique to that country or city. By adding your logo and the city name, you can, in some instances, suddenly increase the value of your products, especially internationally.

I spoke to Andreas Keese, Director and General Manager of the beautiful Sacher Hotel located in the heart of Vienna next to the Opera House. Today, you might be able to buy a Sachertorte in many cafés and department stores around the world. Still, originally it was a recipe created by the Hotel Sacher in Vienna, Austria. He told me that authentic Original Sacher Torte sales have now grown to an incredible 360,000 units per year. The hotel sells them in beautiful wooden boxes (carefully gift-wrapped in hotel-branded paper) of different shapes and sizes through their own retail store in the hotel, which has direct street access, as well as at Vienna airport and online. Remarkably they have achieved annual revenues through these sales to rival the revenues generated from the hotel rooms at the luxury hotel itself. Now that is some very good retail brand extension!

Let's now look at brand extension and diversification in an emerging economy. In this case, Sri Lanka is a country that has a rich history and incredible landscapes and where tourism represents an important part of GDP.

CONVERSATION WITH

Malik Fernando, Director of Dilmah Tea, MJF Hotel and Holdings, Sri Lanka.

Sacha: Dilmah Tea is famous worldwide and is a branded breakthrough product from a less developed country to Europe, the United States, the Middle East and beyond; tell us more about your retail strategy.

Malik: Globally we sell in about 105 countries in a combination of retail and food service providers, including airlines and hotels groups such as Qatar Air, Emirates and Marriott Hotels. We have 13 dedicated retail outlets (including three in our own luxury hotels). Then there are the major supermarket chains that stock Dilmah, such as Walmart and Carrefour. The product is a single-origin Ceylon Tea – and we use different types of presentation from mainstream to speciality tea bags and loose-leaf tea.

Sacha: How much of your product in Sri Lanka is sold to tourists?

Malik: I'd say about 20 per cent of our volumes in Sri Lanka are sold to tourists. Our local sales are not a significant proportion of group profits as the vast majority of our production is exported. Actually we started selling overseas initially and launched in Sri Lanka much later. The products sold in mainstream retail in Sri Lanka are largely loose-leaf of the strength locals like, as well as a limited selection of speciality tea bags. The focus of the tourist and upscale local segment is our global range, which includes the fancier packaging and the speciality teas with a wide selection of black, green, Oolong and white teas.

Sacha: How do customers go beyond merely purchasing your teas to experiencing the product and engaging with the brand?

Malik: The journey starts in our own retail units and those to whom we distribute. We encourage customers to touch and smell and even taste the product. We provide them with photo opportunities by ensuring the product is beautifully presented with in-store merchandizing that creates a differentiated environment and a relaxed sharing experience between friends. Customers are encouraged to visit our tea plantations, watch and learn how the crop is harvested, and see how the factories produce the different blends. They become more attuned to the nuances of teas, and are able to come away with a deeper appreciation of what high-quality tea can be.

Sacha: Could you tell us a bit about your family's travel and tourism businesses and how it all works together?

Malik: Sri Lankan tea producers and Dilmah Ceylon Tea were conceived by the Fernando family in the last century. Ceylon's Collection of Hotels is a new line of small luxury resorts that offer a remarkable circuit across Sri Lanka, with a range of authentic experiences, while contributing towards local communities, tea plantations and the environment through the MJF Foundation and Dilmah Conservation. This 'best of Sri Lanka' circuit currently features three distinctively original resorts, and we are the sole Sri Lankan members of Relais & Châteaux, the global fellowship of individually owned and operated luxury hotels and restaurants.

Sacha: How are you working with the government, suppliers, local communities and your customers to overcome the recent challenging economic and political situations in Sri Lanka?

Malik: Dilmah is exposed to tourism, through our high-end Relais & Châteaux hotels that we own. I have also spearheaded the Sri Lanka Tourism Alliance, which is the first time the private sector has come together to communicate the ground situation to travellers and travel agents overseas, and much more besides. Our website is at www.sriLankatourismalliance.com. We also set up a retail site, www.LoveSriLanka.org, to help serve tourists directly.

EXPERIENCES ARE THE NEW PRODUCT

- Many people travel for special events such as concerts and sporting fixtures. There are many brand extensions and partnerships available for this.

- People travel to experience new things. Tap into the reasons for their journeys and the memories they want to create.

- Great retailers have been creating customer photo opportunities since well before the advent of social media. So what will your international customers, and more importantly, the people they want to influence, be awakened by?

- Can you provide additional value add beyond a mere physical product to imparting knowledge to the customer? Providing experiences that infuse them with knowledge gives customers storytelling power.

- What experiences are going on near your retail space that you can tap into? For example, international marathons, sporting events, theatre or music festivals. Can any of your products, messaging or in-store activities align with those?

- Engage with your shoppers' younger children and teenagers – they will otherwise pull their parents away from shopping with you.

- Millennials are spearheading the move from owning things to experiencing things. This is prompting a dramatic increase in international travel.

- Look to tie retail experiences into trips involving hotel partners, factories, agricultural facilities and community charities. These are all part of the extended supply chain that provides customers with knowledge and experiences, which will help your brand and attract new customers.

References

Amondson, C (2014) 30 most technologically advanced hospitals in the world, *Top Master's in Healthcare Administration*, 24 March, www.topmastersinhealthcare.com/30-most-technologically-advanced-hospitals-in-the-world/ (archived at https://perma.cc/2DRT-DBH6)

Arthurs-Brennan, M (2019) Peloton share prices plummet as spin bike brand unveils losses of $49.8 million, *Cycling Weekly*, www.cyclingweekly.com/news/peloton-share-prices-plummet-spin-bike-brand-unveils-losses-49-8-million-441993 (archived at https://perma.cc/HN46-26EE)

Blake, B (nd) Art Basel, *Citizen Planet*, http://citizenplanet.com/?p=8241 (archived at https://perma.cc/JNT3-3ZJT)

CB Insights (2019) 12 industries experts say millennials are killing – and why they're wrong, *CB Insights*, www.cbinsights.com/research/millennials-killing-industries/ (archived at https://perma.cc/GB4F-4M2H)

Geldfeld, V (2018) Americans already packing their bags for 2019, *AARP Research*, www.aarp.org/research/topics/life/info-2018/2019-travel-trends.html (archived at https://perma.cc/X3N5-U7XP)

Said, S (2013) The cheapest places in the world to get plastic surgery, *The Richest*, www.therichest.com/location/the-cheapest-places-in-the-world-to-get-plastic-surgery/ (archived at https://perma.cc/3GP8-SA87)

8

Digital and online technologies

This is an area that many businesses struggle with. So much money can be wasted, yet never before have organizations that have mastered digital technology profited so much from it. So how can retailers, particularly those seeking to attract and engage with international shoppers, use digital and online technologies to their advantage? Let's start by looking at what luxury brands like LVMH are doing.

CONVERSATION WITH
Jonathan Chippendale, CEO of Holition Technologies and former Managing Director of De Beers Diamonds (Middle East).

Sacha: You work on innovative technologies for Hermès, Covergirl, Cartier, LVMH, Shiseido and many other great retail brands. Can you explain what you do?

Jonathan: Well, our clients are mostly luxury fashion and beauty clients, and we are sort of creative technologists, responding to the particular needs of our client base. We've been in business for 14 years. We are a practice-based consultancy, using our understanding of the future relationship between humans and technology and what that means for each brand. We consider the technology channel of communication no different than any other marketing vehicle and we help our clients harness it to tell stories (brands are stories). As we know, a Louis Vuitton bag does not sell on its buckles, but on its personality. Both Jason Holt, the owner of the company, and I come from a luxury retail background and we wanted to study the fear and anxiety of the industry, and help our clients with the long-term movements in the business and how technology affects this business. We are like a digital anthropology lab, studying the ways technology supports, augments and helps humans in this particular purchasing area.

Sacha: How do you do this specifically?

Jonathan: We help brands ask the right questions and think about what they hear from their customers. The brand no longer simply presents a product line to the customer; the customer tells them what they want and what they should be designing. So, using technology, they can see what trends are considered cool, and get into this infinite loop of designing, listening, designing and so on. It used to be that brands pushed out content, now it is reversed. So we track megatrends, how mobile, for instance, is changing the business, how mobiles will be able to read our faces to help brands know what it is we need. Brands will have to adjust their trends according to the voices and gestures they perceive. These will affect colour patterns and so on, responding to how the customer feels. The mind of the customer will be in the nerve of the hand and brands need to know how to convert these impulses to the Internet of Things.

Sacha: What do you think of technology in stores?

Jonathan: We have seen that 80 per cent of the current technologies put barriers between people and the shopping experience. We anticipate a major overhaul of how we use technology in stores. What has been done so far may be an example of wasted investments. We have partnered with leading brands to pioneer the use of augmented reality apps and in-store kiosks to superimpose items from watches to make-up on their wrists and faces, but this is just the beginning.

Sacha: What about omnichannel marketing?

Jonathan: There should be a ban on it. Humans act differently on different platforms. You cannot put mobile marketing in-store. The key is not to look at one bit of content and put it everywhere, but to understand how people have differences and different ways of shopping and celebrate these differences, rather than trying to mash them all together.

Sacha: What are you seeing right now in the retail environment?

Jonathan: As the demographics of people acquiring wealth change, people don't want to follow the herd. They may want a Louis Vuitton product but they want it to express their individuality and personal sophistication. Or people might want a cool handbag made by a small manufacturer instead. Since we are all fundamentally different, technology has to lose the Amazon idea that 'If you like this, you will like that'. People want to be marketed to individually.

Sacha: How can the brands listen to people?

Jonathan: As an example, we did a study asking 'what is the London look'? We assessed over 1 million images from Instagram for colour, cut and fit, grouping them together, second by second and, by analysing those, we got the trends of London, which were pulled from consumers. From there, we could see the individuality in each look and how brands need to be aware of this and individualize their products. Max Factor did the same second-by-second scanning on mobile phones of face shapes, eyes, physical properties, and were interested in the differences. Then they blended these faces with the weather at the time and specifically selected what products were to be individually marketed to the consumer accordingly.

Sacha: It sounds like you are saying that future purchases and marketing will be based on the consumer's emotions. How do you see this translating to the international traveller and tourist shopper?

Jonathan: The retailer has to stock items that reflect the emotional state of the traveller, and also each brand must have a global presence. As an example, certain pop-up stores raised this question: Do you adapt your American brand in Korea to Korea, or keep it American since that may be what the purchaser wants? The current trend is to do a bit of both. So stores cater to the traveller's nationality and interests, combined with the rarity of the product in the country the traveller is visiting. Also the retailer has to understand whether their customers want a fast transaction or they want to be catered to leisurely in the store, with items being gift wrapped or individualized and so on. Does the customer want to be pampered? A store is like a personal relationship. You cannot force yourself on someone. You have to find out what your customer wants, what style of transaction they want, and provide that to them.

Make your website dynamic and alluring

From the moment someone thinks of travelling to the moment they step off the aircraft, people are on their phones researching what to do and where to go at their destination.

Your website and marketing must be forward thinking – mobile friendly, easy to navigate, making every convenience and saving clear and enticing. Years ago, it used to be that you needed to have your website in various languages. But now, with web browsers translating languages so rapidly and accurately, this is not really needed anymore.

While many websites will try to sell online, in our context here it is more about encouraging the customer to visit you in-store. Many big brands achieve this by having only a limited selection online. For the really great merchandise, you have to visit in-store. You could create a benefits system that includes pre-arrival perks in your store to draw customers from afar. Your customers should feel at ease on your website and be able to navigate around it easily. In other words, make it engaging. An engaging tone can be 'fun' with attractive promotions and creative incentive schemes that are original and relationship-oriented. Getting customers to visit your site is, of course, one of the hardest parts. So we use a variety of techniques, including search engine optimization (SEO), social media, Google adverts, PR companies and, most importantly, partnerships with companies who refer customers to us from their websites. This can include retail travel partners and larger local groups, such as home insurers, banks and shopping malls. The outbound travel market can be easier to connect to digitally, with many airlines and travel sites providing opportunities to advertise in a targeted way, either with direct partnerships or through Google adverts. However, targeting inbound tourists from all over the world can be much more difficult.

Reviews are also important, although users are becoming increasingly sophisticated and distrust sites that don't publish negative reviews. TripAdvisor and similar companies were losing market share at one time due to the perception that they removed negative comments and that some reviews were fake. According to TripAdvisor, this issue has since been remedied (Stimmler-Hall, 2016).

All over the world, action has been taken against fake reviews. For example, a man was sentenced to nine months in prison in a landmark fraud ruling by an Italian court. 'The owner of Promo Solento was convicted of selling fake reviews to hundreds of hospitality businesses across Italy in order to raise their profile on the website. He was also ordered to pay £7,100' (Giuffrida and Wilson, 2018).

There have also been court cases (in connection with TripAdvisor and other review sites) where damages have been awarded to companies that have had negative paid fake reviews posted about them. Pascal Lemy, the chairman of the UN World Travel Organization Committee on Tourist Ethics, said: 'Online reviews play a major role in tourism and consumer purchasing decisions, but it's important everyone plays by the rules' (Squires, 2018).

For those of us in travel retail, reviews through TripAdvisor and other sites are incredibly important. According to the European Commission, 82 per cent of people read consumer reviews before shopping, with estimates suggesting that 1–16 per cent of reviews are fake (Valant, 2015).

It is essential for the retailer to have a team responsible for monitoring reviews. Encourage happy customers to leave good reviews so that any bad ones seem incidental. Reply to negative reviews apologizing for what happened and explain what you have done to provide a solution to the problem.

Consider devoting some of your website to information about the local region, streets and shops around you (with links) so that you can also be an information centre. For example, partner with a weather app so your customer can follow the weather conditions and make informed decisions on whether to visit an indoor attraction or go to a shopping street. Become an authority online for the product and services you provide.

You may need an outsourced social media team who can act as a concierge and jump on any positive or negative issues. If your online 'concierge' is responsive, you will be known online for great customer service, making your brand seem like a trusted friend. Google, in particular, watches whether negative reviews are responded to promptly and penalizes slow or non-responding companies by reducing their rankings on Google search pages.

Figure 8.1 shows the AIDA model, which I find to be one of the simplest and most helpful models for promoting a business. This is an acronym for the stages that a new shop or a brand goes through to get the consumers' Attention, secure their Interest, arouse Desire, and finally lead the consumer into Action by making a purchase. When creating advertising messages, posters and in-store displays, think about the state of mind you want to

FIGURE 8.1   The AIDA model

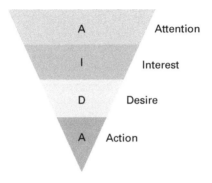

create in the consumer. It's a bit like sending out a party invitation. You want people to be excited, to want to say yes, and to turn up. Use technology to attract and serve customers. More and more travellers are increasingly comfortable with digital assistance. For instance, as of 2019, QuoraCreative reports that around 50 per cent of Google searches are instructed verbally (Butt, 2019). Many travellers use digital assistants to choose what to do at their destination, and this trend will only increase as smartphones and smart devices proliferate. This means that your online information has to be structured differently to consider voice search and other digital aspects. It goes without saying that you must make your site mobile-friendly and make your physical location clear on mobile maps. Here are some suggestions on how to optimize your website for voice search:

- When writing content for your website, use a conversational tone and ensure copy is written in a natural way that responds to questions that customers might have. This is different from the old concept of focusing on website keywords; semantic search is key, as is having content that answers questions so that Siri or Alexa can use your phrases, which they then read out to people.

- Explore the intent behind customers' questions in voice searches, and then expand the content to the most important ones. You then use some of the keywords in this expanded content as part of your AdWords spend on Google, Facebook and other online campaigns.

- Use structured data, and use a schema mark-up in the hidden parts of your website. This is important, as it optimizes search results and provides the so-called 'cards', which are the answers displayed or spoken to the person doing the voice search. This also allows search engines to use your information as part of their knowledge graphs (Olson, 2016).

Reaching your target audience

Having a great-looking website is one thing. Getting people to visit it is a whole other issue. In terms of the online world, there is much that can be done to bring in local and foreign shoppers. More and more stores, shopping malls and even airports hire an influencer to come in to help get their name out there on social media. The cost per post varies and can be astronomical depending on the scale of the influencer, but this method can reap huge rewards (WebFX, 2019). CNN reported (Street, 2017) how Helsinki

International Airport ran a fantastic campaign with a Chinese influencer, Ryan Zhu, who lived for one month at the airport and used all the facilities and retailers, vlogging about his experiences while living in a cabin next to the departure gates.

If your market is inbound, you can place ads in airline magazines, tourist maps and pamphlets in hotel concierge areas. Advertise what is unique to your business for tourists. For example, if you have access to a quiet prayer area, or offer halal cuisine or halal products, feature it in your ads. (Given that there are over 2 billion Muslims on the planet (World Population Review, 2019) and that more and more are travelling, this is a good business idea.)

If your market is in outbound tourism, you can advertise on travel advisory sites, Google AdWords and TripAdvisor, or place an advertorial in travel magazines or in the travel supplements of popular newspapers. A good PR person can help with this to a dramatic positive effect.

Google reviews and Google maps must be in top shape

Google, of course, is everyone's first stop when researching anything in the West. But how you position yourself on the internet is all about knowing your audience. For example, if your target audience is Chinese tourists, they don't use Google; instead, you would be wise to have a site on WeChat (similar to Facebook) and a Chinese-registered site searchable on Baidu (similar to Google) with your information in Mandarin. Likewise, information on your store, entertainment venue, hotel or restaurant must be on TripAdvisor, Yelp and Google for countries other than China. But if you are after the tourist segment, you must present your offering in the language of the tourist you are trying to reach, such as Chinese, Arabic, Spanish or Russian (you can put a translate button on your site). None of this requires genius but is surprisingly often overlooked. While most searches are conducted on a smartphone, the trend is very much towards voice search, so make sure your site works well on Apple's Siri, Amazon's Alexa or Google Assistant.

If a customer wants to find a sushi restaurant near them, chances are they will not be looking for it on a desktop computer screen but rather on a phone, which will typically show a map of the three closest restaurants with the highest ratings. This also applies to other search terms, such as convenience stores or for any product or service. If your business does not come up in these top three options (let alone not come up on the first page of Google), you will have problems attracting international visitors who are often time constrained. Getting yourself visible online can be a difficult task, and web designers can help. But if you really want to do it well, I recommend you engage professional digital search agencies who can get your name out there on all the relevant sites, such as Google, Foursquare, Yelp and so on, in ways that are relevant to your business and product.

Cater for disabilities, even online

As I learnt rather expensively, having a website that can be read even by partially sighted or fully blind people is a legal requirement in the United States. Make sure your website is Web Content Accessibility Guidelines (WCAG) compliant. Visually impaired people use voice search and 'screen reader software', and failure to apply this standard can result in court cases. Law firms representing visually impaired plaintiffs have won substantial damages against businesses in class action cases (Randazzo, 2019). When considering WCAG compliance, it is important to consider the use of alt-text tags on photos, which Siri and other systems cannot describe otherwise. Failure to use alt-text tags could result in customers being denied access to special offers because they cannot see your promotional offer of 30 per cent off today, failing to find out your store opening hours, or a job seeker need-ing to understand images on your site as part of their application.

On a related note, think about universal design. Universal design is paying particular attention to the design and composition of an environment (think a shop, restaurant or any physical space) to ensure that it can be accessed, understood and used to the greatest extent possible by all people regardless of their age, size, ability or disability (National Disability Authority, 2019). Universal design assumes that everyone, at some point during their life, is likely to suffer an injury, be unable to properly walk for long periods, use their hands at full strength, or use other parts of their bodies properly because of age, disability or injury. Making sure door openings, seats, merchandise and other aspects of the retail environment are available for all customers to use and feel welcome is essential, not just for the good func-tioning of society but because it also opens up a much broader range of customers for businesses, especially as those people not working full-time, such as retirees, have the desire and often the means to travel! With longer life spans, in 2022, some 31.9 per cent of Americans aged between 65 and 73 are estimated to still be working and earning money, and by 2050 the population over 60 is estimated to have doubled (Anzilotti, 2017).

Loyalty point schemes – not for inbound tourists

Loyalty points and other techniques to lure back regular customers are great for local customers. They are, however, just a source of irritation for foreigners who rarely, if ever, will return. As I know I probably will not revisit the shop for at least a year or two, this attempt to engage me becomes a source of frustration instead. It's like getting too many emails from a store you have visited. Also, GDPR regulations in Europe are very tough, and you can only hold and use data that customers explicitly give you consent for.

Push your shiny new app to local customers if it is appropriate. But don't think that everyone wants your app, especially if they are never or rarely returning to your store. My experience is that apps and loyalty schemes are great if your product or service is likely to be used at least monthly or weekly. They are great for coffee shops, fast-food restaurants, dry cleaners, department stores and the like. If, however, your customers are only going to visit twice a year, then a loyalty scheme is unlikely to be very effective.

In attracting international travellers, realize that a particular individual may not come back for a while. But if you help serve them well, they will be part of a continuous wave of valuable customers coming to you. They may not want to be in constant contact, though.

Translation apps – can your staff use them effectively?

On a recent trip to Shanghai, I asked the plane stewardess to write out my hotel address in Chinese characters. This was because I knew the hotel confirmation I had printed out in English would most likely be unreadable by a local Chinese taxi driver (don't scoff, how many taxi drivers in Paris or New York can read Chinese characters?). I was completely dependent on my phone for most of the trip for maps and information about where to go. In particular, I was looking for a great clothing store I knew from Hong Kong called Shanghai Tang. The hotel concierge gave the address to the taxi driver, but when we arrived, the store was boarded up and had obviously shut down.

This reminds us how important it is that retail websites are kept up to date. As mentioned before, you can engage professional digital agencies to manage this and ensure that your opening hours, location and reviews are all kept up to date on Google, My Business, Yelp, Four Square, Bing and so on. If you do not keep your website information on store opening hours and locations up to date, people will get frustrated and harm your brand's reputation. Training your staff to use their mobile phones to access translation apps is absolutely a core skill and something I have only occasionally seen applied in the West.

To portray the usefulness of these translation apps, during the same trip to Shanghai I came across an attractive light-up world globe in a shop for my son and needed to know what voltage it used and other technical details. The sales assistant used an app to very successfully translate all this technical information. Because of that, I was able to make the purchase. Despite the language barrier, she acted as if working with me was seamless and natural. This is a good salesperson! Now, can you imagine the same thing happening in your retail stores? Would your staff be as helpful and welcoming and able to use translation apps for customers of different nationalities visiting you? And would your salespeople know how to handle the different customs that are in other cultures as well?

Use market research as a way of engaging important clients

Even though we live in a technological world, people still enjoy being served by real people, want to be treated as special and be invited to what is unique or private. But above all, people want to think that their opinions are valued!

Whether you communicate in person or online with your customer base, it is crucial to spend time with your top customers and top social media influencers (paid or unpaid), listening to them in focus groups, thus making them feel special and valued. Then tell them what you plan to do as you evolve your concepts. If you can do this in person, create a personal focus-group-type atmosphere, with drinks and canapés, where your top customers can express what they want and find out what you are doing especially for them. Offer them private showings. Introduce them to designers or special people involved in your product and get their feedback. Private offerings and special sales or yet to be released products just for your best customers are all ways to keep customers returning. I recently attended a book signing for a book on the perfume industry that was being sold in a perfume store. The discussion centred around the industry's evolution and helped make the clients who attended feel they were part of the process of trend development. The store gifted the books with the clients' perfumes, which all made for a great experience.

On-street marketing techniques

Some countries, like Denmark, do not allow people to hand out flyers. Conversely, New York's Broadway area has many cast members dressed up to promote their shows and distribute flyers. For example, the play *Chicago* often has a character from the play handing out flyers for the show and performing a short dance. The tourist becomes part of the spectacle, and it is as if they are meeting an ambassador for the show, increasing the likelihood that they will go on to purchase tickets. Each country is different, and understanding local laws is important. I once was told to remove a display board I had placed outside our shop in Austria. To my annoyance, my competitor 50 metres away did not, but my complaint to the same official was ignored with the phrase, 'Sir, some people speeding on the motorway get stopped, some do not.' Clearly, life is not always fair, and rules may not get evenly enforced.

If you want to know where to position your signage, observe the people. Do they walk to your premises more from the left or right? Where are their eyes, up or down? What other things do they tend to be looking at or distracted by close to you? I spend a lot of time observing people in the streets because I learn so much! For example, Disneyland wanted to know where to position new waste paper bins, so they handed out wrapped sweets to visitors at the entrance to their parks and observed how many steps customers took on average before they had unwrapped their sweets and were looking for somewhere to dispose of the wrapper. The answer is 10 steps. Hence you will find a row of enticing waste paper bins 10 steps from the entrance of all Disney Parks (McCormack, 2019). The same applies to where to locate other facilities for your customers. Where do they stop and look around to decide where to go next? Would information boards be helpful?

Multilingual branding

Recently I was at JFK airport and saw billboards advertising Chopard watches in English but showing their brand in two versions: one with Chinese characters and the traditional one in the standard western alphabet. Many Asian brands have been using both Western and Eastern characters for decades in their local markets. Think of Sony, Samsung or LG, who use western characters even though they are Asian.

As more and more Asian shoppers visit the West, the need for us to adapt and incorporate other languages into our brand logos and retail storefronts becomes important. As unusual as it sounds, I predict we will see more western brands adopting some Asian characters in their brands for global purposes in years to come.

Use third parties to promote your business

Some businesses buy space for leaflets in a hotel to promote their businesses or pay a fee to the hotel concierge to recommend them. Many restaurants worldwide now pay international apps like Open Table (part of Booking.com) a referral fee for their booking service. Referral agents are nothing new, and partnerships with online brands like these can be beneficial.

Tag onto destination marketing

Almost every country in the world has a minister for tourism, with a budget for a range of marketing initiatives. Getting involved with them can be very lucrative as they can highlight your products or the areas of the city where you might have a store. In addition, national and state marketing departments may struggle to come up with unique tourism stories, so if you can provide an interesting story about your customers, the services you offer, or something that can be in any way newsworthy, this is something they may grab onto and mention as part of a wider online media campaign.

Link your business to entertainment and special events

Tourists fly in specifically to go to sports events, giant concerts, nightclubs, bars, theatre shows, outdoor operas and other events that are unique experiences. Entertainment tourism is a multi-billion-dollar business. One of the largest music festivals in the world is Summerfest in Milwaukee, bringing in 1 million visitors, the carnival in Rio brings in 500,000 international visitors, and London's Notting Hill Carnival brings in 1 million overseas tourists. The Montreux Jazz Festival in Switzerland has 2.5 million attendees (one-third are tourists) (Wikipedia, nd). Clearly, these events do a lot of online marketing and being involved in local events can make a big difference to the number of people that can find you online.

Across the world, from Munich and Vienna to London and New York, Christmas markets are set up to sell a wide range of goods. Special seasonal retail events like this pull people to the city and are promoted by national airlines. Milan has a world-famous furniture and interiors fair called Salone de Mobile, and retailers across the city take part, selling far more than furniture. As Craig Robins (owner and developer of the luxury Miami Design District retail area) describes in my interview with him in this book, these events pull in vast numbers of international visitors, as do similar events in Paris for interiors, or Basel in Switzerland for art. Retailers in city centres benefit by promoting special demonstrations and discounts in their window displays. All these major events tend to have sophisticated websites to promote retailers exhibiting there and help customers find what they are looking for. Often these events are used as demonstration opportunities for new tech, such as augmented reality, to help sell furniture, art and other items to people travelling from afar, enabling them to imagine what it is like to have purchased these items and placed them in their homes.

Communication with customers

Fifty-seven per cent of travellers feel that brands should tailor their communication based on personal preferences or past behaviours. Thirty-six per cent of people will pay more if a trip is tailored for them based on this data (Torres, 2018). For tourists, this personalization of communication with brands is particularly important since they buy something and then leave the country. So using technology to stay in touch is ideal. The brand has to engage with the consumer when they leave and when they return so that the consumer feels like their previous experience is remembered and the conversation can continue. International brands – which are often decentralized – will have to find better ways to co-ordinate between offices so that a customer, say, in Paris, has an uninterrupted experience when they walk into the Berlin store. Blockchain has exploded in the travel world. Some companies have already started using back-end tools that employ blockchain to streamline booking, flight planning, payment and other functions that competitors can only use through third parties. Blockchain platforms avoid many of the costs that come with payment processing, booking and management. For example, customers can use tokens to rent accommodation with zero per cent fees and other overhead fees saved by hosting on a blockchain. These savings can be passed on to users even as hosts enjoy higher margins.

Technologies impacting travel

Fortunately, so far, one technology that some people predicted to disrupt the travel and retail space and end people leaving their homes entirely has not done so – VR headsets that enable visitors to explore a city or shop rather than go there themselves. Instead, these technologies and platforms, such as the metaverse, can serve to improve the experience of travellers who are time-poor when they are at their destination – so they can now prepare for their trip by seeing it beforehand and planning it out, e.g. where to eat, shop, be entertained and stay.

However, what will the next incarnation of the metaverse bring? Will this be a competitor to international travel and its associated retail, or will it be just another space that competes for our daily work and recreation time? Selfridges department store predicts that they will not sell a single thing in 10 years from a point of sale, but the store will be a theatre, an experience, people trying things and being social. You can buy the sweater or shoes on your smart device. After the purchase and after you leave the store, the brand will want to communicate with you and have a relationship. But in the physical retail space, it will be all about sights and sounds, not just selling things.

The role of gatekeepers, the giant Silicon Valley companies with major consumer interfaces in travel distribution, will continue to grow, notably through the use of virtual assistants, payment technologies and integration into social media. They will be the ones making money off the international traveller. The size and power of 'mega-meta-OTA' hybrids (online travel agents with meta-search capabilities and global brands) are likely to continue growing. Consequently, their influence will penetrate deeper into the airline, hotel and restaurant distribution chain, with the ability to negotiate better content and conditions while still receiving commissions from travel-related retailers like you and me. Technology is also making travel much easier.

Kevin McAleeman, Commissioner of US Customs and Border Protection, talked recently about seamless travel using biometric data – check-in, security, aircraft boarding (and, later on, car rental, hotel check-in and door entry). Facial recognition works exceptionally well now, and since 2017 the US Customs and Border Protection Agency has processed 15 million passengers this way. The current match rate is 98 per cent, typically taking just one second to process a match (Vincent, 2019). London Heathrow Airport is about to deploy it, as are many others. This will reduce friction in international travel and make it easier for retailers to engage with a more relaxed potential customer who has more time to shop.

Interestingly, of all the recent technologies discussed at a recent World Travel and Tourism Council meeting, 5G was cited as the biggest disruptor. It is a quantum leap forward in data speeds, making it 100 times faster and 1,000 times more capable (Thales, 2018). 5G will provoke a massive explosion of data creation, which will be a huge enabler of cognitive intelligence, ranging from individual appliances with AI capabilities to customers with a wide range of augmented information available to them about your stores and products, and the supply chains that create and distribute them.

Where will your international customers be coming from?

Data is also helping drive the supply of new destinations. Desiree Maximo, Group Head of Government Policy at Air Asia, says that 70 per cent of airline traffic in Asia is low cost (Tani, Tan and Sun, 2018). Using search history and social media data, they are working on private–public partnerships for new international destinations. New long-range aircraft from Boeing and Airbus will be deployed from 2021 onwards (such as the A321XLR with an 8,700 kilometre range and 30 per cent lower fuel costs per seat) (Airbus, 2019). These will enable airlines to open new low-cost routes from countries such as India or Latin America to Europe, China or Australia, which previously were only available to expensive wide-bodied aircraft. These technological shifts are occurring simultaneously as economic growth changes the number of visitors from specific regions. This is important – where are your customers going to be coming from? Clearly not from the same places they used to come from. Look carefully at the chart shown in Figure 8.2, and you will realize where you should focus your attention.

According to the Brookings Institution, there will be over 3 billion middle-class people in Asia by 2030, far outpacing Europe and North America (Figure 8.2). Rising incomes and the growing middle class in countries

FIGURE 8.2 The size of the global middle class, 2000, 2015 and 2030 (in billions of people)

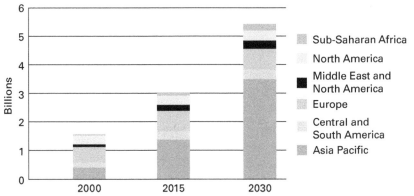

SOURCE Adapted from *The Unprecedented Expansion of the Global Middle Class* report (2017) https://www.brookings.edu/wp-content/uploads/2017/02/global_20170228_global-middle-class.pdf

around the world, from Mexico to India, means that more and more people will have the means to travel, which can be brilliant for your business (Kharas, 2017).

Dynamic pricing and AI

Ryanair is one of the most profitable airlines, moving around the largest number of passengers of any airline in Europe. They happily trim off any additional service they can to remain a low-cost airline. They frequently use tiny hangars as terminals or their own stepladder (rarely do you see a climate-controlled jet-bridge tunnel to connect the aircraft to the terminal). So what if you get wet while getting onto the plane? You are still saving money. Priority boarding at Ryanair still means possibly being kept in a queue for a long time while the speedy turnaround of the aircraft is prioritized. This is fine for a particular customer demographic. They restrict the amount of hand luggage tourists can bring so that they can charge extra for hold bags (which is bad news for retailers at the airport and in downtown stores, of course). Their penny-pinching image represents cost savings to the customer. Every new outlandish suggestion they even pretend to contemplate (from stand-up-only aircraft to charging to use the onboard toilets) gets them column inches in the media, which helps their sales (Shakespeare, 2018).

Yet they and many other airlines are adept at charging higher prices for the same product. As a result, one person can pay as little as $20 for a seat while the person sitting next to them has paid more than $200. Airlines and hotels dynamically adjust those prices according to complex algorithms, looking at current and anticipated demand levels to maximize yields.

Technologies impacting retail

In December 2017, Facebook filed a patent for facial recognition in retail environments and would be able to provide social media data to retailers (Gibbons, 2017). However, Maja Pantic, Research Director Samsung AI Centre Cambridge, voiced concerns about this during her presentation at the COGX conference in June 2019. She imagined a world where a camera in a shop recognizes you and sees what you do. Using facial recognition, it could then look up your social media profile and see your emotional states when looking at images, including seeing what things you have pressed 'like' on (Silver, 2017). It could then use that information specifically to make adjustments to digital pricing displays and tags on store shelves to increase the price of what you shop for more readily and decrease prices of things you do not normally shop for, to try to get a spontaneous purchase. Economists traditionally call this price discrimination (The Financial Times, 2017). Of course, dynamic pricing tech is not just for the giants. Allotz, the Australian-based group, has recently been awarded a patent for their AI-driven dynamic pricing and yield management software and is aiming to sell it to people in the travel and tourism world (Hospitality Net, 2019).

How can retailers and consumers manage their relationship with Facebook and other social media giants in this situation? First, consumers have to reclaim ownership of their data so that stores that use social media technology do not have a special commercial advantage at the expense of the consumer. This requires regulatory reform. Only Facebook or another preferred social media platform would know what, for you, is an abnormally dilated pupil in response to admiring or desiring an object. Only this platform would have all your data on what you like and don't like online. Standard, generic AI that does not know you will not know what is normal for you without this personal information collected from social media.

Many developments are occurring in robotics and AI that will enable AI to assist customers at specific stress points where they are confused and need more help and guidance. Robots will be able to move around a store and offer customers additional information in different languages and respond in a way that displays empathy to calm people and help them with their choices by providing additional visual and verbal information. But going beyond this here is another ethical problem for the near future. If the use of online AI is hidden, and an AI interaction is masked as human interaction, then the potential for manipulation will increase. For example, it can be argued that using AI to exploit people's emotional states to get them to pay more for the same products and services would be wrong – it would no longer be a matter of dynamic pricing but an issue of possibly misleading and emotionally manipulating the consumer. With huge budgets at stake, the travel and tourism industry is likely to be an early testing ground for these technologies. Tremendous advances have been made in using a variety of data points from cameras and other devices to assess human responses to advertising. Companies such as realeyesit.com provide marketing departments with near-real-time analysis of the reaction of potential customers to videos and static digital adverts. Different versions of the same material can then be created that most appeal to a specific target audience's tastes and background and can help tailor the images customers see in-store. CCTV from companies like Hikvision can already easily identify ethnicity, age and other demographic data. In the near future, we will be able to use those data outputs to adjust the images displayed on in-store TV screens and other displays to be most appealing and persuasive to the customers in that section of the store.

Travel distribution channels will continue to shift

In my opinion, we are going to see new players in the market – SAP, Google, Facebook, Apple – really get involved in the overall experience of booking and arranging travel. What enables that is the data and the ability to provide this data in real time. Companies that have the data will be the ones who will ultimately be selling travel and capitalizing on the purchasing power and actions of international travellers.

AI, as discussed, will be making a huge impact in travel – finding locations and destinations, gaining data from Expedia and Google searches and making recommendations for tourists. AI is also lowering the cost of providing services since more and more services can be automated.

Many restaurants around the world, such as Shake Shack in New York, Caliburger in California, Spyce in Boston, and others in China, are experimenting with robots, using them for burger flipping, pizza making, shawarma kebab meat slicing and, maybe in the slightly more distant future, home delivery to the masses. Robots are already extensively used in warehouses and distribution centres, which is likely to accelerate. I suspect that in time 3D printing of certain items for on-the-spot fulfilment, as is already being experimented with fast-food services, will appear in retail.

How to buy into next-stage technology businesses

Corporate buy-ins are a great way to access skills and competitive advantages that are difficult to achieve on your own. According to Boston Consulting Group, corporations contribute a greater share of overall travel start-up funding than just a few years ago. In 2018, for example, corporations participated in 21 per cent of travel start-up financings (which raised a total of $13 billion) compared with 14 per cent in 2013 (Boutin et al, 2019). But they cite two important warnings when buying into tech companies: don't let them run away with all the innovation and deplete your tech capabilities, but also don't tie them up contractually to provide services exclusively to you. Instead, open it up to competitors so that innovations spread across the industry, helping improve the industry and making you money from the investments. Where to find good companies to partner with? Apart from heading to Silicon Valley and competing with so many others looking for opportunities, take a look at Slush, a gathering of 25,000 curious minds, including 4,000 start-ups and 2,000 investors, held annually in Helsinki with offshoots in Tokyo and Shanghai (Slush, 2019). In addition, there is a myriad of elite side events, such as Knights of Nordic. There are great tech conferences in the UK, such as COGX, which attracted over 15,000 people from around the world in June 2019 to discuss AI and meet new companies and experts (COGX, 2019).

Before the war in Ukraine, I might have also suggested considering Russian technologies and innovations by visiting the Skolkovo start-up village in Moscow. There they hold an event annually in May, which used to attract people from 80 countries, including 1,000 investors and 4,500 start-ups (East West Digital News, 2018). However, today such visits are heavily restricted due to sanctions. Hopefully, peace will prevail, and reconstruction can start sooner rather than later.

To name a few recent technological advancements adopted in the travel sector, many airports now have basic robots providing friendly information in any language. In Terminal 2 at Munich Airport, 'Josie Pepper', a humanoid robot developed by SoftBank Robotics, has been directing passengers to their gates and answering questions about restaurants and shops. The robot uses IBM Watson internet cloud-based AI technologies. The robot does not just deliver predefined texts but can also answer each question individually. Of course, robots will begin moving products around premises, from laundry items to retail stock items. This may affect low-skilled employment but will also encourage upskilling. Those in the luxury business will still appreciate professional, highly trained human interaction. What does the increasing availability of AI technologies mean to the average retailer? It lowers the cost, which currently only the very large multinationals can afford, with global supply chains and larger global customer bases. Smaller individual stores can have meaningful dialogue with their potential and actual customer base, both in listening to and sending out messages. A small shop will be able to target inbound Koreans, for example, and speak of their in-store experience and what would be relevant and appealing to that customer base. It would serve small shops to work closely with companies such as Hubba (see interview overleaf), which helps new cutting-edge brands find their customer base and where to place their products. They can help you identify products and services that will appeal to inbound and outbound travelling customers who are in your area. In other words, you can use their AI to curate the best possible retail experience for your customers. You will know where your customer is coming from and what you need to provide them with, now in-store and later online, to maintain a relationship with them.

Using data mining for your retail locations

Data mining and the application of AI to find meaning in the terabytes we humans upload in images, transaction data, GPS co-ordinates and search histories are growing. The value of this data is such that companies offer considerable incentives to attract users to allow access to their data. So how can you profit from these trends and not be left behind by the big players? So let's explore some other areas of innovation. One hot subject is personalization, so I reached out to Ben Zifkin, one of the leading experts in using data for retail.

CONVERSATION WITH

Ben Zifkin, President of Hubba, based in Toronto and New York, is part-owned by the Goldman Sachs Venture Fund.

Sacha: What are the core challenges that retailers face today when trying to attract new foreign customers and repeatedly draw in local customers?

Ben: We focus on working with small and medium-sized retailers and helping them compete in today's competitive world. That means ensuring that their stores provide a wonderful and unique experience. The best way to do this is to ensure that they have the right products for their customers. One of the things we help our own customers, the brands, with is to understand their data. They have to know who their customers are and what their customers care about. They also have to overlay that with macro trends that are out there, such as desire for sustainable products, healthy products and charitable products. Then, finally, they need to overlay all of that with what other retailers, who are similar to them, are doing to be successful. Most retailers are not that sophisticated. Even if they are, they are challenged by not having this data. It is no longer acceptable to have a store in New York simply selling the 'I Love New York' paraphernalia; they need to get more sophisticated both to service their local customers and to attract foreign visitors.

Sacha: How does Hubba and its competitors help smaller retailers?

Ben: We put retailers and interesting brands together. We also empower retailers with additional data. We can help them figure out who their customer is by using mobile data to let them know who is walking by their store, who is coming into their store and where that person was before and after visiting them. We also have great trending data on what types of products are selling at a global level. Our data is wholesale data, so we learn many cycles before things ever hit store shelves. Finally, owing to the size of our network, we have great information on what other similar stores are buying, down to the SKU level. That helps us recommend products to lookalike companies.

Sacha: How can smaller retailers compete with larger ones, who often have better-quality buyers and more buying power?

Ben: Technology comes into play here. Historically, it has been very hard to compete. Every brand was looking at getting a huge purchase order from Walmart or another large retailer. Nowadays, many emerging brands don't want to get into the big stores because it dilutes their brand. The issue has always been that it is impossible to manage and scale the independent retail channel. With a network like Hubba, though, brands can get that reach at little to no effort. On the retail side, there are huge benefits too. An individual high-street retailer may not have a lot of clout with a brand, but the consolidated buying power of thousands of these retailers pooled together in a marketplace can be quite impactful.

Sacha: In the West, much has been said about Amazon competing against its own customers by launching its own branded products and pushing other brands down the search results, with disastrous impacts. Alibaba in China seems to have brought e-commerce more fairly to smaller retailers in China. What are your thoughts on all this?

Ben: Both of these companies are formidable in the world of e-commerce. Amazon is clearly dominating the West while Alibaba is dominating the East. Although both companies are pushing to be more global, I foresee each retreating to their stronghold regions. In addition to regional strengths, Amazon, which has historically been a consumer player, has been working to build an infrastructure backbone to support their users. Alibaba, which was historically a B2B player, has grown to be a massive consumer player. While Alibaba has been great at connecting manufacturers to brands and Amazon has been great at connecting as a retailer to end consumers, there is a huge area in the middle – connecting brands to retailers – that is completely untapped. Retailers buying products to stock their shelves are a $20 trillion industry with no dominant player as of yet. This is where Hubba plays.

DIGITAL AND ONLINE TECHNOLOGIES

- Make your website usable for voice search, which typically involves being able to respond to customer questions.

- Respond to negative reviews with how you have listened and taken positive action.

- Consider outsourcing your social media presence. It's a complex job.

- Use AIDA to make your messaging as friendly and attractive as inviting someone to your party.

- Your website and personnel should sell to outbound tourists as well as to inbound ones.

- Make sure your staff knows how to use translation apps such as Google Translate or Microsoft Translator apps when speaking to tourists, particularly in Mandarin or Arabic.

- Consider branding your name with Chinese or Arabic characters so that your brand communicates with the tourist, and use digital signage as much as possible so you can have relevant messages in various languages.

- Use focus groups as a way of bonding with top clients, allowing them to feel they have influence.

- Link your business to entertainment offerings and special events.

- Many software companies will be selling solutions for retailers to hook into and benefit from these technologies.

- Virtual reality, through the metaverse and other platforms, will become the norm – where people can see where they are going and what activities and shopping they might do.

- There will be the continued growth of mega online travel-booking platforms that will impact where tourists go.

- SAP, Google, Facebook and Apple will increasingly get involved in travel and omnichannel retail, harnessing their data.

- Robots will eliminate many low-skilled jobs while speeding up fulfilment in restaurants, hotels, warehouses and retailers.

- Small and medium-sized companies can utilize AI-driven platforms to compete with larger retailers to pinpoint the best items to stock for the type of customers shopping with them.

References

Airbus (2019) Airbus launches longest range single-aisle airliner: the A321XLR, *Airbus*, www.airbus.com/newsroom/press-releases/en/2019/06/airbus-launches-longest-range-singleaisle-airliner-the-a321xlr.html (archived at https://perma.cc/R7QB-WT2W)

Anzilotti, E (2017) Our aging population can be an economic powerhouse – if we let it, *Fast Company*, www.fastcompany.com/3068543/our-aging-population-can-be-an-economic-powerhouse-if-we-let-it (archived at https://perma.cc/PVP7-CYXX)

Boutin, N et al (2019) Innovation in travel must put the traveler first, *Boston Consulting Group*, www.bcg.com/en-gb/publications/2019/innovation-travel-must-put-traveler-first.aspx (archived at https://perma.cc/J5GF-MT4Q)

Butt, A (2019) 75 voice search technology statistics and trends, *QuoraCreative*, https://quoracreative.com/article/voice-search-statistics-trends (archived at https://perma.cc/3R7P-M6EU)

COGX (2019) CogX – the Festival of All Things AI and emerging technology, *COGX*, https://cogx.co/awards/ (archived at https://perma.cc/W6WJ-3UNT)

East West Digital News (2018) 20,000 participants from 80 countries expected at Russia's startup village, *East West Digital News*, www.ewdn.com/2018/05/15/20000-participants-from-80-countries-expected-at-russias-startup-village/ (archived at https://perma.cc/8S42-WSTB)

Gibbons, K (2017) Facebook develops facial recognition cameras that feed shop staff their customers' profile details, *The Times*, www.thetimes.co.uk/article/facebook-develops-facial-recognition-cameras-that-feed-shop-staff-their-customers-profile-details-58lx0jckt (archived at https://perma.cc/Y5HG-ZY34)

Giuffrida, A and Wilson, A (2018) Man jailed in Italy for selling fake TripAdvisor reviews, *The Guardian*, www.theguardian.com/world/2018/sep/12/man-jailed-italy-selling-fake-tripadvisor-reviews-promo-salento (archived at https://perma.cc/82BB-XJCD)

Hospitality Net (2019) US patent awarded for dynamic variable pricing in real time, *Hospitality Net*, www.hospitalitynet.org/news/4092650.html (archived at https://perma.cc/P8B6-P7UT)

Kharas, H (2017) *The Unprecedented Expansion of the Global Middle Class*, The Brookings Institution, Washington, DC

McCormack, M (2019) 5 things you won't believe about Disney trash, *AllEars.Net*, https://allears.net/2019/02/26/5-things-you-wont-believe-about-about-disney-trash/ (archived at https://perma.cc/GP2N-AWLW)

National Disability Authority (2019) What is universal design, *NDA*, http://universaldesign.ie/What-is-Universal-Design/ (archived at https://perma.cc/SMA8-76F8)

Olson, C (2016) Just say it: the future of search is voice and personal digital assistants, *Campaign Live*, www.campaignlive.co.uk/article/just-say-it-future-search-voice-personal-digital-assistants/1392459 (archived at https://perma.cc/M8YP-ZWBM)

Randazzo, S (2019) Lawsuits surge over websites' access for the blind, *The Wall Street Journal*, www.wsj.com/articles/lawsuits-surge-over-websites-access-for-the-blind-11550415600 (archived at https://perma.cc/C8TT-HJNP)

Shakespeare, S (2018) Ryanair's brand perception falls – but purchase consideration stays firm, *YouGov*, https://yougov.co.uk/topics/resources/articles-reports/2018/08/01/ryanairs-brand-perception-falls-purchase-considera (archived at https://perma.cc/567R-J65Y)

Silver, C (2017) Patents reveal how Facebook Wants to capture your emotions, facial expressions and mood, *Forbes*, www.forbes.com/sites/curtissilver/2017/06/08/how-facebook-wants-to-capture-your-emotions-facial-expressions-and-mood/#32fa346014cc (archived at https://perma.cc/NRT7-THHD)

Slush (2019) The quirkiest startup event in the world, *Slush*, www.slush.org/events/helsinki/why-visit/ (archived at https://perma.cc/Z67H-7LQD)

Squires, N (2018) Owner of Italian business that sold fake TripAdvisor reviews jailed for nine months, *The Telegraph*, www.telegraph.co.uk/news/2018/09/12/owner-italian-business-sold-fake-tripadvisor-reviews-jailed/ (archived at https://perma.cc/YX5A-ZXSU)

Stimmler-Hall, H (2016) what you don't know about TripAdvisor, *Medium.com*, https://medium.com/choking-on-a-macaron/what-you-don-t-know-about-tripadvisor-15d31d745bdc (archived at https://perma.cc/9D3F-4VCC)

Street, F (2017) 'Life in Hel': Man to live in Helsinki Airport for 30 days, *CNN Travel*, https://edition.cnn.com/travel/article/helsinki-airport-30-days/index.html (archived at https://perma.cc/Q56F-Y9FL)

Tani, M, Tan, C and Sun, N (2018) Asia's airline wars: the great profit squeeze in the sky, *Nikkei Asian Review*, https://asia.nikkei.com/Spotlight/Cover-Story/Asia-s-airline-wars-The-great-profit-squeeze-in-the-sky (archived at https://perma.cc/5SX3-CELH)

Thales (2018) What is the difference between 4G and 5G?, *Gemalto*, www.justaskgemalto.com/en/difference-4g-5g/ (archived at https://perma.cc/AAQ8-872U)

The Financial Times (2017) Privacy is under threat from the facial recognition revolution, *The Financial Times*, www.ft.com/content/4707f246-a760-11e7-93c5-648314d2c72c (archived at https://perma.cc/78CN-7VTL)

Torres, R (2018) How to win travellers in the age of assistance, *Think With Google*, www.thinkwithgoogle.com/intl/en-154/insights-inspiration/industry-perspectives/how-to-win-travellers-in-the-age-of-assistance/ (archived at https://perma.cc/6V6A-WEYY)

Valant, J (2015) *Online Consumer Reviews: The case of misleading or fake reviews*, European Parliamentary Research Service

Vincent, B (2019) How facial recognition is changing CBP operations, *Nextgov*, www.nextgov.com/emerging-tech/2019/07/how-facial-recognition-changing-cbp-operations/158704/(archived at https://perma.cc/7ZRD-DXL5)

WebFX (2019) Influencer marketing pricing: how much does it cost in 2020? *WebFX*, www.webfx.com/influencer-marketing-pricing.html (archived at https://perma.cc/SL55-LQ7X)

Wikipedia (nd) Music tourism, *Wikipedia*, https://en.wikipedia.org/wiki/Music_tourism (archived at https://perma.cc/KPD9-MJLB)

World Population Review (2019) Muslim population by country 2020, *World Population Review*, http://worldpopulationreview.com/countries/muslim-population-by-country/ (archived at https://perma.cc/6BPZ-PR7B)

9

Location, location, location

This is true in the housing market, it is true in the online market (top search result on the first page of Google), and it is definitely true in the world of retail. Location really is key. Of course, what is key for one retailer is not necessarily key for another. Putting mass-market products on a super-luxury street with low foot traffic is futile – you need high foot traffic and a different demographic. Landlords worldwide invest a great deal of money trying to optimize their tenant mix to maximize returns. However, what the company Value Retail has achieved by taking under-used land outside of cities around the world and turning them into luxury shopping villages – that attract vast numbers of international shoppers with significant funds to spend – is taking this art to another level.

CONVERSATION WITH
Desirée Bollier, Chair and Chief Merchant of Value Retail, which owns Bicester Village Shopping Collection, and has some of the highest retail sales per square metre anywhere in the world.

Sacha: Can you tell us how many luxury shopping villages you now have?

Desirée: The Bicester Village Shopping Collection is the 11 villages created and operated by Value Retail; two in China and nine in Europe. In 2023 we open the twelfth village, the first in the United States, Belmont Park Village.

Sacha: What are your key customer groups – luxury or everyone?

Desirée: Each year we welcome more and more guests who visit from all over the world. In 2019 the collection welcomed 45 million guests.

The collection appeals to high-net-worth customers, be they domestic or international travellers. Our guests come from wide and diverse markets – Middle Eastern, Chinese, Russian, Korean, Latin American, Indian and, equally, the domestic guest seeking an ultra-sophisticated shopping environment.

We attract a discerning guest looking for a specific type of shopping experience, someone who is familiar with the international superbrands but who is also motivated to explore the authentic design, culture, hospitality and emerging brands from the local region – something that he or she may not find at home, nor online.

Sacha: What changes have you seen in customer demand for products and services?

Desirée: A recent independent survey found that 47 per cent of guests in the villages in Europe and 80 per cent of guests in the villages in China are under the age of 35 – we are attracting tomorrow's travelling luxury consumer, today.

Millennials together with generation Z are driving the most significant changes we see. They have gone through – and are still going through – significant social changes and generational, cultural shifts. They look to luxury as a means of social advancement and self-differentiation.

Individuality, emotion and self-development increasingly matter to how millennials and generation Z choose to spend their money and their time. They seek products and services that speak to them as individuals and look for experiences that excite, demanding a more personal service than previous generations and value clientelling beyond the transaction.

Sacha: How do you attract customers to the villages, which are often in unusual locations?

Desirée: We engage with our guests on many different levels. We are tourism professionals. We partner with local tourism bodies to welcome a new global guest, leveraging more than 400 partnerships with airlines, hotels, luxury travel providers and digital payment platforms including Alipay and WeChat, which simplify and expedite the payment process to ease the guest's journey.

We share business intelligence to ensure that our source-market marketing strategies are nimble and remain relevant to our target customer. Digitally, we are very active in China on Weibo and WeChat and in Europe on Instagram and Facebook, often using film to allow guests to immerse themselves in the village experience before they travel.

The Bicester Village Shopping Collection's net promoter score (a measure of customer experience satisfaction, loyalty and willingness to recommend to others) ranks as high as flagship full-price environments. Our most powerful asset is word of mouth: when a third party talks about you, it is by far the most authentic marketing tool. Our job, therefore, is to deliver a superb experience, one that encourages repeat visits and provides stimulating content to help others engage with our brand and tell our story first-hand.

Sacha: How are brands adapting their offerings in the villages to what they offer in major cities?

Desirée: Brands understand that the Bicester Village Shopping Collection is their trusted partner. From the moment they sign with us, we work with them to ensure they achieve exceptional results.

We offer an elegant environment that mirrors their full-price experience, a boutique as close to their flagship store as possible and we deliver a discerning new customer, many of whom will be discovering the brand for the first time while they are with us.

Latest research shows 78 per cent of guests physically experience a luxury and fashion brand for the first time in the villages and 27 per cent of all customers are converted to the full-price luxury channel. This is extremely compelling for our brand partners, many of whom have their top-performing outlet stores at the Bicester Village Shopping Collection.

In reaction to this, we are seeing a conscious shift with several leading international luxury brands sending their excess merchandise directly to the Bicester Village Shopping Collection as they move away from celebrating sales periods in their full-price city locations, allowing them to offer a consistent flow of newness on their full-price shop floor.

Sacha: How do international shoppers behave differently when they are on holiday from how they behave at home?

Desirée: Guests on holiday are far more relaxed and time rich. It's their time for themselves, and their families. Their priorities have shifted as they travel for leisure. They are open to exploring, to indulging. That means they spend more time discovering local culture and more time shopping.

Located in culturally rich regions, the villages are all within an hour of a major city. From day one we have been introducing these regions to the discerning international travelling consumer. By the time the guest reaches the village, they have already committed to spending, since they have made an investment of time and money to visit.

Our international guests typically spend up to four hours with us, a far greater dwell time than that of a department store. It is our job then to deliver a stress-free shopping experience with the thrill of discovery that they cannot find at home, as part of their holiday.

Sacha: What do you see changing for you in the retail business?

Desirée: The most significant impact for retail continues to be the disruption by the digital age. We view digital technology as an enabler, to connect with our guests and enhance a seamless customer journey. Yet, it can never replace the emotion and memories created from the experience of physical retail.

Nevertheless, digital retail has provided access and choice and has challenged high streets the world over. To compete, bricks and mortar must offer an artistic elevation for all the senses, and this requires money, imagination and a continually evolving nimble approach. It is no longer enough to have a glossy store filled with beautiful products, to open the doors and hope people walk in. Our guests are looking for layers of visual and sensual engagement, the 'wow' moments that they can share on their social channels – Instagramable moments to share.

Being customer-centric is key to success. The elevation of service will continue to provide a significant opportunity for retailers to command customer loyalty. Our private clientelling services deliver exceptional levels of personalized service to engage our guests before, during and after their shopping experience, enticing them to return time and again, by building a unique community that delivers increased value to our brand partners.

Sacha: In which locations are you looking to grow?

Desirée: In 2019 we broke ground on our first site in the United States, at Belmont Park Arena, New York, to be followed by Belmont Park Village in 2023. The 350,000-square-foot village will form part of a dynamic new destination located in Long Island. In addition to the village, Belmont Park Arena features a 19,000-seat multi-use arena, home to the New York Islanders and which will play host to the biggest names in international music and entertainment, a 250-room hotel, 10,000 square foot of office space and parking, and a new station on the Long Island Rail Road (LIRR). This move may sound counter-intuitive, since the United States is over-retailed per person per square foot. But the United States is undersold in our product lines because of the massive number of malls that are uninspiring, with no service or hospitality to offer to high-net-worth guests. Belmont Park Village is poised to transform this flagging retail landscape. The United States is, for us, an excellent opportunity, in addition to the organic growth of existing villages including La Roca Village and Kildare Village.

If you are intent on capturing the tourist shopping market, you may want to reposition your business to airports, ultra-prime shopping malls and popular city-centre shopping streets, and close down any loss-making locations in your portfolio that are being eclipsed by online sales. When considering 'place', the key focus must be ease of access for the target customer and the amount of stock and range of stock you can keep on the premises, which will, of course, have to be balanced with the cost of that extra space in retail rents and property taxes.

Of course, if you are focused on inbound tourists, take a look to see if there are any auxiliary services. These could be currency exchange branches around your chosen location because this will significantly impact the number of tourists you will be able to serve and the amount of spending power they will have. (Research we conducted with LEK showed that more than half of the money customers exchanged in bureaux, such as ChangeGroup's, was spent within 200 metres of the currency exchange locations.)

To help analyse where you should be, your staff can note, simply by paying attention, what socio-economic groups they are currently serving, their gender, whether they are local or foreign residents, and what kind of spending power they have. This data is important as it can highlight some unexpected results. For example, in England, research shows that it is women who purchase a significant proportion of men's underwear for their partners (this is not meant to be a reflection on the whys and wherefores of the inclusiveness of women in the workforce, just a statement about the retail customer journey). Hence many stores selling these male-oriented items repositioned their stock locations and marketing to service the female shopper.

Clearly, the same applies to many other products, so defining the purchaser and user as separate is important. Items targeted at children are a case in point; gifts are another example. 'FREE NOW', the taxi app, is a competitor to Uber but uses the traditional local licensed taxis found in most cities. It has a version of its app targeted purely at hotel concierges. Now, when a guest asks for a taxi, the hotel simply presses a button, a taxi arrives as a priority, and the customer pays for the taxi (and does not need to have the app). The customer relationship, as far as the app is concerned, is with the hotel. This means that while they are serving tourists, their target for their advertising and sales budget for this app version is not the tourist at all but local concierges instead. The same applies to many sightseeing, shopping and dining experiences that are recommended by or booked by hotels. Clearly, the relationship with the hotel is vital.

Shopping mall demographics

While I have met and negotiated with countless shopping mall designers, developers and management agents, rarely have I encountered a mall that did not need significant changes after it opened. This applies to malls in Europe, Australia and the United States, from the multi-billion-dollar Westfield-run Occulus at the World Trade Centre to various designer outlets and mega malls in Europe that failed to bring in the expected customer numbers. Even if these locations are close to sought-after national monuments, museums or other attractions that receive millions of tourists, this does not mean the tourists will walk to a nearby shopping mall. I have seen this from malls near St Paul's Cathedral in London to Niagara Falls in the United States. Yes, great museums like the Guggenheim in Bilbao or Abu Dhabi pull in millions of people, but the local malls might not change in demographics as much as their owners might hope.

Be prepared to challenge the claims of the real-estate brokers pushing the vacant tenancies on nearby streets. It is in their business model to exaggerate. It is in their business model to get people to rent space, and they will not necessarily mind putting competitors right next to you. Ask them who else is renting. Ask for specifics on mall traffic. Talk to other tenants to hear what they have to say. Don't always believe what the mall-centre manager tells you. I once signed up for a group of shopping malls for 10 locations in the United States (luckily, I was only compelled to open three). Unfortunately, the customer traffic was not at all what was promised, and I had to bring in Peter Lynch, a heavyweight in the real-estate industry (who also runs YPO's Global Retail Network), to get me out of the deal and negotiate to pay the landlord an amount to exit the contract.

When malls work well, they encourage a curated experience that flows naturally and encourages browsing, resting and purchasing. Shopping centres should be designed to have easy intra-tenant communication and involvement to help each other create exciting experiences for the shopper. Where they are designed to attract tourists, it is about the services and range of shopping they offer that is more important than their proximity to tourist locations.

This philosophy can also be used to create city-centre areas with specific 'street themes', with tenants working together to foster a creative concentrated mall effect. Good examples of this abound, such as Via Monte Napoleone in Milan or New York's Fifth Avenue for fashion, Wangfujing Street in Beijing for food, and Les Puces market in Paris for bric-a-brac and antiques. Barcelona has a 5 kilometre shopping experience that starts by the sea, runs along La Rambla and its surrounding streets, and then connects with Passeig de Gràcia and Plaça de Catalunya. There are shops side by side; some are famous international retail stores, and others are local brands with local products. Essentially the stores are competing for tourist dollars. Yet, the store owners can work together tacitly and find ways to help each other rather than hinder each other, and to create an attractive shopping destination.

This even works in the medical field in London, where leading experts have historically set up consulting rooms along the famous Harley Street and thus attract medical tourism to treat people from around the world in search of a range of expertise. Some Middle Eastern states have even rented office space to service the needs of their nationals who are visiting Harley Street.

Be near currency exchange services

Foreign tourists travel with a lot of cash. This is for a variety of reasons, such as privacy, fears of card cloning, identity theft, discounts on cash purchases and for flexibility. Because of this there must be currency exchanges and ATM services so tourists can exchange money and then start shopping. Some mall designers place them at the back near a range of general customer services, which is not helpful for retailers who need to attract tourists to spend money. (I have heard arguments of 'well, in time, customers will get to know where things are', which just doesn't work for the majority of tourists who will probably only visit once or twice in their lifetimes.)

Mall designers often assume that people will download apps with directions, or get to know an area after they visit a few times and learn where services are. But, in my experience as an inbound tourist shopper, that could not be further from the reality. Just look at how airports carefully position currency exchange branches at the start, middle and end of the retail experience. They place multiple ATMs in the heart of their buildings in prominent locations – because this is what the customers need.

Most importantly as a retailer, being close to a currency exchange branch means you are near customers who suddenly have local cash in their pocket with a strong desire to spend it. Once customers shop they can also go back to a bureau de change and obtain a tax refund and receive even more cash instantly. Indeed, data from ChangeGroup's own surveys shows that more than half of the money exchanged is spent within 100 metres of a currency exchange location in busy shopping streets such as the Champs-Élysées in Paris or New York's Times Square.

The desires of customers varies with location

Look at how much popcorn costs at the cinema! The retailers know that their customers are in a happy mood; they are in a closed environment in a location without direct competition. Cinemas worldwide have learnt how to use these factors and can charge premium prices accordingly.

We noticed that many people arrived at our location in Marble Arch in London hungry and thirsty, and the first thing they did when they exchanged money or took out cash from our ATM was to search for a food outlet. So we spoke with Alexander Troullier and Rikos Leong-Son who own Wafflemeister, and took out a franchise. We placed their premium-branded waffles, gelato and luxury coffee concept next to us. Now we have extremely satisfied customers ready to walk and shop. Most interestingly, and contrary to what fintechs and banks talk about in the media, 45 per cent of our sales are in cash. The Member of Parliament for Westminster, Nickie Aiken, was so pleased with the collaboration and investment, coming right after Covid-19, that she even came to officially open the new shop for us (Twitter, 2021).

I learnt the hard way that your product cannot only be about what you like. You have to see what works, excise what doesn't and cater totally to your marketplace with profound determination. Be obsessive about this, and challenge yourself and your team to be better and greater than anyone else. Because the market is constantly changing and adapting, your team needs to be fleet of foot.

In Estonia, we used to do a roaring trade with the millions of Finnish customers who arrived every year. Then when Estonia joined the euro, our focus for growth became British and German tourists on party trips. When they tailed off in search of newer and less expensive destinations, we focused on growing by serving people visiting on the many cruise ships. As customers' needs and desires constantly evolved in our locations, we adapted too. To adapt, your teams need to be fleet of foot.

Store design from the point of view of tourists

Exterior signage and store windows are so important that I believe that along with staff attitude and presentation, it is one of the key things to focus on wherever I travel to visit our branches. I tell our managers that if they have an idea for signage, forget the budget: we will always approve additional improvements to signage to attract customers. Of course, we might require some control over the back-office areas to keep general costs down.

But we will put any amount necessary into signage and displays because that is how you get the international traveller in. This is all part of what our shop windows look like to the customer.

Despite 400 million people seeing our brand every year, most people do not necessarily remember us, and we have to use various techniques to pull in our millions of customers. If you have not noticed it yet, a signage war is going on outside in retail (often restricted by local authorities and land-lords), and I expect my managers to win that war.

Retailers who have poor signage are just not going to attract enough new travel retail customers. For example, when you arrive at Heathrow Airport after going through Customs, there are various ways to get to central London. The fastest option, the Heathrow Express train, really struggled to get market share since they are not the cheapest way to go, and they had to compete for business with cars, buses and the slower local underground metro system. After a slow start, they instituted various new mechanisms to appeal to tourists with no prior knowledge of the Heathrow Express. The company stationed representatives at critical points, after passport control and just after Customs. That is when tourists start to see signs for the tube (metro), buses and taxis. Heathrow Express representatives stand there in smart uniforms with hand-held devices selling tickets next to a purple sign with their fundamental proposition, 'Heathrow to London in 15 minutes'. They advertise that they accept every type of payment option and make it as easy as possible for the customer to interact. They also advertise at many departure airports, such as at JFK airport in New York.

Many brands can learn from this approach. Brands such as the Gray Line/Julia Tours' Hop-On Hop-Off sightseeing tour buses operating around the world (and their competitors such as Big Bus) use a variety of manned sale points and pop-up displays along routes that customers walk or where they are likely to be.

Pret a Manger's renowned sandwich shops have had great success in dominating the high foot-traffic locations of the cities they operate in, from Hong Kong to New York, London and Paris. They have an excellent strategy of focusing on locals and tourists in city centres and airport loca-tions. They don't hide in side streets; they take the most prominent positions, so people see them and make a spontaneous purchase. So too, does WHSmith newsagents – a convenience-focused business that has been around for over 250 years and is still growing internationally at airports and city-centre locations. Today they have 1,700 WHSmith stores worldwide, comprising 1,019 travel outlets and 576 high-street stores (WHSmith, 2022).

Digital signage to improve location attractiveness

Modern LED signs can easily display visual symbolism with multi-language translation that is easier and quicker for tourists to understand. The content, of course, is critically important, and some investment is required to get the messaging and video content right. However, despite the huge investment, I believe digital signage is vital in attracting tourist shoppers as it allows you to explain your services when the shoppers might not be familiar with your brand.

On the subject of digital retail content, the digital information kiosks that you often see in shopping malls often get their content wrong. So far, after many years of deployment, I find most of them are poorly thought out and difficult to use. First, they rarely work in multiple languages; second, the search terms are often restricted to the letters of the brand name or company name. These digital information kiosks (either in shopping malls or on major shopping streets, such as in London's Oxford Street or on the Champs-Élysées in Paris) should include technology for multiple languages and a system that allows one to search for a service visually and with key service descriptions – searching should be as simple as using Google.

For example, at the Westfield Mall complex in Shepherds Bush in London – which is Europe's largest shopping mall, attracting millions of local and foreign visitors alike (Clarke, 2018) – if you try to look for a service and not a brand name, say, a bowling alley, my experience is that it is challenging to find. Yes, I must admit that I was running late for a kids' party there, so I felt slightly exasperated and maybe mentioning them in this book isn't fair. But, eventually, I found it in their digital system, where it was buried under the company's name. But if you don't know the name and want to find the service, you wouldn't find it.

There is an important wider lesson here for your retail business. You must show potential customers, especially tourists, what you are selling. Consider how much emphasis to place on your brand over your product. Work with information kiosk operators to ensure your business is properly promoted to maximize the chance of new customers.

Floor signage as a navigational tool in airports and other large public places is effective since it is language-neutral and easy to understand. It works well even at hospitals where infrequent visitors need to find their way rapidly to the X-ray department or accident and emergency. Some malls allow floor signage, and some don't, but if you don't ask, you won't know. Anything that helps you catch the customer's attention is worth considering.

Think about how you can smell freshly baked bread every time you walk past a Subway sandwich shop, even though nothing is being baked – take a closer look. You will see a small air vent in the storefront blowing out a fresh bread aroma from a fragrance atomizer into the street. The mechanism is a great winner to get people to notice their branches. Other brands, such as Hollister, and Abercrombie & Fitch, use attractive young people outside their branches with impactful music and great-smelling perfumes wafting into the street to make their clients notice them. Shops across Spain selling candied nuts have chefs making them there in front of you in big copper bowls, allowing your visual, auditory and olfactory senses to be engaged.

Why are these attention-grabbing techniques so important? Customers can often interact with your brand in a variety of ways: telephone customer centres, online, third-party vendors of your product, through your own stores, apps, Google, or even YouTube videos. But on the street, it should be made easy for people to see your product, with an almost telepathic way of telling them what you offer or do. When creating signage for the retail travel market, you should not just focus on your brand but also on what you do (unless you are world famous). We at ChangeGroup advertise our brand less prominently than our service – that we change money. For example, we show lists of flags, with numbers on them, an international symbol for currency exchange. People have a sixth sense for their own flag when abroad. We make it simple. Just like when you see a knife and fork on a sign, you know it is telling you where a nearby restaurant is located. Show an image associated with your product. In high-traffic areas, like Times Square or the Champs-Élysées, you have a microsecond to get the tourist's attention. Your image should hit them multiple times during their line of travel and be instantaneously clear and concise.

Retail summits

To form connections in this field, there are great events to meet developers and property managers, such as MAPIC in Cannes, every November. This is a premier event where retailers and property professionals from around the world meet to exchange ideas and make deals happen. Of course, there are also many great retail summits in China, Singapore and across the United States, such as the CIO Retail Summit and The Retail Summit. These can be found online. I encourage you to attend them if you are serious about expanding your retail footprint, as you can speak to many developers in a short space of time – just beware of the hype and try to get actual data. Another great event to focus on for partnerships and accessing tourist customers is the World Travel Market in London, which draws over 50,000 professionals across the world in travel, providing businesses with quality contacts, content and communities (WTM, 2020).

Other organizations for inspiration on international retailing you might want to look at are:

- WSTN (World Shopping Tourism Network), headed by Antonio Santos del Valle
- ETRC (European Travel Retail Confederation) and UKTR (UK Travel Retail), which represents travel retail at regional levels, and where Nigel Keal was elected president of both
- AIR (Association of International Retail), headed by Paul Barnes

But, obviously, a lot depends on actual retail locations that your brokers in each country can find. It is no secret to say that finding great real-estate brokers is not easy. Developing good relationships with real-estate agents takes time. They need to know and trust you and that your company can deliver on your expansion plans. Unfortunately, too many companies promise the world and then cannot deliver the authorizations to proceed when it comes to signing retail lease contracts.

Airports are highly successful retail villages

You may want to open a branch of your business at an airport. The Airport Council International (ACI) is an organization that represents all major airports worldwide. They host regional events called Commercial and Retail Exhibitions in Asia, Europe and the United States, enabling you to meet key decision makers. What differentiates airport retailing is that they like to run tenders for retail locations, which means a longer, more complex process of presentations, concept designs, market research and financial analysis than you would engage in renting a non-airport shopping mall or prime street location. Rents also tend to be a mixture of a fixed-base rent called minimum annual guarantee (MAG) and a percentage of your sales, plus additional costs to cover airport marketing (Heathrow, 2019).

Airport retailing is highly competitive, so your product offerings and operations need to be extremely slick. Rents are very high because the demand for access to international travellers wanting to shop is so high. Specialist companies can help you optimize what you do. Craig Mackie, General Manager at Moodie Insights Consulting, gave a presentation at the 2019 ACI conference on driving confectionery income at Singapore Changi Airport. He noted that travellers have different 'shopping missions' (such as Treat Missions or Gifting Missions) at different times of the day, and by using Agile techniques, they were able to test hypotheses and increase income from some important segments. It helps airports access data on flight destinations and origins, minute to minute. You can request customer boarding cards and track who your customers are much more closely than in a typical retail environment.

You can see what add-on purchases and in-store advertising work with a given customer group and adjust accordingly. Small changes make a big difference at airports because of the large numbers of tourist shoppers. At airports, a location before or after security is a major differentiator, and trends are moving for airport retailing to be done after security. After duty-free, food and beverage retailing becomes a big part of customer behaviour. Generally, brands want to be located in areas with dwell times, not where customers are rushing. Metrics such as airport-zone dwell time, time to gate, and peak demand periods for certain products from specific types of customers going to certain destinations throughout the day are carefully measured, all under the watchful eye of the airport landlords who stringently control what retailers do; hence, having good relationships with them is critical. Over the years, our group has successfully tendered for many airports such as Sydney, Melbourne, Helsinki, Vienna, Washington DC, London Gatwick, and many others.

Tendering for airport opportunities

We have lost far more than we have won, which is why putting together a very experienced team to seek out opportunities is so important. Most tenders are available on public websites, but not all are. Developing a relationship a few years before a tender will appear is important; showing how you will be able to service the strenuous demands of long opening hours, strict security, fire and health and safety is vital. You will need outstanding internal and external control procedures and a solid financial balance sheet. Your retail designs for the store fit-outs will need to capture the imagination of airport management and the public. They will also ask a lot about your pricing strategy, on the one hand asking it to be competitive, but on the other, realizing that customers in a rush are looking for convenience and last-minute shopping often can command a higher price point.

The key question that will be asked of you and your team is, why do you think you can operate this concession better than anyone else? And will you be able to pay the airport more rent than other bidders over the contract term? Your financial modelling around this will need to take into account a range of KPIs such as average basket size (number of items sold and their value), as well as hit rate/penetration rate, which basically means how many customers out of the entire body of people visiting the airport you will serve. At the end of the day, airports have to invest vast sums of money in CapEx to keep the facilities looking attractive and operate the business's aviation side smoothly. In some countries, airports are required to consider the level of local ownership of the business and also consider if you have any other benefits for them as a responsible owner/operator of the airport.

A good source for information on what is going on in the airport world is to subscribe to online media such as the Moodie Davitt Report, which covers a whole range of airport retail news internationally every month. All major travel retail announcements are reported there by a diligent team overseen by Martin Moodie and Dermot Davitt. Of note also is the Airports Council International (ACI), where Kevin Burke is the president for the United States, and Oliver Jankovec is the director-general in Europe.

If the financials in the contract are set up right, it can be a tremendous win–win for brands, consumers and the airport owners. But beware of over-promises and the impact of sudden changes in flight destinations and customer dynamics. In the financial crash of 2009, our group lost millions of pounds of income at our airport. Passenger numbers at the airport dropped, and average spending by each passenger on retail took a nosedive. We were locked into rents that nevertheless kept on increasing with inflation indexes. Clearly look carefully at proposed contracts, especially in light of Covid-19, since the airports themselves never guarantee passenger numbers. Both airports and concessionaires need to work together for the long-term health of the travel retail industry. MAG rents are not viable anymore – we as retailers cannot be expected to insure them against issues such as Covid-19, terrorism or other events outside our control.

Dealing with airports has other unique challenges as well. Obtaining permits from the airport to build the retail locations you have won can be difficult. Construction work can be slow due to the need only to make noise when there are no flights. Attracting good people at an economic wage to work in retail locations seven days a week at unsociable hours and far from where they live can be challenging. Having hired staff and then obtaining their security passes can take months. Even what seems like a great location at an airport can change. Flight departure gates vary, thus shifting your key customers. Redevelopment of lounges and security checkpoints also moves passengers around, and suddenly, what was a great location can become almost useless.

So let's now look at things deeper from an airport's perspective and hear from one of the leaders in the field.

CONVERSATION WITH

Stewart Wingate is CEO of London Gatwick Airport, one of the world's largest international airports, serving 46 million passengers per year to 230 destinations in 70 countries pre-Covid. There are more than 90 shops and services units and over 30 food and beverage outlets based at the airport, which combined pay around £200 million to the airport per year (compared with £450 million in aeronautical revenues).

Sacha: What happened during Covid-19, and how are you finding passenger numbers returning again after the pandemic?

Stewart: From the end of March 2020 to the end of the year there was a collapse in passengers due to Covid-19, with just 1.5 million people going through our airport instead of what should have been around 40 million for the same period. We had to close down one of our terminals entirely and furlough or make redundant a lot of great staff. We went into 2021 hoping it would pick up with the vaccine rollout, but it didn't. We served just 0.5 million passengers for the first six months. We could not believe it would be so bad. We expected the UK government to work with other governments and eliminate restrictions where there were vaccinations, but this did not happen.

We also hoped that the government would restore the slot utilization rules but they did not. The temporary slot measures that remained in place effectively saw Heathrow take most of the available traffic. However, that is all in the past now, with the recovery faster than anyone predicted. Already in the summer of 2022 we achieved over 85 per cent of pre-Covid passengers, which was well in excess of the government's modelling.

Sacha: Rebuilding such a large business must have been difficult. How has London Gatwick Airport coped with hiring so many staff post-Covid?

Stewart: Pre-pandemic we had more than 25,000 staff at the airport. Many people who were sadly let go did not want to return, so we and our partners had to recruit and train thousands of new people. We had to totally change our recruitment process because the airport vetting process is very onerous with references needing to go back for five years. We decided to give unconditional offers to people while waiting for the references, which meant we could flex up quicker. The rapid increase in demand was truly unexpected with us returning to 85 per cent of capacity by summer 2022, which was a huge challenge. Airport handling companies at the airport, however, struggled to find enough employees to operate the airline check-in desks, or do the ground-handling and baggage-handling duties for arriving and departing aircraft. Our retailers also had significant issues hiring staff, who often dislike the unsociable hours that are needed at an airport, and there has been wage inflation to attract people. We had dialogue with the airlines to make sure they recruited more staff, but we also proactively cut the number of planned flights for summer 2022 to ensure there were not sudden flight cancellations due to staff shortages.

Sacha: How are consumer spending levels in retail outlets at the airport different for pre-Covid versus post-pandemic?

Stewart: That is a very good question. We think patterns of consumer spending are still transitioning to what is the new normal. The signs are very encouraging, with spend per passenger on retail 45 per cent higher than before Covid-19. We expected with mass tourism opening up that the spend per pax on retail would drop, but actually it has remained at a similar higher level. People are also checking in earlier, so dwell time has increased, which helps retail spend. Passengers seem to want to engage with our retail offerings, which is exciting.

Sacha: How does Gatwick airport differentiate itself and encourage consumer spending in the face of the Ukraine war and the cost of living increases?

Stewart: Our fundamental core strength is our passenger base. Fifteen million people live within one hour's journey time of the airport. We have a very wealthy demographic with four times the European Union average per capita income. We have excellent transport networks with trains once every three minutes. We have a network of competitively priced long-haul and short-haul destinations. Hence we are in a very strong position. It is interesting comparing this to the 2009 financial crisis when I first came to the airport as CEO of Gatwick. Then we saw a 10 per cent drop in passenger numbers and a big hit to retail income, but even in the current financial challenges with the Ukraine war and cost of living squeeze, we believe there will be strong growth going forward.

Sacha: How are the duration of trips and types of destinations changing?

Stewart: Customer demand is higher than we can meet. Post-pandemic, we almost immediately went up to 100 per cent of our pre-Covid passenger levels for short-haul European flights, with long haul achieving only 60 per cent. Now new start-up airlines as well as the big national airlines are expanding their long-haul flights so the initial rush to short haul post-Covid is moving to longer-haul destinations. With people not being required all the time to work in offices, they are also taking longer trips and working from travel destinations, which is also changing the peak days and times of the week for the airport.

Sacha: What are the plans for investment to grow capacity and facilities at London Gatwick Airport?

Stewart: Pre-Covid we were investing around £250 million per year. During Covid-19 we had reduced it to just £1 million per month, which was hard to do. Now we are planning for major development in the retail areas of the terminals. The footprint is heavily utilized and we need to provide customers with more space and increase retail opportunities. We are improving rail, car parking and adding the northern runway into permanent service to increase significantly the number of flights (subject to planning approval in 2024). This means going from 50 flights per hour to 70, so from 46 million pre-Covid to 70 million passengers.

Sacha: How important are sustainability issues for you?

Stewart: They are crucial given that people in the local area, our customers and regulators want aviation to have as low an impact as possible. We have been buying all our energy from renewable sources since 2014 and we want to reduce by 50 per cent the usage of water, and ensure airlines use sustainable aviation fuels. For our retailers and anyone doing construction, by 2030 all materials used at Gatwick must be repurposed for beneficial use, i.e. repaired, reused, recycled or converted to fuel.

LOCATION, LOCATION, LOCATION

- Focus on location. Go where your customers are, and figure that out. Pay the extra rent to be where your target market can find you. It will come back in kind.
- If you decide to go into a shopping mall, verify any landlord promises by talking to other tenants and asking for specifics.
- Try to be located close to a currency exchange branch, this is where tourists will suddenly have significantly more cash to spend.

- Go to retail summits (some are listed in this chapter) and learn what the current trends are and what they are projected to be.

- Airports are exciting environments with a great demographic of the customer with time and money to spend.

- Say no to traditional MAG rents that are not linked to passengers – airports need to deliver the passengers, and you cannot insure them against pandemics or terrorism.

- Think about how your customers feel at a particular location and price accordingly. For example, water costs more where people are walking in the sun, so does ice cream. Where is the best area or timing for you to have premium pricing?

- Don't stint on signage or window design. Be visible at all costs, literally. If no one sees you, no one will come.

- Consider if digital signage is right for you. If so, make sure it is as intuitive and clear as possible.

References

Clarke, J (2018) Westfield London now largest shopping centre in Europe with launch of £600 million extension, *The Independent*, 20 March, www.independent.co.uk/news/business/news/westfield-london-white-city-largest-shopping-centre-europe-expansion-john-lewis-hm-a8265071.html (archived at https://perma.cc/RH29-5LTW)

Heathrow (2019) Heathrow partners and suppliers, *Property*, www.heathrow.com/company/partners-and-suppliers/property (archived at https://perma.cc/382L-NTPQ)

Twitter (2021) https://twitter.com/wafflemeisteruk/status/1410971345802964998?lang=en (archived at https://perma.cc/L7FX-ZZDV)

WHSmith (2022) Our locations, www.whsmithplc.co.uk/our-locations#list (archived at https://perma.cc/6YGZ-YCKD)

WTM (2020) Why visit WTM London, *World Travel Market*, https://london.wtm.com/visit/ (archived at https://perma.cc/2WDX-USF2)

10

Partner with local and state governments

If city governments contribute financing to your area by upgrading it or promoting your business on their travel promotion sites, it can be tremendously helpful. City governments have helped in the transformation of many districts, turning them into tourist destinations. It's good for business, increases tax receipts, and is a win–win for everyone. There are various ways to work with local government, including getting them to expedite tourist visas quicker with fewer costs and encouraging them to allocate financing to improve street policing or street layouts so that your business district becomes a larger destination point. Let's examine a few specific ways in which a city or state government can help businesses like yours by having a deeper conversation with one of the top luxury retail landlords in the United States.

CONVERSATION WITH
Craig Robins, founder and owner of the Miami Design District Development, a major luxury retail area in Florida.

Sacha: How has Miami changed over the past 20 years?

Craig: Miami has become a global city of cultural substance. It began with the revitalization of South Beach in the late 1980s and the 1990s. But when Art Basel came in 2002, it put Miami on the map as a place for global cultural happenings. Miami is, in fact, an international city as a central hub for South Americans and a destination place for Europeans, and for people from all over the United States.

Sacha: What was the district like before you built Miami Design District, and what was your inspiration?

Craig: The Design District is a historical neighbourhood that showcased mass-produced furniture design as well as luxury furniture. It fell into disrepair, and we ended up buying property in the neighbourhood in the mid-1990s. We were one of the largest property holders in the historic district of Miami Beach and we contributed to its regeneration. This renaissance of South Beach and Miami Beach began an overall transformation of Miami, converting it from a sleepy town to a dynamic global city. In the mid-1990s we began revitalizing the Design District, and we initially focused on bringing back design showrooms. Then we began thinking, 'How often do people buy a sofa?' Furniture alone does not attract a lot of people. I visited Salone, the furniture show in Milan, and was amazed how the entire city that week celebrated design with all kinds of exhibitions, parties and cultural happenings. At the time, Salone was a unique global event. A short time thereafter, I met Sam Keller, the director of Art Basel, who was interested in bringing Art Basel to Miami Beach.

From its inception in 2002, the Design District became one of the central hubs for exhibitions and parties during Art Basel in Miami. It was exciting and interesting and set the new course for the Design District. We began making it a place for art, design, food and culture. This led to us founding Design Miami/, a show to exhibit and sell limited edition and historical furniture and collectibles. This was a catalyst for the transformation of the Design District. Grounded as an important cultural destination, it became a happening place for commerce and culture. Our show, Design Miami/, was, in part, inspired by Zaha Hadid, the world-famous architect whose iconic buildings have amazed people around the world. A site-specific installation called 'Elastika' that she did for Design Miami/ in 2005 remains inside the Moore Building in the Design District today. This in turn attracted great furniture designers from around the world – we were having amazing events with international visibility and participation and the neighbourhood was getting better and better.

The inclusion of luxury fashion brands and world-class dining destinations made a big difference. Some brands opened flagship stores, such as Christian Louboutin, and in 2011, an affiliate of LMVH, L Catterton Real Estate, acquired 50 per cent ownership in the Miami Design District. With L Catterton Real Estate, we brought in flagships for many great brands, including Hermès, Louis Vuitton, Dior, Gucci and Cartier. Because these were not typical stores and not just commercial outlets, the brands expressed themselves in different ways and made their stores artistic experiences. This has contributed to the unique cultural fabric of the community and distinguishes it from other destinations.

Sacha: What are the best retail concepts you are seeing at present?

Craig: The best concepts are those where the brands do something interesting and special to express their unique creativity and style. Our sales and traffic have been growing by about 50 per cent year on year over the past 24 months. Our goal has been to make the neighbourhood a must-see destination for art, architecture and design, with incredible stores and cultural sites. The stores are highly creative, free-standing, two- and three-storey global flagships showcasing a full expression of what the brand does, which fits harmoniously with the cultural dimension of the neighbourhood. Unintentionally, it has become selfie heaven.

Sacha: Who do you view as the Design District's target customers?

Craig: I think it is everyone on the ground in Miami. We aspire to offer the kind of experience that makes people say: 'You gotta go see the place.' That's our goal. It's the fastest-growing retail location in the United States.

Sacha: How does the Design District attract new international shoppers who might not have heard of it before?

Craig: It takes time to discover something new. It's not instantaneous but an organic process. We have 350–400 events per year, including major art exhibitions. Bono came to auction Red last year. Art Basel also put the Design District on the map for people from around the world. Many consumers are also interested in the rare watches and jewellery events in the neighbourhood that often include product debuts. We host an international-calibre show that features collectible cars on the street. We have amazing concerts produced by Emilio Estefan. These are free for the public. We also do events for families, often in partnership with the ICA Museum. Generally, there are ongoing arts-related experiences. More and more people are discovering our creative neighbourhood and keep coming back. When visitors to hotels ask their concierges what to do in Miami, the Design District is usually their first recommendation.

Sacha: What is the future of retailing for you?

Craig: Combining bricks-and-mortar experiences with digital platforms. The digital lets you get to know the brand, but we still need the physical experience. One of our stores is Rapha, a bikewear company. I bought a couple of things from them online. Later, when I went to the store, the sales team guided me, and I realized that I'd bought all the wrong things. The future is combining these experiences. The physical store has to know how to work with customers, knowing when to engage and not engage. Having them there is helpful, but they also have to know when to back off.

Sacha: Was the Mayor of Miami helpful to you?

Craig: Our partnership with the city, including the Mayor, has only been positive. The city has supported our adventure since the outset.

Safe walking streets

It seems obvious, but shopping tourists rarely drive cars. They might take a tour bus, but if you are in retail, you need pedestrians – people willing to walk in and out of a range of stores, feeling safe and relaxed as they carry bags of items they bought, putting them down next to their chairs in cafés and restaurants without wondering if it will be safe to do so.

In the early 1980s, Times Square and its surrounding streets were not considered safe for tourists. Prostitutes, drug dealers and pickpockets harassed anyone there. So when the local government announced they would work with developers on a multi-million-dollar effort to clean up the area with targeted policing and redevelopment of street seating and lighting, many were sceptical (Chakraborty, 2016). Later on, our company, ChangeGroup, seized the opportunity and worked with the leading developer, Forest City Ratner, to place our currency exchange services at the heart of their development in order for us to exchange international tourists' foreign cash into dollars to spend in new neighbouring tenancies such as Madame Tussauds' Wax Works, Hilton Hotel, and the many other new retailers and food outlets. This even required the picking up and moving of an entire historically protected Broadway theatre. But it was worth it. As more and more tourists found the Times Square area and 42nd Street safe, fun and inviting, our business and those of neighbouring retailers blossomed.

Of course, things can go the other way. San Francisco saw a dramatic increase in street crime and vagrants in 2018 that scared large numbers of tourists, who posted images online, and that also resulted in the cancellation of business conferences, including a 15,000-person medical convention that had been due to bring $40 million in income to the city (DailyMail.com, 2018). As an aside, tourism is interestingly San Francisco's largest industry (that's right, it is not tech), generating $9 billion a year in San Francisco, $725 million in local taxes, and providing employment to around 80,000 people (DailyMail.com, 2018).

Similarly, changes in local safety considerations have greatly impacted tourism in destinations ranging from Egypt to London, where increases in knife crime made headlines worldwide thanks to President Trump's Twitter exchanges with London Mayor Sadiq Khan (Gage, 2019). Clearly, street safety for locals and tourists needs constant investment, and businesses need to pressure local authorities to maintain spending on providing inviting retail streets for tourists to shop in.

See your city in the movies

How would a film that featured a city your business is located in help your business? Well, if your town or location is shown in a film, viewers might say, 'I want to fall in love there too.' Many people will be inclined to visit the destination after seeing it used in a film. This goes back years, from black-and-white films like *Casablanca* (1942) in Morocco or *The Third Man* (1949) in Vienna, where even to this day, walking tours and memorabilia is still available to purchase. Lovers like to meet up at the Empire State Building in New York, just like they did in *An Affair to Remember* (1957) or *When Harry Met Sally* (1989). *Notting Hill* (1999) transformed the tourism, retail and real-estate prospects of a rundown part of London, and these are just a few examples. I recall watching the film *Absolutely Fabulous* (2016) and seeking out the hotel they depicted in the film in the south of France and then booking to stay there. Netflix series *Drive to Survive* (2022) has resulted in a huge fanbase of people wanting to follow F1 car racing and visit stunning locations like Monte Carlo.

On screen, the hotels, retailers and hospitality venues come alive. Brands have a contextual boost, and people at home can get inspired to travel and shop. Personally, I think filmmakers and TV series makers should be contractually required to list in more detail the retailers, restaurants and hotels they depict as part of any permits or assistance packages they get from the government and local communities.

Have a voice in travel visa issues

There are consequences to state and federal actions that can very much affect the retailer. For example, sanctions against the Russian Federation have hurt retailers across Europe due to the drops in the number of Russian tourists. We have felt it strongly in regions near the border where there has been a dramatic change in the number of Russians coming for regular shopping trips.

As a retailer, you must stay on top of global affairs and be involved either as an individual or as part of your trade association to represent the retailer's perspective to your government. Before the invasion of Ukraine in 2022, Russia aimed to double the number of tourists it receives by 2025 to 50 million and was targeting visitors from China, India, the Middle East and the United States. This was drawing on the success of the visa-free programme it had for the 2018 FIFA Football World Cup when 5 million additional tourists visited the country during and after the event. There was an easy electronic eVisa programme at major ports of entry to the country. Russia's head of the Federal Agency for Tourism, Zarina Doguzova, is looking to extend the visa-free programme it already has in place for groups of tourists from certain countries such as China (Mallick, 2019).

Moving to the United States, the major retailers and hospitality industry in New York, California, Florida and other coveted locations need to be proactive with the government in helping them remove obstacles to visitors. For example, the US visa waiver programme for South Koreans immediately doubled visitors from 400,000 to 800,000 per annum (Bird, 2008).

Western tourists are often not very concerned about visa restrictions, but they can be a huge barrier to tourism globally. I was attending a recent Young Presidents' Organization (YPO) conference (representing 20,000 top CEOs from around the world) in Shanghai. A couple of weeks before I was due to leave, I thought it would be nice to surprise my wife by inviting her to join me so that we could spend a few days afterwards enjoying the city. My PA had already filled in the Chinese visa paperwork for me months before; it included detailed data about my financial and personal situation, which felt very intrusive and not at all pleasant (western governments ask the same of people from Asia too, so I kept telling myself not to feel too annoyed). When we called the consulate helpline, the idea of getting an appointment and completing everything for my wife in seven days was declared practically impossible. In the end, we found an external third-party company that offers a 'visa expediting service' (which is available for most countries and, while legitimate, seems a little unfair). This cost several hundred pounds but ensured my wife got a tourist visa. If she hadn't, the travel retailers would have lost out on the revenue from her flights, food, shopping, and so on, and that is just one person. Imagine how many trips worldwide by millions of people don't take place because of countries' visa restrictions.

City/state area development and tourism planning

Niagara Falls is located between the US and Canadian borders. Interestingly, the Canadian side is more commercially developed, with hotels, restaurants, shops, and much more visual communication with the tourist. The US side is operated as a state park but under-invested in, with rundown buildings, poor quality restaurants and very few shopping options available. So, naturally, the destination of choice for honeymooners and other tourists is on the Canadian side since they maximize the experience with a casino and great restaurants.

Approximately 331 million people visit US national parks each year (Statistica, 2018), and national and city parks are popular all over the world. The more remote areas surrounding these parks may have wonderful local communities but often face challenges to survive. Sensitively designed, eco-building projects that provide space for locally sourced products and services can attract and serve more tourists much better.

Regent's Park in London, with its clear signage around the park, is an example of local government working with an enterprise. They literally dug down into the ground and built The Hub: a food and beverage court, sports and toilet facilities, and rooms for parties and training, all integrated into a park environment with grass coverings and plantings hiding the building. Signage, design, communication and services all work together with a range of businesses, resulting in great success for tourists and locals alike.

Retailers can engage with government bodies (for example, Visit California in the United States or Visit Britain in the UK) to promote themselves as places that welcome tourists. These government bodies have quite large budgets for international promotion. They can really push your business, but they have to understand what customers you are looking for and what you can offer. You can also attend marketing events they host internationally. For example, part of Visit Britain's tourism action plan sets out how the government is delivering on its priorities and announces a significant 'Discover England' promotional fund. The Visit Britain report states: 'This fund promotes food, music and heritage to literature, horse-racing and the coast, the projects showcase destinations and experiences across the country to overseas markets, driving inbound tourism and boosting the domestic market' (Visit Britain, 2013). This builds on the success of the GREAT campaign, which was launched in key markets to promote Britain as one of the best places to visit, study, work and invest in. It shows how people can work together. An esteemed group of British fashion industry insiders launched a 'GREAT' Britain-branded subway train in New York. Victoria Beckham was joined by the likes of Anna Wintour, Tamara Mellon, Marcus Wainwright and Jourdan Dunn to draw attention to Britain's world-renowned fashion designers, the magnificent range of shopping on offer and the distinctive British style (Visit Britain, 2013).

Another example in London is how the New West End Company worked together with its local authorities to identify and address key issues of importance to the West End. For example, the business improvement district members, the mayor and Westminster City Council collectively agreed to the Oxford, Regent and Bond Streets action plan, a programme of activities for improving the West End. All these different entities combined to ensure that the West End remains one of the world's most popular districts to live in, visit and shop.

London, with its traditions in men's tailoring, has also worked on being recognized as the global capital for men's fashion, hosting a 'men-only' fashion week and looking to cement its position ahead of the likes of Milan, New York and Paris. As a result, menswear has become a big business for Britain's economy.

Naturally museums represent a major part of government expenditure in the tourism sector. The museums quarter in Vienna, with its impressive buildings; the museum triangle in Madrid – the Prado, Thyssen and Reina Sofia (where the giant *Guernica* by Picasso hangs) – all generate vast numbers of international as well as local visitors. These people spend vast amounts of money and the same can be said for the areas around the Louvre in Paris or the Egyptian Museum of Antiquities in Cairo.

Governments should promote their monuments

President Obama said at the WTTC Tourism Industry Conference in Madrid in 2019: 'Visit national monuments abroad. When people see you have seen and recognized their culture and stories, then they can be more open to yours.' Iconic buildings in cities across the world need proper promotion; don't assume that people from other countries know what your landmarks are. Fred Dixon, CEO of NYC & Company, which promotes New York as a destination and provides a range of tourism services, was reported in the *New York Times* as stating that he is focusing on hyper-local experiences, creating new destinations within the destinations for the 67 million annual visitors that come to New York (McGeehan, 2019).

NYC & Company educates hundreds of small and medium-sized enterprises (SMEs) about how to promote themselves to tourists. It is not just about having visitors but how to make more money from a given number of tourists. They have pushed the government to improve transport, such as using local ferries to transport commuters so that more options are available to them, adding more services and ensuring more people-power is available in designated tourist destinations.

Governments can change the future of an economy

Desiree Maxino, group head of government policy at Air Asia, speaking at the WTTC conference in Seville 2019, highlighted that 70 per cent of airline traffic in Asia is low cost. In terms of private–public partnerships for new international destinations, Air Asia is pushing for low-cost terminals, not big ones, so that the airport terminal and landing fees can be kept very low. In addition, Air Asia has been instrumental in working with the local Indonesian government to increase shopping tourism. Improvements to local airports have enabled direct international connections from places such as Kuala Lumpur and Singapore to airports such as Bandar Airport in Bandung (Kompas.com, 2010). The place is popular with local Indonesians, who can purchase quality clothes, shoes, bags and so on from various famous brands from factory outlets such as JL Riau or JL Dargo, as all these products are cheaper than what you would find in your own region. Airbnb and various hotels have opened up, and direct flights from Singapore and Malaysia bring much-needed foreign tourist shoppers to improve the island economy (All Indonesia Travel, 2019).

Looking at strategic investment, The Mall of Dubai and Mall of the Emirates have taken the spectacular to another level, becoming so huge and opulent that this oasis of shopping has become a major attraction in its own right in the United Arab Emirates (UAE). It is remarkable to think how much the Dubai government has achieved in a few decades by reinvesting their relatively modest oil deposits into building an economy for the future. People now come not just as tourists, but stay as investors and managers for a burgeoning range of high-tech, healthcare and financial firms. How many citizens in other resource-rich countries must look at these achievements and wonder why their leaders have not done the same?

At the opposite end, there are cities actively trying to halt growth in tourism, worried about the impact of issues such as driving up real-estate prices for locals and changes to the nature of the city. This seems unfortunate, as a better investment in additional facilities for tourists would spread them out more across the city and region. The money earned in taxes could be used to provide better services to local residents.

Caroline Beteta, President and CEO of Visit California, said in a keynote speech: 'As you get further and further away from California – Chicago, New York and, of course, overseas – it's like Coca-Cola or any other retail product. Just because you have awareness and you're in demand, that doesn't mean Coca-Cola stops marketing. We (Visit California) are a consumer product, and people have choices' (Anderson, 2016).

Pier 39 is located in California and is one of the most visited tourist attractions in the United States. I have worked with them for many years in attracting and serving international shoppers. Let's now hear from their CEO.

CONVERSATION WITH

Taylor Safford, President and CEO of Pier 39, San Francisco, California, a leading tourism retail and entertainment venue with 105 independently operated shops, attractions and restaurants.

Sacha: How many US and international people visit Pier 39 annually?

Taylor: San Francisco Travel Association estimates that 15 million visitors a year come to Pier 39. From our research, almost one-third come from California, and of this number, about 20 per cent are from the local Bay Area. Another one-third of our visitors are from the United States outside of California, and the final one-third are international. From our most recent intercept study, we found that about half of our 15 million visitors are repeat visitors, and the average number of prior visits from this group was nine.

Sacha: How do you promote Pier 39? Do you have a central marketing fund?

Taylor: We do a lot of print advertising in local publications and on our local mass transit, TV and radio. We sponsor advertising on San Francisco Travel Association's website, which is a popular site with visitors, and social media is of course important. We have a marketing fund into which all the tenants pay a percentage of their revenues.

Sacha: What makes people come to Pier 39? What is the experience they are looking for?

Taylor: We market family-friendly activities. When locals have visitors come to town, Pier 39 is always a great destination to bring them to because it is a clean, safe, fun place with incomparable views of the bay. It's like a mini vacation for locals where you can eat sweet treats and fun things you wouldn't normally eat at home, and watch our famous herd of California sea lions. We have a wonderful tenant mix that attracts visitors because they can enjoy unique shops, restaurants and attractions that they won't find in their local malls back home. We like to create a sense of discovery here in our beautiful, open-air shopping centre. We are a quarter of a mile from Alcatraz and have stunning views, which makes the experience delightful. We also have a set of piano stairs that are fun to play on. Our mix of shops, restaurants, attractions and views are unlike anywhere else in the world and creates a uniquely San Francisco experience here at Pier 39.

Sacha: How do you see your marketing activities for Pier 39 evolving in the coming years?

Taylor: The natural progression is from online digital to mobile. We want to deliver a high-quality digital experience for visitors that works in tandem with our Victorian-themed architecture.

Sacha: How has the business changed in the past five years?

Taylor: Visitation has increased from 12 million to 15 million visitors, as mentioned. San Francisco faces many challenges, such as its burgeoning homeless problem, and the general retail landscape has become more challenging. So we need to remain a safe, fun and friendly place to visit in San Francisco.

Sacha: Are the customers different in their behaviours than before? Are they looking for a different buy?

Taylor: We do think people want a more modern retail experience. I don't put stock in the 'death of retail' point of view, but I do believe people want an experience that includes intuitive shopping, easy access to information and simplified purchasing. Visitors don't want to feel accosted by salespeople. Visitors are more health conscious as well. Retailers must also understand the power of social media and the fact that whatever they are doing right or wrong, guests will share it on social media, so there has to be more attention to doing what is right for the customer.

Sacha: If there is something at Pier 39 you would like to add in, what would it be?

Taylor: We are in discussions with Aquarium of the Bay for a complete renovation of its aquarium at Pier 39. They would like to expand it to be a significant attraction, scientific research and environmental studies centre here in San Francisco. If we can bring something like this to Pier 39, we can create another iconic destination along the waterfront. We are still in early discussions, however, and it may take several years before this can become a reality.

Sacha: How do you and your team work with local authorities and agencies to protect the retailers from crime, improve transport links, improve the general environment, and make good decisions at a government level that promotes healthy retail tourism?

Taylor: Pier 39 actively participates with the community, serving on influential community boards and associations to ensure and promote the safety of its visitors, employees and tenants. As CEO, I serve on the Board and the Executive Committee of the San Francisco Chamber of Commerce. The chamber is a 170-year-old organization that is the voice of business in the city, whose work includes everything from driving important legislation at City Hall to fast-tracking the approval in 1995 to launch the vitally important and wildly successful F-Line Streetcar system that serves Pier 39 and Fisherman's Wharf. Members of the Pier 39 executive team represent the company and its tenants on the boards of the San Francisco Travel Association, the Fisherman's Wharf Community Benefit District, the San Francisco Bay Harbour Safety Committee, the San Francisco Chamber of Commerce Foundation and the San Francisco State University Foundation. The company is also active on state and federal issues by serving on the boards of the California Travel Association, the Passenger Vessel Association and the US Travel Association.

PARTNER WITH LOCAL AND STATE GOVERNMENTS

- Enlist city/state government to help you succeed by upgrading tourist destinations and giving licensing for well-designed retail in those environments.

- Lobby and write to your national government representatives to ease tourist visa restrictions and simplify paperwork.

- Have politicians promote monuments and tourist attractions well so that people come to your locale.

- When your location is used in a feature film or video, ensure the credits properly mention you so that viewers can find you more easily.

- Government can work with you on planning regulations and opening up new areas for development to increase retail traffic. In addition, they can provide tax incentives that bring in investors to create thriving retail locations.
- Above all, ensure effective policing and push local law enforcement, local government and national government representatives to invest in clean, safe streets.

References

Absolutely Fabulous: The Movie (2016) [Film] Directed by Mandie Fletcher, BBC Films, UK

All Indonesia Travel (2019) You can't miss these 7 things to do in Bandung, Indonesia, *Sher She Goes*, https://allindonesiatravel.com/top-10-things-to-do-and-what-to-see-in-bandung/ (archived at https://perma.cc/DXX9-JHS3)

An Affair to Remember (1957) [Film] Directed by Leo McCarey, 20th Century, USA

Anderson, C (2016) Visit California chief earns spot in travel industry hall of fame, *The Sacramento Bee*, www.sacbee.com/news/business/biz-columns-blogs/cathie-anderson/article96531922.html (archived at https://perma.cc/2GWU-HTU6)

Bird, J (2008) Visa waiver program to double number of Korean travellers to US, *Visa Bureau*, www.visabureau.com/news/visa-waiver-program-to-double-number-of-korean-travellers-to-us (archived at https://perma.cc/2D5H-TGU2)

Casablanca (1942) [Film] Directed by Michael Curtiz, Warner Brothers, USA

Chakraborty, D (2016) When Times Square was sleazy, *CNN US*, https://edition.cnn.com/2016/04/18/us/80s-times-square-then-and-now/index.html (archived at https://perma.cc/U3HL-ZBBM)

DailyMail.com (2018) 'I come from a third world country and it is not as bad as this': San Francisco's homelessness and opioid crises drive away business, as $40m convention cancels because members are too scared to walk alone, *Mail Online*, www.dailymail.co.uk/news/article-5914425/Big-convention-cancels-meeting-San-Francisco-citys-problems-homelessness-drug.html (archived at https://perma.cc/AL3T-VR4E)

Drive to Survive (2022) Series 4 Episode 8, first aired March 11, 2022, Netflix, Box to Box Films, United Kingdom

Gage, J (2019) 'Knife crime': Trump responds to London mayor criticizing him for golfing, *MSN*, www.msn.com/en-gb/news/world/knife-crime-trump-responds-to-london-mayor-criticizing-him-for-golfing/ar-AAGKz9Z (archived at https://perma.cc/KHQ2-RF4M)

Kompas.com (2010) Perluasan Bandara Husein Sastranegara Ditargetkan Juli
    2010, *Kompas.com*, https://money.kompas.com/read/2010/01/26/10522985/
    Perluasan.Bandara.Husein.Sastranegara.Ditargetkan.Juli.2010 (archived at
    https://perma.cc/JJ8X-PYLE)

Mallick, S (2019) Russia to position India as its top-priority market, *Travel Trends
    Today*, www.traveltrendstoday.in/people/inconversation/item/7787-russia-to-
    position-india-as-its-top-priority-market (archived at https://perma.
    cc/875Y-A8WF)

McGeehan, P (2019) NYC is on pace to draw a record 67 million tourists this year,
    The New York Times, www.nytimes.com/2019/08/19/nyregion/nyc-tourism.
    html (archived at https://perma.cc/RKT6-AXE6)

Notting Hill (1999) [Film] Directed by Duncan Kenworthy, PolyGram Filmed
    Entertainment, UK

Statistica (2018) National Park tourism in the US - statistics and facts, *Statistica*,
    www.statista.com/topics/2393/national-park-tourism-in-the-us/ (archived at
    https://perma.cc/D5TG-V58H)

The Third Man (1949) [Film] Directed by Carol Reed, London Films, UK

Visit Britain (2013) Foresight Issue 112, *Visit Britain*, www.visitbritain.org/sites/
    default/files/vb-corporate/Documents-Library/documents/Foresight_112.pdf
    (archived at https://perma.cc/WNF7-NUXS)

When Harry Met Sally (1989) [Film] Directed by Rob Reiner, Castle Rock
    Entertainment, New York

11

The leadership of change

Effecting change means co-operating with your teams of people; in many countries, that means working with labour unions. Let's now hear from one of the world's most important leaders of labour union organizations.

CONVERSATION WITH
Frances O'Grady, Secretary General of the Trades Union Congress (TUC), the UK, which represents 6 million employees through 48 large unions across a wide range of industries, including retail, hospitality, logistics, supply chains and manufacturing.

Sacha: Retail across the globe seems to be having a tough time, yet some unions and governments have been trying to stop the use of flexible contracts/zero-hour contracts. What upsides are there to employers in not using them?

Frances: At the TUC we believe the use of zero-hours contracts, under the guise of 'flexibility', is something of a red herring.

In the short term, there may seem to be some advantages for employers from a pure immediate cost-reduction point of view. But in the long term, not only do they harm the well-being of staff, but they also reduce productivity, engagement, skills development and motivation. Presentism and higher staff turnover are ultimately bad for business too.

Giving employees guaranteed hours and a decent level of pay, so they know they can pay their bills and put food on the table, is a basic right, but we know that nearly 4 million people in the UK are in insecure work – many working in retail. Research for the UK shop-workers union shows that for 4 in 10 retail workers, 20 per cent of their hours are not guaranteed, and 1 in 10 have relied on foodbanks to feed themselves or their families.

This is wrong. It is common sense that this has a huge impact on people's performance when they are at work. The worry and exhaustion caused by not knowing how you will live week to week leads to sick days caused by stress, lower productivity and demotivation of staff.

A 2012 poll found that 77 per cent of retail staff were not engaged with their brand, and this costs the retail sector around £628 million a year in the UK.

Partners of The Living Wage Foundation – which advocates decent pay and decent work – have found that by paying staff a decent wage, not only has it given them a competitive advantage by improving their reputation and distinguishing them from competitors, but crucially – 75 per cent have found that it has improved staff motivation and retention rates. In retail, where customer service, product knowledge and engaging people are so crucial to the sales floor, seeing employees as an investment, not a cost, is a vital part of future-proofing the industry.

Sacha: Sudden sickness and other absences can cause huge problems for retailers. In Sweden, the law is that the first day of sickness is unpaid to discourage poor behaviours. What other approaches should employers consider to reduce unnecessary absences?

Frances: At the TUC we believe everyone has the right to a decent job. This means being paid a living wage, secure hours, having a voice at work, manageable workloads and a safe workplace, and having the opportunity for training and development. When looking at unnecessary absences, employers should really consider if they are providing the fundamentals for staff well-being at work.

We know that in the UK alone, across all sectors, 70 million working days are lost each year due to poor mental health, costing the economy around £2.4 billion annually. Employers should be looking, wherever possible, to support their staff by creating a good working environment. This will help with staff engagement and productivity and reduce the costs associated with absenteeism. As well as ensuring the basics of good pay and good jobs, this may also include things like introducing well-being policies such as flexible working, and ensuring there are mental health first aiders and support lines to help employees deal with personal issues that may be impacting on their work.

Employers also need to ensure they are not (intentionally or unintentionally) creating a culture where, when people are genuinely ill or in need of time off, they are too scared to take it.

The Chartered Institute of Personnel and Development (CIPD) found in one of its reports that most organizations surveyed had witnessed presentism regularly, and a quarter had said they had seen an increase in the last 12 months. We also know from our own research that 2 million employees in the UK are not taking their full annual leave entitlement, and retail has one of the highest rates of untaken leave (302,000).

Unions fought hard for holiday rights and employees must be allowed to take them and not made to feel guilty for wanting a bit of downtime. In the long run, overworked, exhausted, stressed employees are not good for people and it is not good for business.

Sacha: In countries like France, you are required by law to have a union once you reach 50 employees. After resisting unionization for years, I found that having a trade union in New York sometimes acted as a great sounding board for our employees in our retail outlets and improved morale. Do you have any examples of where unionization has helped improve profitability in a retail environment?

Frances: The shop-workers union in the UK, which has over 420,000 members, works with multiple retail partners. Some you may have heard of, such as well-known supermarket brands Tesco, Co-op and Sainsbury's, and they have worked with IKEA for some time now. Union presence has helped to foster better employee/employer relations in these companies and provided knowledge and expertise when employers have wanted to change their practices or introduce new technology.

Another key role that unions such as the shop-workers union, working with the TUC, play is to lobby government. With the high street and retail experiencing very turbulent times, the Union of Shop, Distributive and Allied Workers (USDAW) is advocating for a retail sector industrial strategy that will not only protect jobs, but help reinvigorate the high street for retailers too.

A range of international institutions are now waking up to how unions can benefit not just workers but business. For example, the OECD, which brings together developed nations, publishes an 'employment outlook' each year with recommendations to government. In 2018 they said that working with trade unions through collective bargaining could 'foster skills development and skills use in the workplace, and allow for the effective dissemination of good working practices', while helping to 'promote a broad sharing of productivity gains'. It recommends that governments 'put in place a legal framework that promotes social dialogue in large and small firms alike and allows labour relations to adapt to new emerging challenges' (OECD, 2018).

Given the scale of the crisis, action from the government has been quite slow, and this industrial strategy seeks to address this, calling for among many things a comprehensive review of business rates, tax reform to level the playing field between online and bricks-and-mortar stores, and investment in transport and town centres to improve footfall and dwell time.

Sacha: How can unions and retail employers work together better to overcome the challenges of unfair e-commerce tax and Big Data advantages?

Frances: As mentioned, unions are proposing that the government should adopt an industrial strategy for retail that brings together workers, employers and unions to revitalize the high street and make it viable and sustainable for the future.

A key part of that strategy is reviewing rents and business rates (UK property taxes) that often make it difficult for bricks-and-mortar retailers to operate in these tough times when footfall and sales are struggling.

We know, for example, that the retail industry (in England) contributes approximately £7 billion of rates annually. This is nearly one-quarter of the total business rates bill, far more than any other industry – rates for online brands are often much lower.

As an example, compare Tesco and Amazon: Tesco paid business rates of £700 million in 2016/17. In contrast, Amazon recorded UK sales of £8.77 billion and paid only £63.4 million in business rates.

Unions are also calling for a review of tax to ensure the playing field between bricks-and-mortar and e-commerce is levelled. The shop-workers union has called for an online transaction tax, with the proceeds being ringfenced for reinvestment into high streets and bricks-and-mortar stores.

Sacha: What is your opinion on the speed of adoption and future impact of robotics in retail (including the supply chain), and how can employers and unions, as good social citizens, help people?

Frances: Technology in general has changed the retail landscape and will continue to do so. If it is used merely to replace staff and reduce overheads, we believe this will have a negative impact on the sector. Retail/wholesale is the biggest private-sector employer in the UK – job losses will create more economic uncertainty, with people having even less money in their pockets to spend.

Although online retailing is growing, in the UK over 80 per cent of sales still come from bricks-and-mortar stores. While retailers do have access to lots of customer data that they can use to target customers, people still want customer service.

We advocate a 'bricks and clicks' approach that encourages people to still make use of their local high street, whether that is to pick up online orders or through more store-based experiences. Tech brands themselves, like Samsung and Apple, have shown through their in-store services – where sales teams offer one-to-one sessions and workshops on how to use new purchases, for example – that people are still key to the customer experience.

It could be a great opportunity, and unions also have an important role to play in helping the industry develop the multi-channel and experiential retailing that will help the industry move forward, while also protecting workers' rights. Developing this strategy will require skilled, well-trained and motivated staff, with good progression paths – good job design and good work organization. Working with unions and the TUC, we can help employees contribute their wealth of knowledge and people skills to discussions with their employers. It is vital that people have a democratic voice at work through our unions.

We can also help to devise training and skills development, lobby the government to support this through apprenticeships and help navigate the introduction of new technology to ensure it benefits employees and ultimately the customer experience.

At the TUC, we also want to ensure that any new technology is not misused to exploit or abuse employees. Inappropriate practices, such as using technology for monitoring and surveillance of staff, which could be used to penalize or bully workers, are unacceptable.

It is really important that any new technology, as it is developed and introduced into the workplace, is done so in consultation with employees. The union movement can support this through collective bargaining and we call on employers to work with unions and grant access to workplaces to allow this process to happen. The TUC and union movement in the UK have strong links internationally and we work with our sister unions to ensure that ethical trading is adopted right through the supply chain, including on issues such as tech adoption and use.

Sacha: Thank you so much Frances for providing us with such deep insight!

As Frances has spoken about just now, retailing is complex and leading people effectively as markets change is vital. You will undoubtedly face many new and unusual challenges when adapting your business to capture the tourist market. These can range from facing inadequate resources or having a lack of clarity of vision as to how to apply the resources you do have, to questioning whether your location is suitable and whether you have the right products to attract additional new consumers. All of this can cause a paralysis of fear in the owner, a business unit leader, or a whole department's team members. The way to overcome these fears is to dive deep into the subject by making use of all available data and skills in your team and wider network.

If there is scant available data, you will need to rely on your intuition (you will need to do that even if there is available data). And, if you're going to take the step forward into successfully moving your business towards the tourist market, you will need to have an athlete's vision, determination and courage.

How do you begin the process of change? First, you need to understand that it will take a whole range of people to assist you. A great idea alone is not enough to take you forward; you need to persuade others to come along with you. Those others can be people who provide funding – such as a head office, banks, your shareholders and creditors. To deploy these funds to change your business will invite scrutiny and judgement on the success of your performance. You will have to rely on staff, suppliers and a host of others. This is part of the art of leadership. Doing nothing is often not an option since it can result in a one-way death spiral. In my experience, you have to be a proactive leader, responding carefully to an environment that is constantly changing.

Lead from the front

There is no better way to inspire loyalty, and no better way to gain vital information on challenges and benefits of a new business line or transformation project than being there yourself. In a new country, this means spending time there and perhaps even living there. I have moved countries so many times as we have expanded the company, and this has helped me to grow as an individual and as a leader. Most importantly, whenever we have looked at opening a new branch or product line, I have tried to make sure I am there and that I even serve some of the customers myself. The feedback I get from the sales team and from the customers is invaluable.

For example, I felt it so important that I truly understood the challenges and opportunities of opening a branch at Harrods Department Store in London that I actually insisted I join their in-house training course. Harrods

HR department could not believe that a CEO would invest three days in going through their whole process of staff induction training, but I felt the investment was really important. To this day I am proud that I still have a Harrods staff card with my photo on it, though sadly I don't qualify for any staff discounts!

Delegate effectively

As CEO, I often have managers in various countries coming to me with their challenges and problems. It might be that sales are dropping, costs are increasing, or an outside influence has impacted their business unit's performance in some other way. To them, things may appear to be out of their sphere of control, and problems may be presented to me as though I am the only one who can solve them.

My comment to those managers is always to step up and come to me with a possible solution. If they can make reasonable, well-thought-out suggestions to the problems, they can advance in their career more rapidly than those who wait for others to make decisions for them.

Of course, having an idea is great – many people have ideas – but making that idea a reality takes hard work and business acumen. So tell your employees to gather as much information as they can. At ChangeGroup, we use what is called the 'Fair Process'. Based on research conducted at INSEAD business school in France, the process encourages collaborative decision making and promises to involve our employees in major decisions. We know, and they as employees know, that their perspectives, knowledge and experience can improve management's decisions and get improved buy-in from all the staff for the changes that are about to occur.

I'll give you an example. When we are planning for a new branch in a city, we listen not only to the key people in the international head office but also to key members of local management. We get their opinion as to whether the branch will be a success in that particular location, how they think the branch should be designed and fitted out, whether we need a different range of products, how we should manage staff recruitment in that area, and whether there are any security risks or other things we should be paying attention to. Sometimes we get pushback, saying that opening a new branch will be completely wrong and that the customer base is not the type we are seeking. Sometimes we in upper management make the tough decision to do it anyway, and sometimes we are right, and sometimes we are wrong. That's just life. If we have never made wrong decisions, we probably are not pushing our boundaries enough. The key is to make more decisions that have a net positive impact than a net negative one.

List the full costs and benefits of the investment proposal

Making an investment to focus more on travel and tourism retail means you need to highlight the improvements in key performance indicators (KPIs) that will measure the success of this project (not just revenue, EBITDA, but other metrics such as total basket size increases, retail margin improvements, etc). Look at other benefits that such a focus might bring, not everything can be measured exclusively by short term results. Things such as reputation, higher quality-staff retention and improved buying power with suppliers are all important factors that may take longer to arise but are very important.

Naturally, you will need to show how observant and aware you are, including showing the risks involved and how you will deal with those. This will help everyone feel that you and your team are in control. At the end of the day, people rely on the capability of others. There is no absolute truth when it comes to business. When it comes to growth and expansion, you are stepping into the unknown, so be prepared with as much research as possible. Making others feel that you have all the key issues covered is more likely to win you their support. As a wise friend in the special forces once said to me, most people have a Plan A, and some people have a Plan B; I choose to have multiple contingencies to ensure my success and at least have a Plan A, B, C, D and E.

Negotiate effective parachute mechanisms

Not for yourself! I mean for your business unit! Here's an example of a simple parachute: you can work with suppliers to test products on a sale-or-return basis. You might find signing a 10-year lease in a new location challenging, so try to get a one-year break clause or the right to pass on or sublet it to another tenant if needed. Sometimes you can even negotiate a rent reduction if sales drop below a certain level (this especially applies if the landlord is taking a percentage of your sales).

Feel free to go back and challenge things that are not working for you. For example, a landlord in a prime New York building insisted we keep our doors closed (as stipulated in the lease contract) because he wanted the front of his building to look streamlined and nice. But we noticed a 20 per cent drop in sales when we did this. So after years of asking, we finally managed to get permission to keep the doors open, as sales had dropped, and it was either that or we were going to struggle to renew the lease in a few years' time. We also negotiated to improve the visibility of our brand by installing some eye-catching LED screens – and enjoyed sales growth as a result.

Culture quotient – bring in role models

I have taken big chances on new products, locations, and even whole new territories and countries. But in each setting our teams have encountered new cultures. Cultural quotient (CQ), or intelligence, measures how well people adapt to new environments. Greg Besner was an early investor in Zappos, the breakthrough online shoe retailer whose culture and customer service standards under Tony Hseih were legendary. Greg is now a professor at NYU Stern and in his book *The Culture Quotient* (2020) discusses in detail how it can be a measure of potential success. Indeed the book also mentions how in my company we have codified our unique international culture, moving people internationally, creating induction videos, putting up posters detailing our vision, mission, values and aspirations (VMVA), and linking them to training and performance reviews. Naturally that means also backing them up with all kinds of incentive schemes (Besner, 2021). Nevertheless, dealing with cultural differences can still be challenging.

I have acquired businesses where I felt the staff were not doing what their customers needed or expected. In those cases, I find it helpful to bring in a great role model or advocate who will appeal to the staff I am trying to develop. For example, once we had a big problem in Reykjavik, Iceland, where the staff were not engaging with customers. They were acting more like supermarket cashiers rather than sales consultants. They were not talking with customers, finding out their needs and wants and driving sales, they felt it was not appropriate to engage with people, but keep a respectful cultural distance instead.

By running training courses, providing effective online materials and, most importantly, having some experienced advocates fly in (typically we ask high energy managers or team leaders to fly in from other operations), we turned around the business. We could effect change in the culture by showing them how to really drive sales day in and day out and have fun. We helped our teams make dramatic improvements and rewarded them for the progress we saw. We have used this technique around the world.

In 2012, Dr Carmen Simon conducted a major research study on memory (Rexi Blog, 2013). Her data shows that 48 hours after a training course has finished, people remember only a fraction of what a trainer said.

That is why we reinforce key messages by role-playing customer situations, issue follow-up recap memos, and create videos with key points and post them on our intranet. We have managers do a walk-through of the sales process and then review real-life footage with the salesperson of how they do it and where things could be better. We conduct mystery shops using our own salespeople so they get additional responsibility and the person on the receiving end feels they are getting a knowledgeable assessment. This all helps our culture be embedded in everyone who joins. How do you do it in your organization?

Planning for different peak trading periods

The question is, will your peak periods change as a result of serving more tourists? There are peak trading periods in the day, of course, but tourist habits are different from those of local people. Then there are the week's peak days, and the weekends are a key part of that. Years ago in Vienna, I was aghast to see that all the retail shops closed from Saturday lunchtime and did not reopen until Monday. What a way to treat tourists who had flown all the way to visit their beautiful city (and poor me when I ran out of groceries!). Things have improved since, but many cities in Europe still have laws forcing most retailers to close on a Sunday, which seems like a lost opportunity if lots of tourists frequent the area.

Then there are the peak weeks throughout the year. These often revolve around school holiday periods when people travel more, as well as religious periods like Ramadan, which greatly impact high-value shoppers from the Middle East. The Orthodox New Year and Chinese Spring Festival are also key dates for travel retail. To indicate the power of Singles Day in China, shopping sales amounted to a record £30 billion in 2019 (Martin, 2019). Sporting, music and other entertainment events and conferences have a big impact. Make sure you have a calendar for these big events and look beyond the usual Thanksgiving, Black Friday or Cyber Monday promotions.

Some of the questions we ask ourselves when planning for peak periods are: Is our pricing correct? Can we adjust our prices dynamically at specific periods to maximize the potential income? How can we improve our point-of-sale promotional messaging? Of course, better data use is needed to help ensure that the latest promotional merchandise is not out of stock in key branches. Also, merchandizing recommendations need to be followed but, at the same time, are not too much in conflict with another product's merchandizing needs.

Major dates driving international shopping

New Year's Day	Summer school holidays
Orthodox Christian Christmas	Chinese Golden Week
Chinese New Year	Diwali
February school half-term	October school half-term
International Women's Day	Halloween
Easter	Thanksgiving (with Black Friday, and El Buen Fin – Mexico's Black Friday)
Ramadan	
Eid al-Fitr	Chinese Singles Day
May national holidays	Christmas holidays

NOTE The above list excludes other gift-giving periods, such as Father's Day and Mother's Day, which change from country to country. Please note that many religious holiday dates change from year to year, so research accordingly. In addition, international shopping can be disrupted during Olympic and FIFA World Cup months.

Ask yourself, how can we make our front windows more enticing, especially at peak periods? Do we have the right products stocked in sufficient quantities and the right staff levels? Do we have the best-performing staff rostered at that peak period? Some people shine in busy branches, and others need quieter environments where they can be slow and methodical.

How to decide what to stock and when? Lots of buzzwords are being used in AI and data analytics. Online businesses with access to good data scientists, programmers proficient in Python or managers with access tools to business reporting systems like Tableau can more easily test price elasticities and new products. However, it is harder for smaller or more traditional bricks-and-mortar businesses because less data is readily available.

Suppose an online business with a large online presence (e.g. on Amazon or eBay) drops the price or increases it. In that case, they can see demand changes almost instantly if there are enough customers actively watching or searching for those products.

There will be significant differences in the elasticity of prices when serving in a retail environment from an online one, especially when serving tourist customers. This is because people have the ability to have their needs served immediately and are often willing to pay a premium for that (just ask any parent trying to get a new sold-out doll or must-have toy just before Christmas!).

Using data enables you to have the ability to push non-performing products away from key high-visibility areas of your stores to free up valuable retail space for products that are more profitable at that point in time.

Choosing people is a tricky business

Managers have a variety of means to select their staff. I have found deploying web-portal tools useful. These explain our mission, vision and values, clearly stating what we are looking for in candidates, so we don't waste the applicant's time or our own. Apart from aptitude tests, we use online psychometric testing based on Myers-Briggs profiles to help assess applicants' motivators and how they might fit in with the team. We find it useful if managers can share their own psychometric profiles with their teams. Some managers like to keep theirs private, but I believe it is much better to allow your staff to get to know you. We all have weaknesses and strengths, and if you know your weaknesses, you can solicit people to help you with them. I don't believe everything in a psychometric test, but I do like to use them as an open platform for discussing certain traits that have been flagged up and how they might help or hinder applicants' effectiveness. Hence I find these tests very useful in stimulating dialogue with an individual, finding out more about how they think and using that open dialogue to build a platform of understanding and trust. (I always believe that having trust in human relations, which is another word for predictability, is absolutely vital.)

As a leader you must ask yourself if you have the right mix in your team. We employ over 80 nationalities in our group, with different cultures, races, religions, genders and backgrounds. Their ability to connect to the diverse range of time-poor, cash-rich customers we serve from around the world is amazing, and I am so thankful to them. But regardless of whether you are a manager or not, we all can improve upon our emotional intelligence. It's a lifelong exercise. Each of us needs to learn how to find out about ourselves and about other people. This will result in a better understanding of how to manage people, especially when undergoing change and stepping into the new. Staff will feel new pressures as you expect new things from them. This needs to be handled carefully, as it will be key to your success. You cannot be everywhere at once, so picking up on where there are people who need your individual attention and individual coaching (even for a few minutes) is very important.

We used to get major pushback from some staff in New York on how we liked to approach things. For example, some thought that relatively new recruits should not be made into managers so quickly when there were longer-serving team members who had applied for those positions. They also felt that some of the bonus systems were unfair, rewarding what they saw as the 'lucky people', who served more customers or more profitable customers (funny thing about luck: great golfers often say that the harder they practise, the luckier they seem to get).

Despite lots of talk and explanations of why we did things the way we did, the staff voted to unionize. At first, we were dismayed; there was much soul-searching at the international head office. Had we failed to communicate what we stood for and why? Then we met with the union and showed them all our data on staff performance and rosters, how decisions were being made, the fair process mechanisms we used to get input into key decisions, and that we paid above-average salaries and benefits, including additional holidays. From both sides having at first been very wary of the other, the union could rapidly see that they were there to achieve the same goal as us: the business's success. This would help employees and shareholders alike. In addition, they could see we operated as a meritocracy, paying well and promoting people based on results, not based on seniority in age or length of service. In fact, the union became an advocate for us, helping staff see that what we were doing was open, fair and the best way forward for them in their careers.

For their good work, we reward our staff with individual and team bonuses, days off, and fun parties so that everyone is as highly motivated as possible. So how can you align your incentives to make the most out of travel customers?

James Berkley consults for executives at 11 of the world's 25 largest tourism businesses, so I asked for his thoughts on staff incentives:

'One of the first questions that crops up in any review of business performance is the company's sales incentive programme, and is it fit for purpose? When I point out that they are looking in the wrong direction, most are flummoxed. What I have observed is that rewards and incentives are equally important to those individuals who exceed, meet or fail to hit their performance goals. For new hires, the absence of monetary rewards is a demotivator but it doesn't directly lead to success. Most schemes merely lead to overpaid under-achievers. The key question for dynamic employers today (with near-zero unemployment in the UK and United States) is whether you are suitably equipped to be a poacher or poachee of the best sales talent. That is fundamentally about the relationship that ensues between the sales manager/director and the salesperson' (personal communication, 2019).

In short, I would say the key to success and to getting buy-in from lots of different people is to communicate, communicate, and when you are done communicating, communicate some more. Communicate your mission, vision, what you as a company are trying to do, and how that filters down to individual business units and people's day-to-day actions. This allows you to be vertically and horizontally aligned with the changes that will be happening in this fast-moving retail sector.

Some investments will not work out

Anyone reading this book is clearly interested in attracting more business – and that comes with risk, which applies to your investments of time, money and resources. Don't be afraid if things don't work out. You will learn from them and move on rapidly. Often it is better to give it a go; hire someone into a new role, bring in a new sales training scheme, change staff incentive schemes, bring in new products, change the store displays, try out a new venture, or offer an unusual VIP event. It will either be a quick success, or you can cut your losses and move on to the next thing. But it is important not to make a half-baked attempt if you are trying something out.

No single person is responsible for everything; everything is a team effort, especially when trying something new. Plan for all of the outcomes. If it fails, be sure to build team morale so you can go on to the next success. Your team probably worked very hard on whatever your launch was, and if it flops, help them to recover by telling them the failure is OK. It's one of the steps involved in getting to success.

Let me give you an example to highlight why preparing for possible failure is also important. I was all prepared to buy a company in Estonia to merge into ours, and I had taken two relatively junior team leaders with me from our operations in Finland to help run the retail branch network. They were excited by the opportunity and, as part of re-creating who they would be in their new roles, they had gone out at their own expense and bought new suits for themselves for their new business roles in a new country. Unfortunately, at the last minute, we had to walk away from completing the transaction to buy the target company. The two team leaders felt so demoralized that they resigned. They couldn't recover. They were not part of the negotiation, it wasn't their fault at all, but the failure of the transaction had such an impact on them that they felt they could not continue in their old jobs. Clearly, as this was one of my first-ever merger and acquisition (M&A) deals, I did a bad job of explaining the process and its risks to them and helping them emotionally. I did not work enough with their line manager to make the return to their old positions in Finland with their old colleagues seem a good option for their career development (which, by the way, would have been great, as a year later I went back and bought that company, turning it into a huge success at the time).

We all take risks in business, and have experienced hiring the wrong staff, people with the wrong attitudes or inflated CVs, or staff who are using you as a stepping-stone. Likewise, staff take a risk believing in you, that you represent the best investment of their time, energy and careers. There is no guarantee, and yet if we don't take those risks, someone else will, and success may appear elsewhere.

There are lots of great techniques you can use in motivating and developing people, and someone who is an acknowledged leader in the field is Christine Comaford, whom I was privileged to interview recently.

CONVERSATION WITH
Christine Comaford, acclaimed writer, public speaker on leadership to Fortune 500 companies and founder of SmartTribe Institute. Her latest book is Power Your Tribe.

Sacha: To shift focus from local customers to international ones, a significant change needs to happen in companies, from the products they stock to how they are designed and how their staff serve customers. How can senior managers and leaders swiftly get everyone to engage with and execute such a plan?

Christine: By first analysing the emotional experiences their customers want from travel. What is the traveller seeking from his or her experience... safety (older people)? A desire to fit in and belong (millennials)? A desire for five-star service (Baby Boomers)? Have the teams sit down and make profiles of what emotional experiences the customer might want and then produce some possible outcomes of what may occur if you provide these experiences. This can be a fun process when engaged in by everyone. Different people will have different insights and this will result in a richer fount of ideas for the business to grow into. By doing so and seeing the outcome of offering such a diverse and thought-out emotional experience to customers, your staff will feel invested, innovative and proud.

Your team should also set goals for delivering that emotional experience and provide benchmarks to show how we will know when we have reached them: will it be reaching x number of customers or a 300 per cent increase in sales in the region? What will be the proof? Get the whole team working on this, and have them take some time to figure out what resources are needed to service this customer base and what side-effects/trade-offs might occur. Then set dates to meet these benchmarks and next steps. When the whole team comes together, with everyone aligned around this outcome, you move from a management of herding cats and fear-based thinking to a leader enrolling everyone into having a stake in the adventure.

Sacha: What does a great retail tribal culture look like, and how can managers create it?

Christine: A great culture is where there is a lot of safety, belonging and mattering (SBM). Where there is open, clear and complete communication, transparency. Where leaders model the company values and are also accountable. Where the company mission and purpose is clear so that the staff can be aligned with these values and not work there if these are not their values. Values cannot be changed easily; they are part of the structure of who we are. You need to protect your tribe, to advertise clearly what your values are, and only allow people to join your company if they truly embody those values. A great company helps people see themselves in a bigger way, as more capable and more valuable. It helps them to see where they are growing and learning. When we bake all this into our tribal identity, people love what they do and are satisfied. The company should not babysit people, but invite them into their culture. If it is the right one for the employee, it clicks with who they are and what they are aspiring for in their future.

Sacha: You talk about the recipe for employee motivation and engagement as a blend of one hormone and two neurotransmitters: oxytocin (feeling of belonging, being cared for), serotonin (feeling good) and dopamine (feeling of anticipating reward). What are the tools for that?

Christine: One of the tools is using the outcome frame to delineate what we would like the outcome to be, what this will do for us, what value we are making and what our next steps are to achieve this. This helps create an experience of SBM. This means not judging but taking the time to understand what someone is asking for. If the person does not feel safe, they will spread fear. If they don't feel they belong, they will step away from the tribe or withhold information. If they are not feeling they matter, they will condescend, be arrogant and stand apart. It is essential for leaders to understand what experience each of their team members needs and provide them with that. The most powerful thing to say is 'Together we will solve this!' or 'Together we make this better'. More details on this technique can be found in my book, *Power Your Tribe*. Ninety per cent of our decisions and behaviours are driven and dominated by our emotional brain. So it is crucial to be on top of the emotional needs of our staff.

Sacha: In retail, there is often a mixture of management and staff capabilities concerning effectively delegating a particular issue. What advice do you have?

Christine: When delegating, managers need to ask themselves if the person they are delegating to has the three Cs: capacity (time), capability and communication (understanding). You cannot just be a 'drive-by delegator', issuing orders and expecting your standards to be achieved. However, saying 'repeat back to me what I just said' sounds rather hostile. Instead, put the onus on yourself, by saying 'I am really trying to be a better communicator. Please can you help me by repeating back to me what you think I said so that I can see if I am doing a good enough job?' Of course, a key part of the process of delegating is providing feedback, and rather than use the basic techniques that employees hate to hear, instead try helping their brain to stay focused by using the two-step feedback process: say 'What you are doing great is xxxxx, and what I need to see more of is xxxxx, just like you did xx months ago.' (NB: please don't say: 'what needs improving is...', as that will cause someone to enter their so-called 'critter' state where blood stops flowing to their prefrontal cortex.) Then pause, so their brain can work on it. (If they have never achieved the positive outcome or behaviour you are seeking, then instead of using an example of where they have done it before, have a brainstorm with them of what success might look like.)

THE LEADERSHIP OF CHANGE

- You will face inadequate resources, a lack of clarity of vision, location issues, and new decisions about whether you have the right products. Do as much research as possible by asking suppliers, staff and bankers about this new marketplace you are going into... and then dive in!

- Work out the cost/benefit of a new investment proposal before you start.

- Negotiate with suppliers to test their products rather than buy and return what doesn't sell.

- Work out a flexible rental contract to protect you in lean times.

- Be flexible about what you may need to attract customers – new posters, new hours, new advertising. Be open to the new.

- Help your staff change for a new target market and bring in advocates for change and role models of how staff should work in this new marketplace.

- Plan for peak trading periods with the right staff (those who can handle busyness) and the suitable hours (stay open later during the tourist season).

- Hire a diverse staff who understand different nationalities and will be able to communicate with your new customers. A diverse staff will understand nuances that you yourself may not.

- Be transparent when hiring staff. Open yourself up to your employees, and they will open up to you.

- Know that some products, some places and some staff will fail. It's natural. Help your team move on to what works.

References

Besner, G (2020) *The Culture Quotient: Ten Dimensions of a High-Performance Culture*, Ideapress Publishing, Oakton, VA

Besner, G (2021) The culture quotient, https://www.theculturequotient.com/-collaboration/blog-post-title-four-dpp4h (archived at https://perma.cc/D6CN-RGZG)

Martin, B (2019) China's singles day nets record £30bn, *The Times*, www.thetimes.co.uk/article/59a5133e-04c4-11ea-872c-a98e8bfab8fc (archived at https://perma.cc/6W59-87JR)

OECD (2018) *Good Jobs for All in a Changing World of Work: The OECD jobs strategy*, OECD, Paris

Rexi Blog (2013) What do we remember from PowerPoint presentations? *Rexi Media*, https://reximedia.com/remember-powerpoint-presentations/#.XcpvUzP7SUl (archived at https://perma.cc/24YL-QH3A)

12

Preparing for emergencies

I started to write this chapter just before Covid-19, and never in my wildest dreams did I think we were going into a global pandemic that would disrupt so many businesses worldwide so heavily. Fortunately, I used the time well to reach out to key people not just for our own group but also to gain their perspectives so that I might share some of them with you. The question I would like to pose to you is this, how can you not just survive a crisis but thrive as a result? So I reached out to the highest-ranking government minister who was representing our travel and tourism sector from the time of Brexit right to the start of the pandemic.

CONVERSATION WITH
Baroness Nicky Morgan served as Secretary of State for Digital, Culture, Media and Sport (which also covers the tourism sector) in Boris Johnson's government until 2020.

> **Sacha:** As Secretary of State, you oversaw the UK's vast tourism industry. How much do you feel the government could really influence the sector's growth?

> **Baroness Morgan**: Government cannot drive tourism growth on its own. Government has convening power to bring people and organizations together. For example, we can create a supportive visa regime for tourists to come into the country easily. We can ensure we portray an open, welcome message to the world. We can build the transport and other infrastructure for tourism to flourish. I took great delight in promoting and protecting our national heritage buildings, art collections and history. As a specific example, we would write letters of support to facilitate bids to host major sporting, art, music and professional conference events.

Sacha: During times of crisis, how can businesses engage with politicians and help them understand the issues they are facing?

Baroness Morgan: Talk to your local politicians and members of parliament. Be in close contact with representatives for your local retail and tourism industry, because they can represent your views to local and national government. Government listens to organizations like Visit England, Visit Britain and other representative bodies. For example, Brexit was a big concern for tourism regarding free movement of tourists and free movement of workers who might need work visas. It was important that we in government heard those views to see how we can help the sector as the rules change. Invite MPs to things you are doing as they will learn more and then tell ministers. There is nothing more powerful than a group of MPs coming together and presenting an issue. For example, during the early period of Covid-19 in January 2020 when the disease had not yet appeared to have reached Europe, a number of MPs came to me to say that Chinese visitors were dropping off and that businesses in their constituencies would be in trouble soon if we did not help.

Sacha: When you originally worked at the Treasury Department, you must have seen many requests for help from companies and business groups. Outside of national crises, what tended to be the types of circumstances where the government might intervene with financial support for companies?

Baroness Morgan: If there was a problem, it was typically a critical national business, like an airline, such as FlyBe, whom we were unfortunately unable to save in 2020. It tends to be market failures where no one else would step in and help ensure key services are provided. But looking beyond bailouts, government will offer support for companies to expand, to try out new things, hire more people. In tourism we try to support how businesses use the data they generate and improve how they market their services abroad, e.g. The GREAT campaign. My opposite numbers in Europe, the United States and Asia will have similar programmes in place. Also retailers are getting better at gathering more data on the customers served in-store and online. This data on where potential customers come from is helpful, because if we know there is lots of interest from Chinese about coming to, for example Bicester Village, everyone can work together to help them attract those customers. Globally, tourism is such an important employer and driver of investment in manufacturing supply chains that it will need lots of support in the coming years from governments around the world.

Sacha: In France and other European countries it might be difficult and costly to make staff redundancies normally. However, they also have laws to furlough staff at home for a few months, with the government paying most of the salary. The UK government adopted this for the Covid-19 crisis, but do you think countries like the United States, the UK and elsewhere should adopt it into normal law for the next crisis?

Baroness Morgan: Unlike the usual shape of a recession, Covid-19 has been a steep economic hit, and so as Boris Johnson spoke about, governments need to support business to ensure skills were not lost through redundancies. In the UK, as in many other countries globally, business has received our support, so they could keep skilled workers and ramp up services quickly. Tourism has always had a flexible labour force, due to the seasonal nature of the business, and Conservative governments would always prefer for market forces to rectify things, rather than use government funds and legislation to cover the normal challenges of the economy ebbing and flowing, but the Covid-19 crisis required a very different response.

Sacha: What should companies and governments learn from the Covid-19 crisis?

Baroness Morgan: Prepare as much as possible for the unexpected. Having reserves that you can fall back on is so important. Government support can help companies keep skills in businesses and help businesses to bounce back again quickly, but it is difficult to know where the next crisis will come from. It could be a natural disaster linked to climate change, huge migration waves, terrorism, cyber attacks, national strikes, all manner of things are possible. There is the saying 'Fix the roof whilst the sun is out.' Having a crisis plan of what to do if something happens is absolutely essential. During the foot and mouth disease breakout in 2001, which actually only affected farm animals, we had to shut down movement of people across most of the countryside and sadly cull millions of cows and sheep. It was a terrible time for livestock, for farmers, and the movement restrictions devastated countryside tourism and even delayed the general election. So prepare for a range of potential events.

Show customers you know how to cope with emergencies

So let's step back for a moment and consider what areas might be on the minds of tourists themselves as they travel. Traditionally security has been looming large in tourists' minds going back to antiquity. Religious pilgrims indeed used to complain of thieves and bandits. Today's tourists worry about pickpockets, cloning cards on payment terminals, fraud in wiring money for larger purchases, and fraud from being overcharged by unscrupulous businesses. And people worry about terrorism. It is your job to make your customer feel that you and your team are trustworthy and will ensure they are not in danger.

There may be a pandemic or, more likely, an armed attacker of some kind. During Covid-19, we learnt the need to protect customers with screens, facemasks, hand sanitizer and regular cleaning. In physical attacks, the situation is different. Tourists are frightened of terrorist attacks, which can come in diverse ways. The Parisian Bataclan attack of 2017 involved armed attackers, the London Bridge attack of 2017 involved knives, and cars/vans have been used for attacks in Barcelona, Nice and Stockholm. Tourists and employees need to feel that the environment is as safe as possible, with CCTV, security guards/police patrols and anti-van bollards lined up along the streets and pavements to prevent attacks.

Your staff may need training in how to react in case of a terrorist incident or a robbery. We have even had a car drive into one of our stores in Sweden as part of an armed raid, like some jewellery shops have experienced. We have had to position anti-vehicle bollard systems at many of our store entrances and provide other systems and specialist training to staff to ensure they and our customers feel safe. Naturally, providing access to mental well-being experts and psychologists after such events is vital to ensure they can return to work fully and feel happy in their roles.

Protests and civil unrest

In the case of the yellow vest protests in Paris, I was in an Uber trying to get to the Right Bank, and our brilliant driver from Ghana said, 'Don't worry. I will make sure I get you to your hotel.' He put on a yellow emergency vest, spoke carefully with the protesters, and we were waved through what seemed to be a war zone with broken fences, barricades and people and cars all over the place. When we got to the Ritz hotel, the hotel team were fabulous. Led by their General Manager, Marc Raffray, about 50 of their normal staff and management were at the front door to help their guests and protect their facilities, including the many boutique shops they have. Both these examples show marvellous customer service to the traveller.

Sadly, the yellow vest protesters did smash the glass in the front of our stores in Paris and destroy the screen of our ATMs, and so we decided to shut down on the weekends for several months.

There may also be other global and local events that disrupt business, such as political actions and protests. For example, when there were big climate change protests by Extinction Rebellion at key London locations, we had very few visitors in some of our shops for weeks but reopened when the marches were over and the tent camps removed. Fortunately, we had other locations in the capital to help tourists.

When deciding how to respond to such events, it is important to be led by the atmosphere at the time. During the May Day protest a few years ago, one of our tourist retail shops in Whitehall, London, was looted. We lost tens of thousands of pounds in fashion accessories, which our insurance company covered. However, the McDonald's next door was even less lucky and was completely trashed by the protesters, with extensive damage done to their fit-out. Cleaning up after such events can be traumatic for staff and working with them side by side is important.

There will be natural disasters

Larger than usual Californian wildfires in 2018 and 2019 hit the local tourism industry hard. The number of cyclones and hurricanes hitting cities and tourist resorts seems to be on the increase. No one can predict these events with accuracy, but your investors, staff and customers have to know that your team knows what to do in case of an event, such as an earthquake or other vulnerability in areas where these are an issue. Disaster preparedness starts with the appropriate design of retail branches but extends to safety training and backup systems.

We lost six branches during the 2011 Christchurch earthquake in New Zealand. We knew it would be a long time before tourists would come back into the stricken city, so we sadly had to abandon our operations there. Unfortunately, we had natural disaster insurance but not business interruption insurance. It was sad to have to let go of so many people in the midst of a crisis. We tried to relocate some staff, but we could not do so for all. So we worked with the local government to help people who chose not to move to Auckland, where we had other branches. Our teams acted impeccably, and with the help of structural engineers we safely recovered much of our stock from collapsed buildings.

During the Icelandic ash cloud problem of 2010, when many flights were cancelled across Europe for weeks on end, retailers helped tourists with essential clothing and toiletries. A number of companies helped people find a way to get to their destination when their flights were cancelled. Helping tourists when things go awry has become crucially important. Now, one sees specialist businesses at many airports that help with rebooking accommodation, vouchers for food and beverages, places to get clothing, supplies and so on.

Similar things happened in Hurricane Katrina in 2005 when much of the US insurance industry let down home and business owners in New Orleans by exploiting obscure technicalities. People and businesses who had insurance received little or no payouts. It seems to me that where large catastrophic events occur the industry always has language in contracts that lets the insurance companies get out of payment, unless you use a good lawyer when negotiating your contracts (and hope in subsequent annual renewals your terms are not watered down). Business interruption insurance is almost always only going to help you with individual catastrophes limited to your business and not if it impacts such a huge amount of businesses that the insurance industry itself cannot deal with it. Fortunately, when Hurricane Sandy hit New York in 2012, the insurance industry and legislation were much better prepared, and payments were much more forthcoming.

In the Asian tsunami of 2004, when so many lost their lives, with the help of our charitable foundation we raised $250,000 and I flew out to help those affected in Sri Lanka. Overall, our charitable work is a key part of our corporate social responsibility and our desire to be a force for good in the world. In the Asian tsunami, as in so many other natural disasters worldwide that affect so many local people, tourists, and businesses, emergency money transfers through companies like Western Union are a lifeline.

As Massimiliano Alvisini, Western Union's Senior Vice President and General Manager, Europe and CIS has talked about to me frequently, remittances are a true lifeline for millions around the world: sending money back home to families and loved ones funds education or healthcare needs, provides a safety net during emergencies and enables businesses to continue to trade when banking systems are not functioning. As Western Union has a strong focus on financial inclusion, they have set up the Western Union Foundation, which provides millions of dollars each year to create economic opportunity for youth and people who migrate, by empowering them with the education and resources needed to succeed in today's global economy, as well as relief during disasters (Western Union Foundation, 2021).

Part of disaster preparedness is business continuity. What happens if some of your key staff cannot get to work (as happened to us during the 2019 Barcelona separatist protests with cars being set alight)? What happens if card payment terminals are compromised, as happened to the entire Visa card network across Europe in June 2018 (Griffin, 2018)? It is widely feared that both private and terrorism-linked hackers are developing online weapons to disable critical infrastructure, including payment systems. The Swedish government has now issued official warnings for all citizens to hold stocks of cash to ensure that daily life can continue and commerce is not interrupted when, as opposed to if, electronic payment systems fail (Palmer, 2019).

How can your organization prepare and help with whatever might be the next disaster you or your customers are faced with?

Data breaches

We talked earlier about the power of data and of the giant leaps forward in its collection and analysis. But beware, hackers, fraudsters and even competitors may want to access your data. European data regulations are increasingly tough, and GDPR laws require customers to consent explicitly to how you hold and use their data. In 2019 British Airways suffered a serious data breach and was fined £183 million as a result (Cellan-Jones, 2019). These laws also extend to data about your employees, so correct handling of personal data of any kind is ever more important. But for all the talk of external attacks, it is internal data breaches we should be vigilant about. A Ponemon report on data found that 75 per cent of employees say they have access to data they shouldn't have, and 25 per cent of employees are willing to sell data to a competitor for less than $8,000 (Shah, 2019). Verizon, a US telecoms group with a large retail presence, found that 28 per cent of all breaches were inside jobs, and three-quarters of these were driven by profit, while 'pure fun' was another top motivation (Shah, 2019). No system is ever going to be foolproof, but investment in IT security is critical, especially if you are dealing with important customer data.

Travelex fell victim to a terrible ransomware attack in 2020 that resulted in the closure of all their branches and ATMs at airports, shopping malls and online for many weeks, leaving customers stranded without any services (Guardian, 2022).

Other challenges – counterfeit goods

With the rise of international tourism there has been a rise in luxury shopping and, with that, a rise in counterfeit goods.

Intellectual Property Office published a report in 2016, which stated that imports of counterfeit and pirated goods are worth nearly half a trillion dollars, or around 2.5 per cent of global imports, with US, Italian and French brands the hardest hit and many of the proceeds going to organized crime (OECD and European Union Intellectual Property Office, 2016). This has impacted the potential profits of local and international brands and the consumers who are defrauded. Across many cities in the world, you might see salespeople on the pavement offering counterfeit sunglasses, handbags, perfumes and other branded products that consumers knowingly purchase as counterfeit items. In Hong Kong and Macau, it is easy to find counterfeit luxury watches where the differences from the real items are increasingly difficult to spot. Companies deal with this issue in varied ways. For example, years ago, while I was visiting Cambodia, I was told that Rayban deliberately sell their products there much more cheaply than in western countries. Thus you were hard-pressed to find any counterfeit Raybans at all! Companies must work with local luxury goods suppliers and local law enforcement. We also need to help customers who have purchased counterfeit goods to file relevant complaints with the authorities and consumer protection agencies. Some countries take a stern view of this illegal trade, while others turn a blind eye and don't bother to put in the resources to stamp out this activity.

Because of the number of counterfeit goods and the switch and bait tactic in some Asian stores, especially with electronic goods, it is not uncommon for retailers to have to allow customers to open boxes to ensure that the item, for example, perfume or make-up they are buying, is not fake, but the real thing. It also avoids any complaints later on.

If you want to keep people coming back, keep being honest with your customers. If you are putting up signs saying 'fine Italian leather shoes', make sure the shoes you sell are Italian and not the stock made in Asia and just packaged in Italy.

Amazon and eBay do what they can to take down fake offers and counterfeit goods, but many remain. We must help our customers avoid this at all costs. Check your suppliers and make sure to take no risks with the reputation of your business.

Don't forget fraud

If a customer finds out they are a victim of fraud, help them get to the right authorities that can help them tackle the situation.

Unfortunately, most popular tourist areas around the world suffer from thieves and fraudsters trying to exploit more vulnerable tourists. There are even con-artist tricks with VAT tax refunds, and the perpetrators prey on travellers. Shops need to be aware of these scams. Where there is money, there will always be someone with an ingenious idea of how to steal it. Cyber attacks, phishing scams, mandate fraud and card cloning are just some of the things we must take rigorous steps against.

Staff need to be properly trained on how to be respectful with customers' payment cards, always keeping them in sight of the customer. They need to ensure that payment terminals and data cables are regularly inspected for cloning devices, and CCTV footage needs to be regularly reviewed (where you are legally allowed to) to see if things are occurring that look suspicious. Mystery shopping exercises can be especially powerful tools, not only to verify the customer experience but also to detect fraud attempts by staff and let them know that safeguards are in place.

Just in the UK, between April 2021 and March 2022, there were 2.3 million bank and card frauds, with 1.4 million occurring in a consumer and retail setting (Daily Mail, 2022).

Show investors you can deal with a crisis

Investors know businesses will be hit with challenges. How you deal with them is what matters. If you can shine now, they might even have greater confidence in you for the future.

Depending on the severity of the incident, you may have a drop in income of anywhere from 10 to 100 per cent. Quick actions are key because you could see your whole business collapse without them, as costs quickly overwhelm your cash reserves. Within days of a major event such as the 2009 financial crash and Covid-19, we put together an emergency committee consisting of finance, operations, HR and property. We would write to all our landlords asking for them to bear part of the problem and give us rent discounts or ideally to stop the rent entirely. We know, of course, that they normally have no legal requirement to do so, but many landlords choose to take a long-term view of having good tenants and understand when things are outside your control. With major disasters impacting us in multiple territories, I have actually run negotiation training sessions for our senior managers around the world. After all, you cannot leave all the negotiations to a few individuals – often, you need a whole team, and they need new skills to deal with the situation. Indeed during both 9/11 and the Covid-19 pandemic, some of the biggest and toughest New York landlords were the most kind and accommodating to us! Investors, bankers and regulators expect to be constantly updated and consulted on what you are doing. I sent out both written memos as well as held regular video calls during the pandemic.

My motto is to communicate, communicate, and when you are finished, communicate some more. That applies to a full 360-degree view where your suppliers, customers and even your family need to know what's happening. One thing they will be looking at in all this is how are you doing? How are you coping? The reasons they take an interest are severalfold, but aside from them wanting to display a caring attitude, they also want to see if you can cope, if you can lead your business unit through the emergency or not.

Dealing with insurance is obviously important. Most of the time, my experience has been that you must inspect the claims very carefully and use specialist lawyers to fight on your behalf if needed. During Covid-19, one area you could also save on is to claim back part of your insurance premium if staff were furloughed and there were no customers, because insurance premiums are often linked to the number of staff employed and revenue levels of business.

One of the key challenging parts of keeping the business afloat is the staff. Most of the time, there will be no assistance from the government – Covid-19 was an exception when governments did assist with some labour costs. So my advice is cut once, cut deep. During Covid-19 we had to make a series of redundancies over many months as the pandemic worsened and went on longer than anyone imagined. Travel recovery was slower than anyone foresaw at the start. That was not good for morale.

I chatted recently with Dinesh Dhamija, the founder of the giant online travel agency ebookers.com; he was also a member of the European parliament. He recounted to me what happened during 9/11: 'Customers started to ask for refunds on their travel bookings en masse. They were running out of cash and had to lay off 20 per cent of the staff. Despite Dinesh never having fired anyone before and feeling terrible about it, the stock market reacted to his news by his share price rising because investors felt he was looking after their investment well. Fortunately, travel recovered quickly in most of the world, whereas Covid-19 has had a longer, deeper impact.'

The immediate period after a horrific attack will be difficult from a retailing perspective. After 9/11, I decided not to sign a corporate lease in San Francisco, thinking that inbound and outbound travel would be affected. But interestingly, we signed to extend a lease in New York, sensing that things would get back to normal eventually. I take this opportunity to thank and commend our various landlords in New York who, after the attacks, stood shoulder-to-shoulder with affected businesses. They offered us significant rental discounts and helped our business to keep going at times when people stopped travelling. Business is often about forging long-term relationships because it is in everyone's interest to help one another. Naturally, we have stayed very loyal to these landlords, which has helped us as we come out of the pandemic into a world where travel is much in demand again.

Clearly getting your messaging internally and externally right in a crisis is vital. Lots of academic research has been done on what works best for businesses. So I reached out to a world expert in the field at INSEAD, which is one of the top universities for MBA and executive education based in France with additional facilities in Singapore, San Francisco and Abu Dhabi.

CONVERSATION WITH
Professor Ian Woodward is Professor of Management Practice in Organizational Behaviour at INSEAD at their Singapore campus.

Sacha: Crisis messaging is clearly a fundamental way for leaders to calm their teams and provide direction. It also is important for people outside the organization to see you are in control. How can this best be achieved?

Ian: Well, I recommend the following 'Golden Rules':

- Crisis message should: acknowledge the problem or issue or update, express empathy, explain the actions to be taken or the process to find the actions.

- Overcommunicate credibly: throughout the crisis, it is much better for your people to receive communication updates in frequent, short bursts. Relying on long, infrequent communication exchanges causes three problems: information overload; increased feelings of isolation or uncertainty; and rumours that fill the vacuum.

- You can meet the different intellectual, emotional and psychological stakeholder communication needs by remaining clear, credible and consistent:

  o Clear (short and to-the-point messages).

  o Credible (stay with the facts): Provide transparency with reassurance. During Covid-19, Governor Andrew Cuomo reiterated that the lessons being learnt in New York would be shared with other states. He always showed key data and demonstrated he trusts the scientific advice. While he offered personal opinions, he repeated, 'Follow the data and the science.' Unfortunately Cuomo was only credible for a short time, ultimately losing his position through a lack of leadership credibility.

  o Consistent (communicate frequently): Provide sharp updates on progress. Explain what is changing, why new moves are needed, and give evidence. In both leaders' communication, we see regular attention to providing the number of cases, tests, recoveries and deaths. Policies change as the crisis has deepened, but each includes explanations as to why a change is needed – backed by science, and is expressed empathetically.

- Make it meaningful: Make messages relevant to your stakeholders' situation. Keep core messages short, accessible and interactive. Be prepared to answer, or anticipate, questions. Your objective is to help people understand what is happening and why, but leadership is also about being a beacon of hope and inspiration when there is fear and uncertainty. Showcase yourself as a leader of competence, composure and clarity to exemplify how and why we will get through this together. Avoid unsubstantiated wishful thinking.

Sacha: Thank you Ian, that sounds like great advice!

Looking after yourself

Often in a crisis, the situation can feel overwhelming as you have to deal with pressures from investors, staff, customers and also your own family, who will have their own personal concerns. You need to be the leader who shows them the way and gives them courage through the difficult times. During the pandemic, what started as a sprint turned into a marathon and getting sleep and rest were as important as handling calls. Looking after yourself physically, mentally and spiritually is key to staying strong. Like many athletes and leaders, I have found using visualizations can be very powerful. Dr Catherine Shainberg has written some outstanding books and runs the School of Images in New York. She has helped coach me through several such emergencies. Her school has some wonderful techniques that look at the conscious and subconscious, which can assist business people and the public alike in making clearer decisions by responding to situations and not just reacting.

Fundraising for growth

How can you think about growth during a disaster? It is exactly in the middle of market turmoil that the greatest opportunities exist. Key assets such as stocks, equipment and prime real estate will likely be priced at significant discounts. Opportunities to enter into important contracts will exist that were not available before. Your competitors may be so weakened that you may be one of the only viable bidders.

Think creatively about funding; banks may be risk averse, and suppliers do not want to extend much credit. In the next interview, you can read about the frustrations of PDS, one of the world's largest garment manufacturers – the CEO Pallak Seth felt he had become a banker to major retailers worldwide!

One route is to use private equity or debt funds that provide mezzanine funding or even normal debt at higher interest. Another is entering into joint ventures. Indeed this is what we did with Prosegur Cash – initially we entered into a joint venture to win and operate all the 15 branches at Gatwick Airport and 80+ ATMs.

Given the large number of stock market investors, suppliers and companies interested in the travel and tourism retail space, I asked Richard Chamberlain, managing director at Royal Bank of Canada Capital Markets, for his views on how his team sources and writes good research on it. This is what he said: 'At RBC Capital Markets, we follow several travel retail companies closely and publish regularly on the sector. For instance, we monitor passenger flow data, forward bookings and various economic and mobility indicators to assess demand for travel. These include proprietary "GOAT" (get out and travel) and "GOAL" (get out and live) composite indices developed by our digital intelligence strategy team. We also model cost lines such as staffing and rentals, plus cashflows and balance sheets to estimate the earnings growth and financial health of travel retailers. Above all, we maintain a regular dialogue with corporate and industry contacts in the sector.'

Obviously not many companies can raise funds on the stock market, but the fact that the sector is so large, and research reports are widely available, will assist you when your organization goes out to raise funds.

Preparing for the next crisis

- Diversify: Part of our strategy as a company has always been to maintain geographic diversification and to have locations spread across a city, region or the planet. This has helped us maintain overall income levels when hit by a number of natural disasters or terrorism events over the course of many years.

- Join a trade association: I have often found industry associations to be talking shops where little gets done. But in a crisis, governments quickly enact legislation that cannot be properly thought through and yet can have devastating impacts on your business. This can range from changing product standards to border controls to taxation. It is at those times that effective lobbying is vital to ensure that you and your competitors get the support and attention of legislators that you need to be able to survive. Trade associations play an important role in this, being the voice of the retail and hospitality industries. Indeed in some countries such as Denmark, legislators are required to seek trade association input to new laws before they are enacted.

- Get good insurance: In the United States during Covid-19, the lawyers and state legislatures took a very different view on insurance and tried to force the market to pay business interruption losses by saying through the courts that it is retrospectively covered and also that their definition of damage is different. This was different to the UK and European Union. So ask your broker if there is a cover for the risks you can't foresee, not just the standard ones.

- Train your managers in negotiation: Not just for customers who are affected, but in dealing with irritable key suppliers and officials who are finding the situation challenging, a great phrase here to calm people down is 'If I were you I would undoubtedly feel just as you do.' After all, you can say this 100 per cent sincerely and honestly because, if you were that person with their body and their thoughts, then, of course, you would have the reaction they are having. Having built a connection and made them feel better understood, you can both calmly look at the situation and find mutual solutions.

As mentioned in the earlier interview with Seth Palak, whose global apparel manufacturing business felt retailers were unfairly treating them during the pandemic, they had to negotiate constantly with their customers. The reality is that unless you have a huge financial pot to rely on, you will need to cut costs and obtain better credit terms to survive. The government, your employees and your suppliers need you and your peers to survive too; it is 'just' a matter of finding a way forward that works for everyone.

I thought it a good moment to speak with an adviser to leading politicians and business people around the world on the subject.

CONVERSATION WITH
Professor Steve Jarding, Harvard University. His 'Running for Office' class at Harvard has twice been nominated as the most influential course in the United States. He is the CEO and Managing Director of Jarding Global LLC, which has worked in a dozen countries on five continents. He also teaches annually at the IESE Business School in Madrid, the Aspire Programme in Romania, and at the RAPS programme in Sao Paulo, Brazil.

Sacha: Travel and tourism retail clearly depends on the free movement of people. In particular Chinese customers and Russian customers have been very beneficial for retailers in the past decade. How do you see geopolitics in the next decade affecting the travel and tourism sector?

Steve: To begin, there is a lot of uncertainty in the geopolitical world. From Russia's invasion of Ukraine, to the instability of democratic governments and the rise of populism worldwide, to the ongoing problems from the Covid-19 pandemic, to the growing refugee issue, the continued rise of income inequality, and many other destabilizing factors, the world is becoming a more unstable and unpredictable place. In unstable and difficult economic times, some people might tend to travel less.

On the other hand, places like China and India have seen their middle class explode in the past 30 years, providing much more financial wherewithal for their citizens to travel more readily than the Chinese or Indian people did in past generations. Couple this with an increasingly intertwined international economic system that makes international travel routine alongside ongoing technological innovation, and the travel and tourism sector does have a potentially good outlook.

Sacha: Most leaders, including myself, were unprepared for the pandemic. Why is it so hard for us to imagine such big events?

Steve: The easy answer is that political leaders today tend to want to invest only in the immediate term so they can reap the political benefits while they are in office. Such benefits do not come with long-term investments.

Look at global warming, the world saw it coming for decades but virtually no government even attempted to prepare for its destructive impact on our planet and on humanity.

Today, there is a growing consensus among scientists that it may be too late to deal with the devastation global warming is bringing us. Experts tell us that in the coming decades or less, global warming will cause oceans to rise significantly, and with 80 per cent of the human population living within 80 miles of major waterways, this is a huge problem because no government will be able to afford the cost of relocating hundreds of millions of people and rebuilding entire new infrastructures.

Couple this with the economic and human costs that come with the projected 1.2 billion refugees that experts are predicting before mid-century as places like Indonesia and Bangladesh – with their combined nearly 400 million people – are underwater.

We are already seeing unprecedented wildfires worldwide, as well as massive droughts and the drying of major waterways worldwide. To make matters worse, the ultra-rich are buying politicians, ensuring that they and their companies are not required to pay their necessary share in tax revenue to pay the price of good governance and a stable world.

As a human society, it is vital we demand more of our political and business leaders.

PREPARING FOR EMERGENCIES

- Have good links to trade associations. They are the ones who can push your point of view to politicians effectively during emergencies.
- Make sure you inspect your payment terminals and data cables for cloning devices.
- Check your CCTV footage for customer and sales staff fraud.
- Beware of data privacy laws and secure your data as much as possible to prevent huge fines.
- Be aware of counterfeit goods. Work with local law enforcement.
- Let customers inspect your goods for authenticity, should they ask.

- Have a plan to deal with natural disasters, both for your business and for your customers.

- Ideally, have several retail branches and outlets in different regions so that if disaster strikes, you can still operate and make money.

- Factor in that city protests and marches may affect your business. Plan accordingly.

- Ensure you can accept cash from customers and pay suppliers in cash if and when banking or payment systems go down next.

- Make helping in disasters part of your corporate culture.

- Practise and plan using the 'Golden Rules' of communication to ensure you can lead your team and the key people you need to influence.

- Demand better actions and preparations from your politicians and leaders. As citizens and businesses we need help to thrive for the long term, not just the next election cycle.

References

Cellan-Jones, R (2019) British Airways faces record £183m fine for data breach, *BBC News*, www.bbc.co.uk/news/business-48905907 (archived at https://perma.cc/3LZH-ACXF)

Daily Mail (2022) Britain is the card fraud capital of Europe as we suffer more cons with the highest losses, new figures show, by Charlotte McLaughlin, 3 August, https://www.dailymail.co.uk/news/article-11077401/Britain-card-fraud-capital-Europe-suffer-cons-highest-losses.html (archived at https://perma.cc/X3FG-BAPX)

Griffin, A (2018) Visa issues: card problems across UK and Europe as payment systems go down, *The Independent*, www.independent.co.uk/life-style/gadgets-and-tech/news/visa-card-payment-down-mastercard-not-working-broken-payment-shop-a8379381.html (archived at https://perma.cc/KZS8-FQBY)

Guardian (2022) How the growing Russian ransomware threat is costing companies dear, by Rob Davies and Dan Milmo, 5 February, https://www.theguardian.com/technology/2022/feb/05/how-the-growing-russian-ransomware-threat-is-costing-companies-dear (archived at https://perma.cc/H4GF-656J)

OECD and European Union Intellectual Property Office (2016) *Trade in Counterfeit and Pirated Goods: Mapping the economic impact, illicit trade*, OECD Publishing, Paris

Palmer, K (2019) Sweden, nation that pioneered living without cash, warns: hoard your banknotes, *The Times*, www.thetimes.co.uk/article/sweden-nation-that-pioneered-living-without-cash-warns-hoard-your-banknotes-6f72jqbf3 (archived at https://perma.cc/6NHJ-UTTG)

Shah, S (2019) The rise of employees stealing data: how do businesses stop this from happening? *Information/Age*, www.information-age.com/stealing-data-123481286/ (archived at https://perma.cc/LSM7-ATXQ)

Western Union Foundation (2021) *2021 Impact Report*, Western Union

13

International expansion

Expanding across borders and making your company multinational is a great opportunity. In my experience, growing internationally can be great for your shareholders, suppliers, staff and for your own career. There is a huge world out there, and you can capitalize on an opportunity in other markets by bringing something new there, be it products, services, experiences, or any of your other unique selling points. Growing internationally makes life fun and often very profitable. It balances out customer flows from season to season, and it protects your business against regional issues. There are organizations around the world, from embassies to trade associations, that have programmes to assist businesses internationally, and you can be a big or small company to access them. Let's get some insight now into some of the opportunities and challenges of working with them.

CONVERSATION WITH
Lesley Batchelor OBE, Director General of the Institute for Export and International Trade in the UK.

> **Sacha**: Your organization helps push companies to expand internationally and export abroad – please could you tell us more?
>
> **Lesley**: We do, indeed. We do that in many ways as a membership organization, encouraging people to join and become a member, where they network with each other. We provide vital services, specific to their membership. That includes a technical helpline and events where they can come and share business experiences and questions. The institute runs topical one-day training programmes, helping with the detail of one or two aspects of international trade, and we also run Ofqual accredited education programmes, which provide qualifications and post-nominals that support the

professionalism of the industry. This education process is divided into four pillars of learning. The first offers people the opportunity to learn how the World Trade Organization (WTO) works, and how the tariffs and taxation system works, linking intellectual property and licensing into contracts, and how international contracts differ. Then, that takes us on to the second pillar, which is all about market research and marketing in a different culture, which is a huge topic. This leads to the finance of international trade, pricing, cash flow and foreign currency. The final pillar is all about compliance and regulation, which is increasingly important; especially when you start going into more and more exotic markets, you have to learn more and more about what you can and cannot do.

Sacha: How many members do you have?

Lesley: We have just under 3,000 members.

Sacha: What kind of companies become members?

Lesley: Any sort of company. Remarkably, we are sector agnostic, so we have large companies like Rolls-Royce and BA Systems, but then we also have the membership for smaller business too. If you are a smaller business, we also offer an international set of terms and conditions that will support you in international trading across the world. We have different types of memberships that help make sure businesses are ready to go to a new market.

Sacha: How are you finding the UK support for companies wanting to expand abroad? What I mean by that is, for example, I've used the UK government's Department for International Trade (DIT) and sometimes asked for help from British ambassadors. Despite having a relatively small retail presence in a country, sometimes they have been tremendously helpful and even gone to key business meetings for us, such as in Iceland, where we had an issue with hidden barriers to winning the retail tender at the main international airport in Reykjavik. The ambassador drove our chairperson to the meeting with the directors of the airport and explained that they needed to provide a fair and level playing field for all companies, and not just Icelandic ones. We actually won the tender to operate our retail units after that! Do you liaise with the Department of Trade or the Foreign and Commonwealth Office who run the UK embassies, have contacts with trade missions, and can link you to ambassadors and commercial attachés?

Lesley: We do liaise with the teams as actually a lot of their outfacing staff are members of ours. A lot of the big banks are members too. Yes, the

Department for International Trade do a great job. They, of course, target specific areas/markets whereas we tend to be process driven. We also do a great deal of work with UK Export Finance, an organization that, I think, is getting better and better as they tune into business needs. Helping businesses to understand the financial aspects of new markets is essential, and trying to get them to work with a credit line, and using credit insurance, makes a huge difference to their risk exposure.

Sacha: Obviously, you're a UK organization supporting UK companies going abroad. How does that compare with similar organizations supporting French, American or Japanese companies?

Lesley: I think the French have a slightly different take on it all, which I quite like. They all have their own ways of doing things. I think that possibly the Germans, and the way they work with the Chambers of Commerce, are probably the most effective that I see.

Sacha: Could you give me an example of what the French and the Germans do?

Lesley: The French have a system of taxation that actually gives you relief on your export expenses (e.g. research and essential training) before you enter a new market. You don't actually start paying extra tax on funds until you have made your first sale abroad. The Germans have a system of using their Chambers of Commerce – membership is mandatory so this means they can actually collectively help exporting businesses more effectively.

Sacha: So those Chambers of Commerce then do individual export work?

Lesley: Well, they all work together. There is a sort of a national system, which ensures they know what companies are doing in a new market, which in turn helps them offer really specific help. Whereas in the UK, for example, it is a choice whether or not you become a member of the Chamber of Commerce. Because it's a choice, not everyone engages, and we don't know exactly what is happening in the world of exporting everywhere. So, if you wanted to talk to everyone in a specific sector, it would be harder to find that information in the UK than in Germany, where they can just press a button to access the data. If you wanted to open a trade mission somewhere, or you felt that you wanted to go into a particular market, they have much better data on their businesses than we do.

Sacha: Brexit is a very hot topic. Everyone has talked about increasing exports worldwide to compensate for the UK not being a member of the European Union and doing less trade with the EU. What do you see as the main challenges for the UK industry?

Lesley: The main challenge is that we have got to get into the habit of learning how to do international trade; people and businesses need the right skills. We need to focus on those areas I mentioned earlier. I would suggest we all need to understand the context of the areas in which we are trying to operate. Increasingly, we need to understand the compliance and regulation issues that businesses face. Obviously, the finance issues remain a problem and trading has always been a mixture of negotiation and common sense. We, as a nation, in the UK adopt a 'wait until the very last minute' approach, which is bad. If a company is exporting their products or services to another country or is trying to set up a retail network in another country, it may have a problem with finance. It is something we tend to leave until only a few days before we need it. The reality is that, really, we need three to four weeks to get the finance resources up and running from banking and governmental support agencies; this then helps to release the necessary cash flow. The great thing about international trade is that you can be absolutely certain that everything takes three times longer than you thought it was going to take!

Together with my parents, we have travelled the world opening new companies and creating joint ventures on three continents over more than three decades. According to Deloitte, 24 per cent of revenues in the world's top 250 retailers come from their international operations (Deloitte, 2019). This is how our company has grown over the years, with over three-quarters of our operations overseas, and it has been a true net positive for everyone involved. It would have been easy for us to just stay in the UK, but we chose a different path, and the result of all our hard work speaks for itself.

Growing internationally requires a step change in your business. Your organization may need to update its vision and strategy for the business. That will need to be communicated to key stakeholders to get their buy-in, for example, banks, shareholders, directors and your management teams. The more the various parties buy into the revised vision and strategy, the easier it will be to execute it. Here are some tips.

Research where to go

Albeit important, reading reports, regional research and industry publications will only get you so far. I find jumping on an aeroplane is the easiest and most instinctive way to do research on a possible new expansion, as nothing beats being on the ground. If someone visits your branch in London one year, then they might go to another country the next year – where might that be? Your taxes pay for your government export agencies and embassies abroad, and they will provide export advice, arrange export finance, help you with tax advice, market assessment, and so on. Some of these professionals will be amazing, some not so. Find people in government agencies who can really help you. Use your lawyers and accountants, who are often part of wider international networks, to refer you to people they know in those countries you are looking at. This is part of the suite of trusted contacts you can meet with. When interviewing these outsourced professionals, test their local contacts' strengths. Pay for good advice. Join local Chambers of Commerce and local business clubs such as the Rotary Club. Time is valuable but be prepared for you and your management team to invest time and effort in developing local networks.

Hiring great management is key

The management team you hire can make a big difference in getting things opened smoothly (though sometimes those skills are very different from the ones needed to run day-to-day operations). It is often harder to hire good top management for a position in a relatively new international group that has limited or no existing local operations. What job security will you be able to offer the talented candidates? How can you reassure them that your group will make good on the promises to invest and grow?

When selecting top managerial candidates consider how they will be able to assess the market and bridge the cultural and technical differences between the new country and your home base. Obviously, they need local experience and people networks in the market you are choosing to enter. However, make sure that they, in turn, do not hire people who are too close to them. For example, it is usually a good policy to exclude the hiring of family members. One thing to help balance them out is to hire non-executive directors locally because non-execs are not involved daily and can offer insights that your full-time employees cannot.

Make sure to have a diversity of opinions and cultures within your team, as that will ultimately strengthen your new operation. Is speaking languages important? Absolutely! Although my brilliant teachers at Highgate School taught me extremely well, it was only when I moved to Austria (and then to France for work and some pleasure!) that I truly became fluent – not just because it was the right thing to do, but because if you really want to get ahead you need to adapt to the local environment and stand up for yourself. I often joke that Eddie Murphy perfected my German since the one video cassette I had in Vienna was of him dubbed into German. My colleague Kasper Larsen and I spent every evening coming back late from work, eating dinner watching Eddie flirt and cajole in German!

Joint ventures

In some cases, using a joint venture (JV) partner introduced by a bank, embassy or market research company can be a good way to reduce risk. Especially in the Middle East or China, you need to have significant share-holdings with local partners. Many organizations start by franchising their brand, then moving to a JV and finally buying out their JV partner after several years when they have learnt about the market. You will have to create a win–win for a JV partner; don't try to take advantage of them.

Make sure your JV partner feels supported about how they will generate an income. Unless you think of the relationship on a long-term basis, it will probably fail and absorb time you won't want to give. You need to prequalify your partners; don't just accept a partner that approaches you. Check references with people they are in business with. Even if you like the proposed partner personally, check what legal entity you are signing with – is that really an entity of substance?

One thing also to be aware of is that even if the local corporate laws do not require local ownership, in many countries, airports and other key real estate is owned by local or national governments. Their procurement policies may require bidders to have substantial local ownership and active local management. For example, most US international airports have requirements that a significant percentage of the subsidiary you use at the airport is owned by a locally registered ACDBE (airport concessionaire disadvantaged business owner).

A legal agreement is not always an agreement

Many countries have differing business cultures. Whether you sign or handshake on a legal agreement or contract, sometimes it doesn't mean what you usually think it means. I once signed an agreement with a large bank to buy some of their subsidiaries, but when the bank was shown to have misrepresented what they were selling me, I was told I was unlikely to be able to get justice owing to the local court system and the lack of recognition of foreign contracts.

I spoke to Nick Davis, partner at the formidable Mishcon de Reya law firm (which also represented Princess Diana in her divorce) for advice on this. He said; 'When starting up in a new jurisdiction it is vital that you appoint the right lawyers to guide you through the rules and regulations. Initial advice needs to focus on how you set up in the new country (for example, will it be a registered branch office or limited liability company and, if so, what type of company). If you already have a trusted lawyer, ask them if they use anyone in the new jurisdiction. Personal recommendations are always the best. Using large multi-office law firms does not always translate into individual office quality. If you do not have any recommendations, then legal directories like Legal 500 and Chambers are worth using provided that they cover the country in question.'

Years ago, before the war in Ukraine, I was in Kiev. There, I was presented with a heavy mace hammer as a gift by a Ukrainian government minister and then immediately told to sign a document in Russian that I could not read; not an easy situation to get out of when surrounded by local officials and your interpreter is provided by their government. Needless to say, I did not sign, but I did agree after much discussion to sign an English translation they hastily created for me, which broadly said I was in Ukraine to create jobs and boost the tourism sector.

Building relationships in a new international location is far more vital than we often realize. Spend time with your local advisers, just having lunches or coffees can provide vital insights beyond just reading legal documents.

Funding

Keep an eye on your working capital. Even if you are not a director or owner, how can you help preserve liquidity in the business? So many great businesses fail because of a lack of proper cash-flow management. Many put all their funds into stock and then don't have enough operating capital to succeed. I once had a business in Austria that started slower than expected, but I had enough liquidity to fund the runway to our eventual success. International expansion often takes more resources (people, money, time) than was planned for. Can you find better local suppliers and banks to assist you? Banks and specialist companies can help with solutions around this, such as asset finance and invoice discounting. Some can save you money when sending money internationally at regular exchange rates. Specialists can also help hedge against exchange-rate risks. Make sure you are prepared for bumps in the road and have the financial resources and the right team of people to jump in and keep the project alive and well.

Culture

Your organization might have a great culture or be working to create an even better one. But, when you expand internationally, you must consider how and to what degree you would like that culture to be exported into your new location. There is no such thing as a completely uniform company culture. In our experience, around 80 per cent of our new countries' company culture is similar to that of the HQ country, but 20 per cent is adapted and flexed to each local country. That way, we have an organization where people can talk across boundaries and not just stay in silos. Having the same core values is key. They help set direction, can be a core part of bi-annual reviews and allow the building of trust across teams. Get staff feedback on the core values and aspirations of the organization; this helps your team and employees to internalize them and feel they are truly a part of them. Once these core values have been agreed upon, make sure you communicate them effectively. Because I don't have the opportunity to meet the hundreds of new recruits we have each year globally, we created an in-depth video that communicates our vision, mission, values and aspirations to these new team members. My belief is that we must be prepared to walk away from opportunities that don't meet our values, no matter how big the opportunity is. Don't blame your employees for walking away from an opportunity that doesn't meet your organization's standards: congratulate them! According to Jean Claude Biver, President of the LMVH Watch Division, the most important condition of long-term success is honesty: if you are honest in life, you get the results in the long term. We are not primed to wait for results in the long term; we are primed to achieve immediate results because business is often driven by the short term. However, remaining committed to honesty brings you success in the long term. And the only success that is valued is the success that comes at the end (Monteiro, 2018).

Staff hiring and development

How do you choose whom to hire? Job adverts that work in one country may fail in another. We use internet job boards and agencies and seek applicants with an inherent desire to help people. Technical skills we can teach, but the desire to help others is vital in travel and tourism retail and cannot be taught. Hire people who respect different cultures and want to give your customers the extra bit they are not expecting. That trait reveals itself in the enthusiasm of their communication style when meeting with your team. The rest will be covered in your training and development, where you might teach your staff the meaning and contexts of language and manners in each country, for instance, and other job-specific skills and knowledge. Our staff at ChangeGroup go through a four-month training programme that involves on-the-job learning and classroom and online sessions backed up by exams to ensure standards are met internationally. Over time we upskill staff and provide learning and development and mentoring to enable people to become the next leaders. Indeed, more than half our management team started as sales consultants. This provides a great pool of experienced talent to support our international expansion.

Variations in sustainability standards in different countries

Different countries have different levels of consumer, supplier, governmental and media awareness. What might be a pressing issue in your home country might not be one elsewhere. For example, in Germany, recycling has been at the forefront of consumers' minds for many decades, and almost all beverages are sold in glass or durable plastic, which has a refundable deposit from retailers.

Some countries focus on carefully using water resources and ensuring that rivers are not polluted by factory waste; most countries now care greatly about climate change and how much carbon the company is offsetting. While each country has specific concerns and laws relating to environmental protection and sustainability, your organization will need to think about adopting both your home country's standards as well as those of the new countries you enter into. Significant damage has been done to brands that only comply with more lax regulations abroad and are then caught out by activists and consumers pointing to violations of home standards abroad. International businesses are rightly held to a higher standard. Your customers and the media will be impressed if your business applies high standards across the board internationally and does not dilute them where more lax regulations would allow. So use this as a point of differentiation from your competitors.

Salaries

Some countries allow you to set salaries according to your preference, whereas countries like Germany operate collective bargaining agreements, which are separate from unions (Berlin Business Location Sector, 2019). Again, you may need a commercial lawyer or an accountant with experience in retail in any new country you expand into. See them with your questions and get them answered in detail so that you can share the information with your senior team.

You can find the right adviser through the local Chamber of Commerce or consulate or embassy in the country you are going to. Lawyers will usually give you an hour's worth of free time to see if they are right for you for a long-term relationship. Ask the right questions, and don't be afraid to ask 'silly' questions. Just ask. There will be a myriad of regulations you won't expect, such as premium hours after 6 pm, overtime limits, different rules regarding how many hours staff can work consecutively, and different maternity and paternity rules. Indeed, in many European countries, there are limits on using mobile phones or answering emails out of hours. Sweden has full sickness pay (part company, part government paid), although the first day of sickness is unpaid, which is effective at stopping the so-called Monday morning hangover 'illness'. In Denmark, you might have to pay for six months for an employee who is ill, which can be a crippling cost to a small business (AngloInfo Denmark, nd).

Motivation and bonuses

As discussed earlier in this book, it is very easy to make assumptions about your employees' preferences and what motivates them, but in most cases, assumptions are just guesswork. Each employee will be attracted to different aspects of your company. Some will like flexible work times, or being seen to do good in the world, or because they aspire to own products of the brand. Our CSR programme donates 3 per cent of our annual profits to charities that help underprivileged children in the developing world access education. In addition to our substantial donations, our employees are invited to get actively involved in collaborations and fundraising for these charities. Although this programme was not created with recruitment benefits in mind, it has turned out to provide us with additional appeal when recruiting and retaining people. Millennials, especially, value choices, flexible working hours, changing countries, and being a force for good in the world. They want fast results and jobs with meaning. Part of the challenge with international expansion will be communicating with and motivating your teams effectively from afar. Listen to them. They have the ultimate responsibility of representing you in front of your customers, and they know what concerns need to be raised. Get rid of unnecessary, tedious or boring tasks as much as possible. Define job specifications accurately with clear responsibilities, objectives and ambitions. Make your staff feel like partners.

HR records

My experience is that hiring and, in very rare cases, firing anyone is always far harder than you imagine it will be. An important consideration is documentation; document interactions with employees, what is good, and what is bad. A manager once came to me and said: 'I have to fire Sam (not their real name) because he is a disruptive influence on the team and doesn't follow our sales process.' 'Show me the documentation,' I replied. But when I looked at it, I could see only glowing performance appraisals on Sam. The managers had shied away from putting negative comments in their six-monthly appraisals because they disliked confrontation, and none of the issues were in HR files. This makes dealing with anyone difficult legally, and Sam might not even have been fully aware of the urgent need to improve!

Suppliers

It goes without saying that you may need to change some, if not all, of your suppliers when you expand internationally. When choosing international suppliers, consider if they can meet your delivery schedules, quality standards, pricing and local labelling needs. Can you easily navigate the relevant regulations and processes if you are importing items? How are the import duties, warehousing and transport costs compared to what you are used to? Are there quasi-monopolies at play, or do you have real bargaining power with suppliers? (In some countries, there might be only one or two suppliers of key items, and this means you might have to be creative in finding levers to negotiate with, such as the possibility of not opening up at all or of importing things from abroad.) Are the suppliers meeting your ethical and moral standards on labour practices, environmental sustainability and corporate governance? Are there anti-bribery processes in place within your organization to ensure things are done for the right reasons? These questions are all answerable, with the right people and good research.

Refine your product for expansion

As you take your product abroad, adapt it to the country you are expanding into. Nestlé's KitKat bar has slightly different recipes in different regions, as does McDonald's and many famous soft drink brands. Hello Fresh serves German food in Germany but changes its menu to include different cuisines in the UK and in Japan. McDonald's even does green-tea ice cream in Japan!

You need to think about your customers' needs in the countries you are taking your product to. For example, furniture resellers have to take into account that their furniture designs may have to be smaller if selling in Japan or Hong Kong since people live in tighter spaces. Levi's Jeans changes sizing according to the local population they are selling to. However, don't lose sight of the increasingly international shopper base that exists in most tourist destinations. As described in Chapter 7, I landed in Tokyo once, with my luggage mistakenly being sent to Moscow. Buying new clothes, even from foreign brands, in a country where most people are much shorter than I am, was very challenging, so think beyond the local market to foreign shoppers too!

Godiva chocolates have recently decided to enable its products to have a more universal appeal by discontinuing chocolates with alcoholic liquor in them. While Godiva could always sell their non-alcoholic chocolates in the Middle East, by making all their products non-alcoholic, it means that millions of Muslim tourists in London, Paris and around the world have the option to go into Godiva shops and concessions at airports and in city centres, buying products that they are comfortable with.

Finding retail units

Let's be honest; this is the make-or-break decision when expanding into a new territory. Take your time. If you can't find the right location, don't compromise; move on to a different area, city or country. We once had a JV partner in Austria who put us under so much pressure that we took branches in locations we should never have accepted, and it took us years to recover from the mistakes. We often find that regulations and planning permissions for property fit-outs vary hugely, especially with historic buildings, which can hugely influence their attractiveness as a potential unit. Also, get advice from property consultants and lawyers on trading permits, as specific activity licences for a building can take months. We often use big international property firms and have them walk us around a new city to show us available units and explain rental prices, and what types of customers walk and shop in different areas. After a while, we sometimes find a more local specialist real-estate broker that has even better local knowledge and can help in negotiating better deals through well-established contacts.

Negotiating rental agreements

You will have to find out what is the norm for negotiation in each country or region. Rental amounts are just the start. Leasehold premiums paid to the outgoing tenant are very common in Europe and can be hundreds of thousands of dollars or even millions. Deposits paid to landlords can tie up working cash flow, and in some countries, the norm is to pay rent quarterly in advance. You will have to find out what common area maintenance charges apply and negotiate those, as some can grow to exorbitant amounts if not negotiated. Some countries may offer the first six months without rent, which can really help, and some landlords will help with fit-out costs. Speaking of which, my advice is to negotiate that the previous tenant must remove their fit-out and leave the premises in 'broom-swept conditions and with white walls' because it can be expensive to have to do that and will take up a lot of time. Also, find out about the local real-estate taxes. In England, these taxes (called 'rates') are roughly half the rent you pay. Don't let local taxes come as a big shock; make sure your advisers keep you informed of any new changes to regulations. In New York, a few years ago, a special tax on properties below 90th Street was introduced, and our accountant based in San Francisco did not know about it – we got handed a huge fine.

Property fit-out permits

Getting new premises built takes time, and things will be done differently in an international location from what you are used to, that is almost for sure. Our Global Head of Design Hans Van Rijswijk was a genius in creating amazing looking branches at more than 200 locations around the world, before he retired. He and my mother Bette Zackariya scoured countless locations on three continents, finding the best way of building branches and dealing with tremendous amounts of bureaucracy.

For example, when opening up a retail store in Spain, here are the typical steps we follow:

- You walk the streets and identify a good retail site you either found yourself or through listings you receive from a broker.

- You call the broker, and apart from finding out the current status and pricing, you most importantly find out if this is a 'heritage building' and the special regulations regarding that.

- You brief your architects about what you ideally want to do; they will create initial plans and do a brief check of the building history and permitted usage.

- You put your financial offer in to landlords (via the real-estate broker – who may not have the landlord's mandate themselves but work with another company) with your plan proposals, subject to various conditions.

- You negotiate and sign heads of terms, then a full contract, which has to be notarized.

- Pay an agreed deposit.

- Now your local engineering and design consultants can look into the property in closer detail, as you might find out that you cannot fit it out precisely as you would like. In addition, the previous tenant may have broken the law for 20 years, or your engineer and design consultants will say that the space is not disabled-compatible – that wall has to be put back, or you are going to have to lose this prime window you thought you were going to have.

- Once you have gone through that rigmarole, you can have the architect draw up your final plans and get them approved by the landlord (which may not be the one you know since the ultimate owner is possibly different from the current leaseholder). The owner may physically have sublet the whole building for 50 years to XYZ Corp, who is subletting to you.

- Then you have to get a permit from the local council to start to construct, which your engineering and design consultants may take care of instead of your architect.
- Then you get your quotes from three builders.
- You sign contracts with them and pay deposits.
- You apply for street parking and a permit for the waste skip container.
- The builder starts work and you inspect regularly to ensure things are done as per the agreed design and help find solutions to the many construction problems that suddenly appear.
- When works are fully complete, the various inspections, from the fire brigade to police to councils, must take place.
- Now you can get a permit to trade from the local council or trade association, depending on the country. This can all take many months, and meanwhile, you are paying rent while the shop is sitting empty!

I recommend you get good legal advice about how to get all these approvals and also to help you negotiate effective signage rights. For example, the shop next to you may have a beautiful sign, but you might not be allowed to have such a sign since they don't issue them anymore. Or conversely, a McDonald's might have a 20-year-old garish sign next to you, and you might only be allowed a sign with silver and black, even though your brand does not have either of these colours.

In Barcelona, we took over a prime unit in the famous La Rambla shopping street, which had the old signage in gold from a musical emporium shop, and that signage was heritage listed. This meant that we, as new tenants, had our signage relegated to a small section underneath the historical sign – hence some people enter our shop thinking it is a musical instruments shop!

By no means is the slowness of this process confined to Spain. It took us two years in New York for the Department of Buildings to process the paperwork for a small external air conditioner to be replaced! There, you may even have to pay professional 'expediters' because the bureaucracy can be so tough that applications get processed extremely slowly without them (Kaufman, 2014).

International data protection laws

Even data protection laws are different in different regions. In the European Union, you have to ask permission to collect a customer's email address, ensuring the customer is positively marketed to. There has to be an easy opt-out mechanism, and you cannot share data with other companies without explicit permission. Certain types of personal data cannot leave the EU, so file-sharing apps like Dropbox can be an issue and must be tightly controlled (Information Commissioner's Office, 2019). Similar laws are being enacted in California, and the fines for breaking these regulations can be in the multi-millions.

Mergers and acquisitions

If all the work involved in organic international expansion sounds like a lot, there is a shortcut. In many instances, we have first bought out a competitor in a new country, complete with an experienced management team, systems and processes to then build upon. This has been very helpful, and although you may have to pay a premium price for the ready-made organization, you then have the building blocks for a great future. Corporate financiers or your accountants and lawyers can help with this. We actually hired a number of graduates from INSEAD business school in France to work on our own M&A manuals and systems so that with each new transaction, we have become better and better at it. To date, we have done 18 such deals, and while I could write a whole other book on this subject, I recommend you consider this a potential mechanism for expansion.

Fundraising

How you raise funding for that expansion is, of course, a key consideration. Raising money from suppliers, banks, private equity, larger conglomerates and private shareholders are all options. At ChangeGroup, we have done all of these. My parents and I started with a friends and family round to open in London, obtained growth funding to open in Denmark and Finland from a second round, and obtained support from key suppliers and contractors with extended payment terms. Our chairperson then persuaded the private equity firm 3i to invest, which boosted us. Later we went into a joint venture with Raiffeisen Banking Group to expand operations in Austria. After that, bank fundraising for both organic growth and M&A became easier in many of the countries we operated in. A key element in fundraising is getting to know one another and seeing if the fundamental values and aspirations are similar.

In our case, we were so impressed by the professionalism and size of Prosegur Cash, which is listed on the Madrid stock exchange with tens of thousands of employees in many countries, that when we were approached, we took their overture very seriously. They had aspirations to grow and enter the travel and tourism sector of cash services and wanted to accelerate that through M&A. With the assistance of Sunil Duggal at Canacord Corporate Finance, and Nick Davis at the law firm Mishcon de Reya, we then negotiated first a joint venture and then went on to complete a deal in the summer of 2022, whereby they invested additional funding and took a majority equity position in the group.

This is enabling us to grow far faster than we otherwise would have. Building trust between the organizations is key, and regular video calls are just not good enough, in my opinion. In our case, all this started because I happened to be in Madrid for my birthday. So I texted the CEO, Jose-Antonio Lasante, to ask if he wanted to have lunch. Unbeknown to me, he was recovering from a serious form of Covid-19. He still said yes and booked a restaurant called 'Sacha', an attention to detail I really appreciated. For me, relationships are key and from that first lunch together we started to build a global deal for growth.

Building your talent pipeline

International expansion is only possible if you have the right people to support growth. Getting approvals internally from those above you for increases in headcount can be hard enough. But even then, will you find the skills you need not just today but for the future? So I decided to interview someone who is a recognized international expert in the field.

CONVERSATION WITH
Jason Holt, Chair of the Apprenticeship Ambassador Network, UK Department for Education, Chairman of Holts Group of Companies.

> **Sacha:** Many companies struggle to find good-quality people who are highly motivated and well trained. Having a good talent pipeline is vital if they are to keep expanding locally as well as internationally. How have apprenticeships helped retailers and brands in different countries around the world?

Jason: Finding the right team is the name of the game in all businesses. What I have seen work well in other countries and being brought into the UK is a change towards educating young people to have soft skills, which I consider essential skills: communication, problem solving, how to behave in life, how to approach people, negotiate. We have tended to focus on getting high grades, and yet graduates have to take jobs that require basic business skills they do not have. What I have seen elsewhere is that employers get involved with education at a very early stage, even primary school, so children actually know what people do. Data shows that when learners have three encounters with employers during their schooling, they are 85 per cent more likely to do better in life. In the apprenticeship world, the recent reforms mean that the programme is far more focused on what employers want. Employers are in control of what is taught. This is a game-changer in ensuring a better-quality experience and a new talent stream available for retailers to tap into. This model is well established in what is known as the apprenticeship block countries, such as Germany, Austria, Switzerland and several in Scandinavia.

Sacha: How does this work in retail?

Jason: Retail has traditionally been a particularly difficult nut to crack in terms of further education and apprenticeships. Retailers for a number of reasons have been reluctant to engage – possibly as routes into employment have been more informal. However, we are seeing many new partnerships between employers and training providers. The likes of Marks & Spencer and L'Oréal are getting together with providers/colleges, and are in the driving seat. They are saying that if you want our business, let's co-create the curriculum you teach so that it fits the needs of our businesses. The institutions who say yes to working in this way are winning the contracts. Places like Fashion Retail Academy are delivering training for Zara (the fashion retailer that is part of the Indetex Group in Portugal). By way of example, they are providing three-year apprenticeships where the learners are getting a university degree, being trained for a job and ending up employed at the company with all the benefits of any employee while they are learning. They end up far wealthier than their graduate counterparts and, of course, debt free. So, the degree apprenticeship in England is a game-changer for retailers. The most successful are those where there is a partnership approach between provider and retailer. These companies are setting the standard for today and tomorrow.

Sacha: How can retailers improve the skills being taught at education facilities since many are unhappy with the output?

Jason: There are two keys to success: (1) sourcing the right educational partners who can really get under the bonnet of your organization; and (2) creating, through those partners, an educational experience where learning and work are meshed seamlessly together so that skills learnt in the classroom are applied in the workplace.

Sacha: Why and how did you get into training and apprenticeships for the retail jewellery trade?

Jason: In 1999, when I joined the family jewellery business in Hatton Garden, it was evident how close to retirement our craftspeople were. So, we embarked on trying to recruit, but couldn't find the right skilled people. This led to setting up our very own in-house jewellery school – the idea being to cherry pick the best ones for ourselves. The ones we didn't pick were snapped up by other jewellers and very quickly we grew into a teaching organization supplying hundreds of students each year to the jewellery sector. After 15 years we were multinational with 1,000 students a year, with the first apprenticeship in the sector for 600 years.

For more information on statistics and reports that demonstrate the benefits that apprenticeship schemes bring to companies (especially retailers), visit these links:

www.apprenticeships.gov.uk/employer/benefits#

https://europa.eu/european-union/topics/education-training-youth_en

What is the long-term goal?

Review your international strategy regularly with your teams and understand the board's and the shareholders' desires. Economic and political events can hit you. Review your competitors, carefully review changes in employment regulations, taxes or import–export restrictions, so you know when to pivot. If needed, go in a different direction and change your business to be successful. Play the long game. Remember to think strategically, not just managing the short term.

I really recommend pushing yourself forward and out of your comfort zone to expand into another country. You will be offering new services and a different way of expressing a brand, and your uniqueness will work for you. If you and your organization (even if you are a small company right now) become international, you will have greater cachet and be able to hire better-calibre people. All this expansion attracts new consumers, as well as investors, bankers and shareholders who see you are not dependent on one market. The profits, cash flow, supplier relationships and brand power that come with it can be hugely rewarding.

INTERNATIONAL EXPANSION

- Don't just read research reports; spend time actually visiting the locations you want to expand into internationally.
- Pay for good local advice and get references from those advisers – don't just blindly believe everything they say!
- Hire a good local manager who fits culturally within your wider company.
- Plan for the unexpected, including having extra cash funding reserves, as things often take longer or are more expensive than planned.
- Retail fit-out permits and the entire construction process may be very different from what you are used to in your home country.
- Your products and services need to evolve when expanding internationally, so rapid testing and reassessment will be needed.
- Invest time in developing strong long-term relationships in your new country, as business growth opportunities may come from unexpected sources.
- Fundraising is key, have great advisers and make sure the funding sources will support your aspirations.
- Look at apprenticeships as a way of accessing great talent pipelines, which you will need to continue expanding.
- Keep reviewing changes to your local and international markets, as you will often need to pivot quickly.

References

AngloInfo Denmark (nd) Benefits and allowances in Denmark, *Angloinfo*, www.angloinfo.com/how-to/denmark/money/social-security/benefits-allowances (archived at https://perma.cc/4227-PNLQ)

Berlin Business Location Sector (2019) Collective agreements for certain sectors in Germany, Business Location Center, www.businesslocationcenter.de/en/labor-market/employment-law-and-collective-contracts-system/collective-agreements-for-certain-sectors/ (archived at https://perma.cc/747N-F9T3)

Deloitte (2019) *Global Powers of Retailing 2019*, Deloitte

Information Commissioner's Office (2019) Guide to the General Data Protection Regulation (GDPR), *ICO*, https://ico.org.uk/for-organizations/guide-to-data-protection/guide-to-the-general-data-protection-regulation-gdpr/ (archived at https://perma.cc/DUV6-MMSR)

Kaufman, J (2014) Renovating? Don't forget the expediter, *New York Times*, www.nytimes.com/2014/12/14/realestate/renovating-dont-forget-the-expediter.html?0p19G=2870 (archived at https://perma.cc/DNL2-QNN4)

Monteiro, F (2018) Three conditions for a successful life, *Insead Knowledge*, https://knowledge.insead.edu/blog/insead-blog/three-conditions-for-a-successful-life-10156 (archived at https://perma.cc/SX6L-7EW9)

Conclusion

Putting together this book has been a labour of love, with input from a diverse range of amazing leaders in their respective fields, from international brands to real-estate gurus and technology pioneers. I have reached across political divides and socio-economic ones, I have looked at countries that are developing to those that are near the height of their power.

Serving international travellers is both financially and personally rewarding. It has lit up my life, and I hope that you and the teams you lead will have the opportunity to experience the exhilaration and sense of connectedness that come from serving people from around the world.

What has become so clear in recent years is that there is an urgent imperative for major brands to make eco credentials in products real and make them visible. Too many brands think of these attributes as unseen and therefore as less valuable to driving customer sales. How can brands make these attributes more valuable to international shoppers? Well, think how Porsche has fluorescent-green brakes on the wheels of their best-selling electric and hybrid models – what other innovative ways can brands use in retail to distinguish the best products that meet customer desires for a responsible impact on the world? Failing to make the eco credentials of consumers visible to their loved ones, and those they want to influence, risks a brand being disintermediated by newer brands. Newer generations of consumers want to broadcast to their friends and followers who they are, and major brands who can help taunt consumers' ESG credentials will be the winners.

This book has many other ideas and insights into how you can make your business more successful, by attracting international shoppers with plenty of spending power. Use them wisely with your teams, I wish you great success in your endeavours.

ACKNOWLEDGEMENTS

First and foremost, I would like to thank my parents Bette and Zacky for instilling in me the joy of travel and a love for experiencing the various cultures the world has to offer. They worked so hard and made so many sacrifices along the way. Together we co-founded ChangeGroup and built it into an amazing company and I am so proud of them both. Thank you very much to my sister Claudia, for being my fellow adventurer on our many early travels and inspiring me to try to write my first book.

Thank you to all the many ChangeGroupers around the world I have worked with over the years. Their dedication, passion and trustworthiness is something I am so proud of. In joining with the team at Prosegur Cash we will now have the opportunity to achieve many great things together. In particular I would like to thank the following people: Alberto Lara, Alex McCann, Alicia de Miguel, Alvaro García Prieto, Antonio Fuentes, Beatriz Montes, Bob Kaciski, Carl Bailey, Carl Knight, Carlos Quintana, Chris Mason, David Lester, Elena Rodridguez Comu, Elias Fullana, Enrique Martinez-Tellez, Eva Fernandez, Fernando Morán, Gary Smith, Gary Parekh, Gavin Wood, Graham Carlton, Gregory Dumartin, Ignacio Cea-Fornies, Javier Hergueta, Javier Lopez Huerta, Javier Ruiz, Jelena Stoskaja, Johan Fransson, Jose-Angel Fernandez Freire, José Antonio Lasanta, José Carlos Villarejo, José Retuerce, Juan-Luis Marin-Carrera, Justin Latter, Louis De Bourgoing, Luis Pereira, Maite Rodriguez, Mar Pedraza, Mario de Vicente, Marina Couso, Michael Jackson, Michael Robl, Miguel-Angel Bandes Gutierrez, Miguel Ángel Elena, Miguel Ángel Yunta, Mike Shipton, Milos Maricic, Minnie Borg, Mohamed Lebbe, Murad Medinakattan, Mustapha Zouaoui, Nathalie Johansson, Neel Kapoor, Norbert Lill, Pablo de la Morena, Pablo de Santiago, Pat Greene, Paul Crombie, Paul Meehan, Pauline Maguire, Rafet Sirjaric, Refet Arel, Rosa Remuiñan, Samy Larouchi, Sebastian Sanchez, Stefan Erickson, Stuart Wilson, Tracie Cook, Vicente Carreras and Kasia Jedrys.

A very special thank you to the exceptional leaders and professionals who kindly gave their time and vast knowledge to be interviewed for this book. I have been inspired over the years by the words of many great leaders in politics and business, and I am honoured to be a conduit for your wise words here. I would like to extend a thank you to Chris Cudmore and everyone at Kogan Page for believing in this book and making the material accessible to so many people around the world. Thank you to Charlie Wadey, Soreh Milchstein and Gay Walley for all your hard work and support throughout this project.

Thank you to my uncle Dr Yehiya, Amal Hashim and the many other team members for all their tireless work in running the Tree Foundation for a quarter of a century, which has enabled so many children to attend senior schools and tertiary education. On a personal note, thank you especially to the many teachers I have had in the many schools I attended around the world – your patient efforts with all my constant questions have provided me with the skills and knowledge to embrace life.

I would like to thank my other amazing friends, business colleagues and coaches who in various ways inspired me to write this book – in particular Professor John Drew, Dr Catherine Shainberg, Jason and Shona Holt, Arnon Woolfson, Junior Akwule, Vick and Augusta Mirchandani, Nick and Claire Cornwell, Rohan and Tess Virmani Arnaud and Jennifer Bachelet, Pekka Viljakainen, Ben Zifkin, Sam Abboud, John Lutzius, Chris Brown, Edward Perry, Sebastian Junoy, Paddy Lyell, Shamshad Ahmed, Chris Chippendale, Bertil Akesson, Hinson NG and Nigel Mumford. Ian Campbell, Jonathan Pollard, Wendy Spenks, Johnny Rayner, Rachel Bulford, Pia Kluck and Nora Immonen, Toby Stone, Rahan Shaheen, Alex Batchvarov, Scott Dowty, Aad and Ron Van Kleef, Dr Ying Xu, Nicola Kravitz, Georg Muzicant, Gilles Hittinger Roux, Paul Berkman, Robert Karin, Princess Caroline Colonna, Prince Mario Max, Daniel Gestetner, Paul Glossop, Mark Horgan, Ted Nussbaum, Dana Stein, Shabir Randeree, Freddie Munao, Peter Sire, Diego Palomo, Nick Scott, Andrew Donachie, Benoit and Lisa Robinot, Roely and Gianfranco Santamaria, Nermeen Varawalla, Orlando Hamilton Biney, the Rotheisens, Axle and Ines Kunzli, Sybille and Daniel Sciamma, Alexandro Rossi, Ali Dajani, Chrisyophe de Taurines, Ramiro Orutiz, Benjamin Rosende, Herbert Schoderbock, Miguel and Mencia Yacobi. I would also like to thank the 'Finnish University Crew' we meet up with in Helsinki every year.

Now, a very important and big thank you to my grandparents, aunts, uncles and cousins from England and Sri Lanka, all of whom have been such a defining part of my life journey in so many ways. Thank you. I would also like to give a special mention to my nieces and nephews: Seraphina, Saahjiy, Mikael, Olivia, Nicolas and Hugo – may you find joy in all the positive things that the world has to offer.

Finally, thank you to my wife Helena, for all her work in making this book so much better, and for supporting all I do. Thank you for sharing your life with me and helping us get through the pandemic, you are amazing.

To my children Xerxes and Ella, whose energy, enthusiasm and persevering minds are so inspiring, thank you. I learn from you every day and I am so proud of you both. Thank you also to Pirjo and Risto Maki-Opas, my parents-in-law, who have taught me so much about Finnish culture and provided such a nurturing environment to our family at their lake house.

INDEX

The Meeting Place   Paul Day 2011.